Barbara Smit is a journalist and has reported on the affairs of big businesses for the *Financial Times*, *International Herald Tribune* and others. Over the past four years she has travelled all around Europe and the United States to investigate the true story of Adidas, interveiwing those involved with the company, declass-ifying documents and unearthing exclusive stories. This book has been translated into five languages.

BARBARA SMIT

Pitch Invasion

Three Stripes, Two Brothers, One Feud:
Adidas, Puma and the Making of
Modern Sport

PENGUIN BOOKS

PENGUIN BOOKS

Published by the Penguin Group
Penguin Books Ltd, 80 Strand, London WC2R ORL, England
Penguin Group (USA) Inc., 375 Hudson Street, New York, New York 10014, USA
Penguin Group (Canada), 90 Eglinton Avenue East, Suite 700, Toronto, Ontario, Canada M4P 2Y3
(a division of Pearson Penguin Canada Inc.)
Penguin Ireland, 25 St Stephen's Green, Dublin 2, Ireland
(a division of Penguin Books Ltd)
Penguin Group (Australia), 250 Camberwell Road, Camberwell, Victoria 3124, Australia
(a division of Pearson Australia Group Pty Ltd)
Penguin Books India Pvt Ltd, 11 Community Centre, Panchsheel Park, New Delhi – 110 017, India
Penguin Group (NZ), 67 Apollo Drive, Rosedale, North Shore 0632, New Zealand
(a division of Pearson New Zealand Ltd)
Penguin Books (South Africa) (Pty) Ltd, 24 Sturdee Avenue, Rosebank, Johannesburg 2196, South Africa

Penguin Books Ltd, Registered Offices: 80 Strand, London WC2R ORL, England

www.penguin.com

First published by Allen Lane 2006
Published in Penguin Books with amendments 2007
1

Lyrics on pp. 218–19 from 'My Adidas', words and music by Joseph Simmons,
Darryl McDaniels and Rick Rubin, copyright © Rabasse Music Ltd and Rush Groove Music,
administered by Warner/Chappel Music Ltd, London W6 8BS, are reproduced by permission

Typeset by Rowland Phototypesetting Ltd, Bury St Edmunds, Suffolk
Printed in Great Britain by Clays Ltd, St Ives plc

ISBN: 978-0-141-02368-7

To Yann and our children
Lisa
Karen
Fanny
Marius

Contents

CONTENTS

Illustrations

(Photographic acknowledgements are given in parentheses.)

ix

PART I

Two Brothers, One Feud

1924–1974

I

The Dashing Dassler Boys

The two young men wore smart suits and proud grins as they posed in front of the newly polished vehicles. At a time when automobiles were the preserve of wealthy families, Rudolf Dassler had splashed out on a Mercedes two-seater. Somewhat more modest, his younger brother, Adolf, had opted for a Triumph motorcycle with a sidecar. Since the take-off of their footwear company in the late 1920s, the Dasslers had become the smartest boys in town.

Adolf and Rudolf Dassler were the two owners of Gebrüder Dassler, which generated unprecedented excitement in the small Bavarian town of Herzogenaurach where it was based. The two had come up with an unheard-of proposition: a business that would make shoes to be worn only for sports. Since sport was still an uncommon pastime, the plan seemed far-fetched. Yet the Dasslers had persisted with such drive that their factory was attracting orders from sports enthusiasts across the whole of Germany.

Made of dark leather, with large nails driven through the soles, the Dasslers' spikes were distinguishable from others by their suppleness and light weight. Adolf, who was both a cobbler and an inveterate sports fiend, perpetually looked for ways to make shoes that were both light and adjusted more closely to his own requirements. Prototypes were subjected to hours of testing by 'Adi' and his friends during lengthy forest runs.

The partnership between the two brothers worked smoothly, based on contrasting characters. A short and quiet man, Adi Dassler relished the time spent in his workshop permeated with the smells of leather and glue, becoming animated only when the subject turned to sports. His brother Rudolf, with his loud and extrovert manner, was better equipped to head up the company's fast-growing sales team. Undeterred by Germany's economic depression, he talked and wheedled until he obtained orders, converting his brother's obsession into money. They could easily afford the vehicles, the suits and the expensive fashionable cigarette-holders that dangled from their lips.

The brothers' venture was a departure from the Dassler family's long-lasting relationship with the weaving industry. Their father, Christoph, was the last in a long line of Dassler weavers from Herzogenaurach, a medieval village just a few miles north of Nuremberg in the province of Franconia, on the northern edge of Bavaria. Until the end of the nineteenth century it was known as a bustling mill town, employing hundreds of weavers and dyers. In keeping with the German tradition of roving apprentices, Christoph Dassler left the village to learn his craft by seeking employment with weavers elsewhere. During a stay in Gera he met his wife, Paulina Spittula. Their wedding was celebrated in October 1891 and their first child, Fritz, arrived one year later. A daughter, Marie, followed in early 1894. However, the revolution that swept through German industries in the late nineteenth century made Christoph's skills obsolete. Following the mechanization of the weaving industry, thousands of skilled workers were replaced with machines, plunging many families into an errant life of grinding poverty.

Christoph and his new family returned to Herzogenaurach, where two more sons were born: Rudolf in April 1898 and Adolf in November 1900. The mill town had not been spared by the industrial revolution, which had reduced its hundreds of handlooms to scrap. It turned instead to shoe production, and scores of small factories soon dotted the cobble-stoned village, most specializing in heavy felt slippers known as *Schlappen*. Christoph found employment at the Fränkische Schuhfabrik, one of Herzogenaurach's largest plants.

While Christoph Dassler learned tedious stitching methods, Paulina complemented her husband's meagre earnings by setting up a laundry at the back of their house on the Hirtengraben. The family biographer, Hermann Utermann, described her as 'a joyous, somewhat plump woman who was always ready for a cheerful chat'. She took care of the washing with her daughter, and the clean laundry was delivered around town by the three Dassler boys using a ramshackle hand-cart. This was quite a rewarding duty, since those people who could afford to have their clothes laundered usually had a spare coin for the couriers, too. The three brothers became known in Herzogenaurach as 'the laundry boys'.

When the Dassler brothers were still at school, at the beginning of the twentieth century, sport as a popular pastime barely existed. Germany had a long tradition in gymnastics but other games had only begun to emerge in the last two decades of the nineteenth century and the thought of playing anything outdoors still seemed incongruous to most Germans. They just didn't have the leisure to care about much else than putting food on the table. To make matters worse, sports were frowned upon by the more conservative leaders of the gymnastics movement. They were particularly disparaging of football, which was regarded as a degrading sport spread by Germany's arch-enemies, the English. Organized since 1900 under the German football federation, the game was rejected by the establishment as an 'English weed' and 'a foreign viper that needs to be rooted out'.

Yet Adi Dassler spent most of his spare time setting up impromptu running races and other contests. His appetite for physical exertion went far beyond boyish exuberance. Fritz Zehlein, an equally healthy friend, was dragged out on long runs in the forests and meadows that surrounded the small town. 'These two were inseparable,' said Zehlein's nephew, Klaus Zehlein. 'Whenever they had a spare moment they roamed around together, making up sports.' They carved sticks to make javelins and picked heavy stones for shot-putting. In the winter they built a makeshift ski-jump and lunged downhill on a pair of polished planks.

While Adi was still at school, his eldest brother Fritz left their medieval home town to take up a position as a bank clerk in Munich, and Rudolf learned the ropes of shoe manufacturing with his father at the Fränkische Schuhfabrik. But the call for mobilization of the Reich's army in August 1914 brutally interrupted their plans. Since the declaration of the German Reich in 1871, Bavaria had retained a degree of independence from the empire's Prussian rulers, with its own diplomatic corps and an independent army, but it had been agreed that this would fall under the control of the Kaiser if war were declared. The two elder Dassler brothers were among the thousands of conscripts who believed they would be back home in a matter of months, but who would spend four long years away in the muddy trenches of Flanders.

As the war dragged on, Christoph Dassler anxiously watched the decimation of Herzogenaurach's shoe industry. Nearly half of the town's factories had to close their doors. To make sure that his youngest son would learn a safer trade, Christoph had an apprenticeship lined up for him: Adi was to rise long before dawn every day and spend eighteen gruelling hours in the blasting heat of a baker's furnace. Usually obedient and soft-spoken, the teenage Adi protested. It took a good deal of hard talking to persuade him to report for work at the Weiss bakery, on the Bambergerstrasse, in November 1914. After three exhausting years the reluctant apprentice obtained his diploma, but he never got the chance to paint his name on the front of a bakery because his services were immediately requested by the army. At the beginning of 1918, the 17-year-old Adolf Dassler joined his two brothers at the Belgian front.

Remarkably, all three Dassler brothers returned to Herzogenaurach hardened but unharmed. There they found their mother's washroom empty. In the post-war misery few could afford the luxury of having their clothes washed and Paulina had given up the business. Adi rapidly made up his mind: there was no way he was returning to the bakery; he would set up his own little shoe-production unit, right there in the former laundering shed.

In the aftermath of the war's savagery, Adi spent many days scouring the countryside, picking up all sorts of army utensils left behind by retreating soldiers. He scavenged any debris that could be remotely useful and hauled it back to his workshop. Strips of leather could be cut from army helmets and bread pouches, to be recycled as shoe soles. Torn parachutes and haversacks were more suitable for making slippers. Among his early inventions was a leather trimmer fixed to a bicycle frame: in the absence of electricity, the device was powered by some of Adolf's more athletic friends.

Established at the beginning of 1920, Adolf Dassler's shoe company began life as a very small business indeed. While Adi crafted, two of his friends took turns at the pedals. Christoph would drop by during his lunch breaks to teach his son the rudiments of shoe production and his sister Marie helped with the stitching. When the employees arrived at dawn they sometimes had to climb over Adi's bed: he had set it up at the entrance of the workshop so that he could rush to his table if he happened to be hit by a brainwave in the middle of the night.

Adolf slowly built up his trade with sturdy footwear that could be expected to last for several years, but he was still most interested in sports shoes. He sold some slippers for gymnastics and eagerly tinkered with samples for running shoes. In those days this part of the business was more or less experimental, the only 'customers' being Adi and his friends. The running spikes were forged and driven through the shoe soles by his friend Fritz Zehlein, who conveniently was the son of the town's blacksmith.

To improve his spikes, Dassler avidly studied the production methods in countries with a more deep-rooted running tradition. By far the most prominent of them was Finland, which bagged a sackful of Olympic medals for throwing and running disciplines in the twenties. The Finns, who ruled the roost in middle-distance running, were led by the impassive Paavo Nurmi, a deadpan little runner who set a spate of world records and won eight Olympic golds. He also generated unparalleled publicity for Karhu, a Helsinki company set up to make shoes for Finland's finest athletes. The Karhu brand name shot to prominence at the 1920 Olympics in Antwerp, where it outfitted all of the Finnish javelin throwers. The brand's triumph was complete four years later at the Paris games, where Paavo Nurmi took five gold medals wearing a conspicuous pair of white Karhu running spikes.

Adi's hard-working crew was soon joined by his brother Rudolf. Upon his return from Belgium, Rudi had not stayed in Herzogenaurach but left to pursue a short police training course in Munich. He then briefly joined the county police but he rightly concluded that his expansive manners would make him a better salesman than police officer. He honed his selling skills at a porcelain factory, then with a leather trader in Nuremberg, before Adolf agreed to employ him in 1923. A typewriter was the only capital asset contributed by Rudolf to the operation.

As things turned out, the Dasslers could hardly have picked a worse time to get their business going. Under the harsh prescriptions of the Treaty of Versailles, the Great War victors seized most of Germany's resources, leaving little to rebuild the battered country. This caused huge resentment and appalling deprivation, with millions suffering from unemployment and hunger. In Herzogenaurach, many of the small shoe factories that survived the war were pummelled by this economic hardship. The small town registered a staggering unemployment rate of roughly 70 per cent. Yet amid this tension and misery, sports and other forms of entertainment began to attract swelling crowds, grateful for

1. The small town of Herzogenaurach, where the Dassler brothers started out, in the 1920s.

any form of distraction. Longing to shake off the country's conservative ways, youngsters most eagerly turned to sports that were regarded as modern and outlandish.

The Germans displayed particular enthusiasm for boxing. They enjoyed the aggressive aspect of the sport that outraged the establishment. When the ban on boxing was lifted after the armistice, boxers, some of whom were former prisoners of war who had honed their skills during their detention in Britain, were among the country's most popular heroes. Adi and Fritz Zehlein formed a boxing group in Herzogenaurach, but this quickly disintegrated when the other members realized that their participation would result only in a weekly beating.

It was football, however, that fast emerged as the most popular sport of all. Germany's gymnastics leaders watched helplessly as football clubs sprang up all around the country. Adi himself became a member of the local club, FC Herzogenaurach, where he played centre forward, and thousands of supporters thronged shaky stands at football matches in the German club championship. The time had come for the Dasslers to launch Adi's inventive sports products on a larger scale.

The expansion was consecrated on 1 July 1924 with the setting up of Gebrüder Dassler, Sportschufabrik, Herzogenaurach. Along with the running spikes they began to offer football boots with leather studs. The early Dassler boots looked much like their English forebears – leather contraptions with thick protection for toes and ankles – although Adi fiddled with each of the components until he managed to make them a little lighter.

Under the troubled economic circumstances, the brothers struggled to make a living from their sales to retailers, but they found another way to get their business rolling. When the Herzogenaurach sports club decided to build an enlarged hall, the Dasslers convinced its managers to order a large batch of Dassler shoes to be offered to club members at a reduced price. The club placed such a weighty order that the Dassler brothers had to hire staff and work flat-out for several months.

From then on, Rudolf exploited the growing sports craze by sending brochures and packages of Dassler shoes to scores of Germany's mushrooming sports clubs. The response was overwhelming. The Dassler shoes were of such undisputed quality that the cobblers from Herzogenaurach began to arouse the curiosity of the country's most eminent sports specialists.

The breakthrough came when a spluttering motorbike skidded to a halt in front of the Dassler factory. On the saddle sat the coach of the German athletics team, Josef Waitzer, a lanky man with a crew-cut and a neatly clipped moustache. He had heard about the spikes made by the sports freaks in Herzogenaurach and he had ridden all the way from Munich to check them out for himself. Waitzer needed the best possible shoes for his team ahead of the 1928 Olympic Games, to be held in Amsterdam.

The unexpected visit turned into an hours-long discussion. Jo Waitzer and Adolf Dassler shared the same enthusiasm for all things athletics. Waitzer himself had taken part in the Games back in 1912, in Stockholm, as a javelin and discus thrower. Waitzer failed to win any medals for Germany, but he moved on to coaching and in February 1925 was recruited as head trainer of the German track and field federation. An utterly precise and dedicated man, he wrote several manuals on the finer points of javelin and hammer throwing.

Josef Waitzer's motorbike and sidecar became a regular sight at Gebrüder Dassler. He was effectively employed as an adviser to the two brothers, and became close friends with Adi. They ran together and spent hours discussing Dassler's shoes.

By then, Gebrüder Dassler had left Frau Dassler's former washroom and moved into larger premises: the vacant Weil shoe factory on the far side of the river Aurach, which had ceased production in 1926. A brick building with tall windows, the plant was conveniently located next to the railway station. The move presented no logistical difficulties: all of the Dassler brothers' equipment and stock fitted into a single horse-drawn cart.

Employing about twenty-five people, the company's sales expanded at such speed that the Dasslers began to savour their success. After the deprivations of the post-war years, the second half of the twenties appeared to herald Germany's recovery. Gebrüder Dassler fully benefited from the upswing. Along with the swanky vehicles, the two brothers splashed out on outings to the nearby town of Nuremberg and short breaks in the Bavarian mountains, just a couple of hours' drive away.

Around the same time, Rudi's bachelor years came to an end after a striking encounter on a station platform in Nuremberg. He was returning from a night out with his brother Fritz in August 1923 when he spotted the 18-year-old Friedl Strasser, her younger sister Betti and their cousin. They began to chat on the platform and sat together in the train. By the time they reached their destination, Friedl, a pretty brunette, had agreed to a date. 'Rudolf was a bit of a peacock, but there was no doubt for Friedl that he was the man of her life,' her sister Betti recalled. Since their father had died, shortly after the war, the Strasser sisters had been brought up by their mother, who ran a grocery store in Fürth, on the outskirts of Nuremberg. The wedding was celebrated there with about forty people on Sunday 6 May 1928.

The newlyweds moved into the cramped family home on the Hirtengraben. Brought up in a Catholic family with hard-working and conservative values, Friedl quickly adjusted to her role as a *Hausfrau*. Nevertheless, the house became uncomfortably crowded with the arrival of the couple's first son, Armin Adolf, in September 1929, so the two brothers decided to start building a much larger residence for the entire family, behind Gebrüder Dassler's factory.

The construction was further motivated by yet more economic gloom. After the apparent recovery of the late twenties, Germany had been struck again by the sudden collapse of the world economy triggered by

2. *The young Adi Dassler stands proudly among samples in his new factory.*

the Wall Street Crash of October 1929. All around them the depression was biting, unemployment still rampant. German companies were crippled by the country's galloping inflation. In the circumstances, the Dassler brothers deemed it wise to invest some of their earnings in bricks and mortar.

This climate, and the impotence of the country's government, paved the way for the rise of extremist politicians. They had been gathering strength since the end of the war, when the imperial regime had been overthrown and the Kaiser forced into exile in Holland. As Germany sank into an economic quagmire, Marshal von Hindenburg, the ageing and conservative war veteran who ran the country, was an easy target for populists on all sides. Support was spreading fast for the radical changes advocated by Adolf Hitler and his National Socialist Workers Party (NSDAP). The Nazis appealed to many who suffered from the country's desperate situation, as well as others who could not stand its perceived humiliation at the hands of the war victors.

The Dassler brothers could not escape the phenomenon. Demonstrations of mass fervour were held in the adjacent town of Nuremberg,

3. When the brothers still spoke: Rudolf and Friedl Dassler (standing left and centre) pose in front of the company truck, while Adi grins at the back (centre).

host to the party's awesome rallies. To supervise the region Hitler had appointed Julius Streicher, perhaps the most insane of his henchmen. Often wearing a tight leather outfit with a whip at his side, Streicher spread his venom through his own Nuremberg-based newspaper: *Der Stürmer* offered a revolting mixture of pulp and anti-Semitic propaganda under the motto 'Jews are our misfortune!'.

As he admitted to the American authorities after the war, Rudolf Dassler began to vote for the NSDAP in 1932 and was among the earliest Nazi supporters in his neighbourhood. While the elections consecrated the NSDAP as Germany's largest party, it obtained just 22 per cent of the votes in Herzogenaurach. Steeped in its conservative mentality, the small town still stood massively behind von Hindenburg. The three Dassler brothers were all registered for party membership on the same day, 1 May 1933, roughly three months after Hitler seized power.

At that time Adi was living in Pirmasens, a small town in the hills of the Palatinate, the German region leaning against the French border in the Alsace. Pirmasens was then entirely devoted to the shoe industry. Although Gebrüder Dassler was expanding at breakneck speed, Adi felt restricted by his lack of technical expertise. All that he knew about shoe manufacture he had learned from his father. In his early thirties, he therefore registered at the highly-reputed Schuhfachschule of Pirmasens. Owing to his experience, Adolf Dassler was fast tracked through the two-year course in eleven months, though he still had to share his room and assignments with other students. In his bid to produce the lightest possible shoes, he showed up at most of the classes with weighing scales. Rudolf was left alone to supervise Gebrüder Dassler, which by then employed roughly seventy people.

One of Adi's mentors at the Schuhfachschule was Franz Martz, an established producer of wooden lasts – the moulds that are used to shape a shoe. It was during an appointment at the technician's home that Adolf met Käthe. Fifteen years old, she was the second oldest of the Martz family's six children. Franz Martz gladly condoned the quiet relationship between his pupil and his daughter. Together with Rudolf Dassler, he was one of the witnesses at their rain-soaked wedding in Pirmasens on 17 March 1934. The bride got a taste of things to come when, for their honeymoon, Adolf Dassler hauled her off to Lake Schlier in the Bavarian Alps and taught her how to ski.

The couple returned to Herzogenaurach and settled in on the ground floor of the family's new residence. (The house on the Hirtengraben was left to Fritz, who set up a lederhosen company, Kraxler, in the former washroom. Marie, meanwhile, had left home and married a former carpenter, Simon Körner.) Rudolf, Friedl and Armin occupied the first floor, while the second floor was reserved for the parents, Christoph and Paulina. It was in this enclosure that the Dasslers fell apart.

2

The Owens Coup

For Gebrüder Dassler, Nazism was a boon. Having effectively run the country since January 1933, Hitler's stooges implemented their theories with haste, and one of the most urgent tasks they had set for themselves was to promote sport. Hitler regarded sport as a prodigious instrument to encourage discipline and comradeship, while German victories were high in propaganda value. Not only that, but widespread participation in sports would help Hitler to build up an army of athletic young men. As he explained in *Mein Kampf*: 'Give the nation six million impeccably trained bodies, all impregnated with fanatical patriotism and animated with the most fervent fighting spirit. In less than two years if need be, the national State will turn them into an army.'

To this end, Hitler resolved to tighten the country's sports infrastructure. Under the principle of *Gleichschaltung* (compulsory integration), all clubs and federations were forcibly merged under a Nazi banner. The clubs previously tended to be affiliated with organizations of diverging political obediences, but under the Nazis there was only one acceptable credo.

The regime acknowledged the excitement stirred by football but it still placed the strongest emphasis on athletics. Josef Waitzer was confirmed by the Nazis as the national track and field coach. The Dasslers' adviser ingratiated himself to the regime as a staunch proponent of *Wehrsport*, or military-style games. Led by Waitzer, a delegation of German athletes travelled to fascist Italy in May 1933, singing Nazi songs and proclaiming themselves representatives of the new Germany.

As Nazi fervour continued to spread, the Dassler brothers benefited from the exploding demand for sports shoes. Gebrüder Dassler was enlarged several times, with extensions and a tower built at the entrance of the former Weil factory. A second plant was acquired on the Würzburgerstrasse. Among the Dasslers' best-selling products were spikes named after Waitzer.

Under the Nazi regime participation in sport came to be regarded as an act of political faith, with a deeply patriotic resonance. Millions of German youngsters were herded into the Hitler Youth, which offered a mixture of sporting activity and political education. Adi apparently decided that in order to cultivate his contacts with the town's sports clubs and its athletic youth, he would have to join it. He became a member in 1935, acting as a coach and supplier. At a welcome parade for a local party leader, Adi was seen wearing a Nazi uniform with the swastika neatly emblazoned on the lapel.

Hitler himself was most enthused about motor racing and boxing. 'No other sport is its equal in building up aggressiveness, in demanding lightning-like decision, and in toughening the body in steely agility,' he wrote. The Führer went out of his way to be seen with Max Schmeling, the heavyweight boxing champion who was emerging as Germany's

4. *Adi Dassler practises the high jump in a T-shirt featuring the Dassler company logo.*

greatest sporting hero in the second half of the thirties. The boxer was invited for tea with Hitler on several occasions, although he staunchly refused to become a party member.

Schmeling, who spent much of the early thirties in the United States, further ignored insistent pleas to sack his Jewish manager, Joe Jacobs. He was confronted with the spread of blatant anti-Semitism in his country when an upscale Berlin hotel manager refused to give a room to Jacobs. 'When this shows up in the New York papers,' Schmeling warned, 'you'll have seen the last of your American guests. Is this room available or not?' The man behind the desk sheepishly filled in the forms.

Having failed to annex Schmeling, the propaganda ministry pointedly refrained from supporting him ahead of his fight for the world heavyweight title, to be held in New York on 19 June 1936. The German boxer looked almost certain to get thrashed by Joe Louis, the stony-faced black American, but the Reich's propaganda supremos changed their tune when Schmeling devastated black America by knocking out the Brown Bomber. Among the telegrams which he found in his hotel room was one from Josef Goebbels: 'Congratulations, I know you fought for Germany,' he wrote. The next one was just as complimentary: 'Most cordial felicitations on your splendid victory,' it read. 'Adolf Hitler'.

Over the next weeks, the two eagerly exploited the supposed Aryan fighter's destruction of *der Neger*. They could not have hoped for a more encouraging prelude to the Olympics that were to be held the following month in Berlin.

The Olympic Games had been given to the German capital two years before the Nazis seized power. However, Hitler came to regard the competition as a matter of utmost priority for the Third Reich. It offered an extraordinary stage on which to demonstrate the superiority of the Aryan 'race'. At the same time, it could serve to appease other European nations, which watched the rise of the new Germany with a mixture of wonder and concern.

Some Olympic committees began to protest that, under the circumstances, the Olympics could not decently be held in Berlin. They pointed out that the regime's anti-Semitic policies were applied in sports with at least equal ardour as elsewhere. Among the prominent victims was Helena Mayer, an Olympic fencer. She had won a gold medal for Germany at the Amsterdam Games in 1928, but because her father was Jewish she was instructed to stay away from Berlin. Theodor Lewald was removed from his post as president of the German Olympic Committee due to his partly Jewish ancestry.

The Dassler brothers anxiously watched the political developments. Aided by their friend Jo Waitzer, the Dasslers' shoes had acquired a reputation beyond the Fatherland. They had reached the United States during the previous Olympics, in 1932, as most of the German athletes sailed to Los Angeles with 'Waitzer' spikes in their luggage. Among them was Arthur Jonath, a sprinter, who snatched a bronze medal in the 100 metres. At the Berlin Games, the Dasslers would be playing on their home turf, with the Nazis' track and field coach on their side.

The run-up to the Olympics, however, was marred by heavy protests from American athletes and mass demonstrations in New York, demanding a boycott of the 'Nazi Olympics'. The debate raged for three years. Avery Brundage, president of the US Olympic Committee, decided to check the situation for himself. Josef Goebbels took impeccable care of his American guest: when Brundage returned to the United States, he was adamant that Jews were indeed given a fair chance to compete in German sports.

This could not have been more blatantly untrue. The segregation was made official by the Nuremberg Laws of September 1935: stripped of their civil rights, Jews and part-Jews were to be banned from sports organizations. Still, Avery Brundage had his way. He staunchly believed that the Olympics should be held every four years no matter what – in line with the principles of Baron Pierre de Coubertin, the French aristocrat who revived the Games in 1896. At a meeting of the Amateur Athletic Union, in December 1935, Brundage silenced his critics and the proposed boycott of the Berlin Games was rejected. Scores of American athletes headed for Berlin.

Back in Europe, the racist bile that rose in Germany caused further outrage. Just before the opening ceremony, Henri Baillet-Latour, the Belgian president of the International Olympic Committee, expressed his disgust at the anti-Semitic posters he had seen around the country. In an uncharacteristic show of defiance, Baillet-Latour told Hitler that the slogans would have to be removed – otherwise the Olympics would be called off. Hitler barely managed to contain his anger but he still ordered a radical clean-up.

Regardless of the concessions, the Führer was determined to turn the Olympics into a spectacle of power. Leni Riefenstahl, his favourite film-maker, was offered unlimited resources to film the proceedings. Hitler ordered the construction of a bombastic Olympic stadium, and still complained incessantly that everything was far too small. The Olympic village was set in a majestic forest, with manicured lawns and artificial ponds. It was dotted with scores of large bungalows, a canteen, a library and many other facilities. For several weeks athletes from all over the world ran, jumped and chatted in the village, oblivious to the atrocities that were brewing just outside.

Among the athletes warming up in Berlin was Jack Beresford, a British rower. This would be his fifth Olympics, and he had never failed to bring back a medal. The 37-year-old would be the flag-bearer of a full British contingent.

On the back of the American protests, some British intellectuals had added their voices to the chorus of dismay about the Nazi Olympics. Fiercely independent from the country's political authorities, the British Olympic association ignored the tumult, but it instructed British athletes not to salute Hitler as they entered the stadium for the opening cere-mony. Athletes from a handful of nations gave a Nazi salute; others opted for an Olympic greeting, which is nearly the same and was inter-preted by the crowds as a sign of enthusiasm for their leader, but the British stuck to an eyes-right. The gesture was viewed as an act of defiance, engulfing the packed stadium in a stony silence.

The 16-year-old Dorothy Odam regarded it all as an amazing adventure. She had never travelled before and wasn't sure what to make of the public's mass hysteria. 'We woke up every morning to the Hitlerjugend marching past our windows with spades on their shoulders,' she recalled. 'We just figured it was all part of the celebrations.' When the English women went shopping with their chaperones, the store owners greeted them with the obligatory 'Heil Hitler!' 'Good morning King Edward,' they gingerly replied.

Dorothy Odam, later known as Dorothy Tyler, went on to win a silver medal in the high jump. The two other women on the podium, the Hungarian winner and the German bronze medallist, both rose an arm in the Nazi salute. 'I just thought they looked silly,' recalled the athlete. One person wrote to her at the Friesehaus, the building housing female competitors, urging her to tell the world about the horrors that were unfolding in Germany. When she showed the letter to her team supervisor, it was taken away from her.

Like nearly all the British athletes, Odam travelled to Berlin under her own steam and with her own kit. She did not receive any financial support from the Olympic association – never mind a pair of spikes. 'My shoes were so worn-out that one of my toes was hanging out,' she recalled.

Only the most fortunate among the athletes in Berlin could afford Foster's spikes. Named after a cobbler in Bolton, they had shot to fame at the Paris Olympics in 1924 on the feet of Harold Abrahams and Eric Liddell, the heroes whose story would later be enacted in *Chariots of Fire*. The scion of a long line of shoemakers in Nottinghamshire, Samuel Foster started complementing his ordinary range of footwear with cricket shoes in 1862, depicting himself as the inventor of the spiked cricket shoe. Samuel's son moved the family to Bolton, where he opened a confectionery, but one of his grandsons eagerly learned the ropes of shoemaking.

A keen runner himself, Joe Foster built on his grandfather's expertise to make lightweight spikes, marketed as Joe Foster's Running Pumps. They became known among runners in 1904 when Alf Shrubb, a tiny long-distance runner from Sussex, broke three world records in a single race at Ibrox Park in Glasgow with Foster's pumps on his feet. But after the British triumph at the 1924 Games Foster's business took off at such a pace that he opened a full-fledged sports-shoe plant called The Olympic Works.

At the Berlin Olympics, Adi Dassler was hoping to pull off a similar coup. The crowds certainly wouldn't care which spikes the athletes were wearing, but the Dasslers had learned just how beneficial it was to be associated with winning athletes. Word of mouth spread quickly in the small group of coaches and club managers who placed the largest orders. The feats of the athletes could be underlined in brochures and catalogues, to suggest that the Dassler spikes contributed to their success. Dassler therefore headed to Berlin and used his friendship with Jo Waitzer to gain access to the Olympic village, armed with several pairs of spikes and a repair kit. Through Waitzer, Dassler could rest assured that many of the German national team would be wearing his spikes, but he had set his sights on the most admired athlete in the world.

The son of an Alabama cotton-cropper, Jesse Owens had obtained a scholarship to hone his extraordinary running talents at Ohio State University. His finest hour came during a university competition at Ann Arbor, Michigan, on 25 May 1935. On that single day, in the space of forty-five minutes, Owens broke three world records and equalled another in the 100 metres. As was written in the American press over the next few days, Hitler himself had asked for details about the record-breaking American Negro who threatened to undermine the German team's medal haul in Berlin.

On the road in the United States, Jesse Owens and his black team-mates constantly suffered racist insults. While white runners wolfed down their snacks in roadside diners, the coach had to smuggle sand-wiches out of the restaurant for the black boys who sat waiting in the car. Predictably, some of Germany's reporters proved just as bigoted. They printed a photograph of an ape next to Owens, and attributed his speed to 'animal qualities'. But the German public at large still revered him for his feats. To his amazement, thousands of admirers had con-verged on Hamburg for the arrival of the American team, and the crowds excitedly chanted his name.

Equally awed by Jesse's unprecedented performances, Adi Dassler was desperate to get his shoes on the runner's feet. Josef Waitzer prob-ably warned his friend that he would be well advised to keep a low profile. Surely, the Nazis would not be amused if they found out that a Bavarian shoemaker had provided the spikes that helped a Negro to defeat their Aryan runners. But Dassler was undeterred. Regardless of the politics, Jesse Owens was a stupendous runner and there was no doubt that he would be the hero of the Berlin Olympics. Once he had found the American athlete, Dassler timidly pulled out his spikes, gesturing and mimicking until Jesse Owens agreed to try them out.

Among the most poignant contests was the long jump. This pitted Jesse Owens against a German, Lutz Long, who could easily have been cast as a prototypical Aryan. After a heated duel, Lutz Long walked down the track to prepare for his last jump. Hitler beamed as the German athlete, in an all-out effort, achieved a remarkable 7.87 metres, equalling the Olympic record set by Owens just before him. But the American was unfazed. As the packed Olympic stadium erupted in frenetic applause for Long, Owens prepared for his last jump. After two long minutes of silent concentration, he powered towards the board at full throttle. He soared through the air with such strength that, for a moment, he appeared to be floating above the sandpit. Owens had destroyed the previous record with a stunning leap of 8.06 metres. Much to Hitler's horror, Lutz Long rushed to hug and congratulate the winner. As they walked past the sulking Führer's lodge, the Aryan and the Negro were chatting, arm-in-arm.

The American's display in the sprints was marred by the same Adolf Hitler, who was accused of snubbing Owens by storming out of his lodge after the American's spectacular triumph in the 100 metres. But Owens ignored the commotion. Stunningly composed, he went on to take two more gold medals for the 200 metres and the 4 × 100 metres relay. Sitting among the rapturous crowd, Adi Dassler could barely contain his pride and excitement: Owens was wearing dark Dassler spikes with two dark stripes of leather running down the sides.

The Owens coup anchored the Dasslers' reputation among the world's most prominent athletes. The brothers milked their success in their catalogues, inserting a compliment by an unnamed coach of the US Olympic team. 'These are outstanding shoes!' he crowed, confirming that Jesse Owens had been wearing them in Berlin. Already established as the country's leading sports-shoe suppliers, Gebrüder Dassler began to receive letters bearing foreign stamps. While travelling in Germany for international meetings, athletes and coaches dropped by Herzogenaurach to check out the shoes worn by Jesse Owens.

5. Jesse Owens and Lutz Long give their own salutes to the German public.

By then, however, tensions had begun to simmer in the Dassler family. While Gebrüder Dassler was taking off, the opposing characters of the two brothers were the source of increasingly frequent rifts. Rudolf, who drove the company's mushrooming sales, rolled his eyes at Adolf's obsessive tinkering. He regularly lost patience with his brother's aloof attitude towards business matters. As for Adolf, he became increasingly disturbed by his older brother's brashness.

While the divergences caused some unpleasant conversations at Gebrüder Dassler, the disputes in the Villa adjoining it, fuelled by the Dassler women, were much sharper. A harmonious and self-effacing woman, Friedl Dassler had won the approval of her in-laws by softly blending in with family life. While taking care of her son, Armin, she was always prepared to lend a hand at Gebrüder Dassler. She tolerated Rudolf's notorious gallivanting with other women and put up with his curtness. By the ultra-conservative standards of the Dassler elders, Friedl was a model daughter-in-law.

Adi's wife, Käthe, was far more assertive. Like most German women at the time, she strove to serve her husband without complaint, waking at four every morning in order to fry his sausages. She watched him patiently as he practised his jumps, and packed sandwiches for football matches at the weekends. However, she was an outspoken woman who liked to take charge and to make her presence felt. Warm and spontaneous, the youthful bride also found it hard to deal with the suspicious and somewhat boorish ways of the Franconians. 'She was a serious person, yet she was used to the relaxed attitude of her environment in the Palatinate,' wrote Adi's biographer, Hermann Utermann. 'The Franconians seemed brusque and hard to talk to.'

Amplified by Käthe's hard-headed character, this unease led to recurrent clashes between Adi's wife and the rest of the family. 'Her brother-in-law's family certainly didn't make things easier for her,' Utermann observed. Others noticed that, shortly after Käthe's arrival, the atmosphere at the Villa began to deteriorate. Betti Strasser, Friedl Dassler's sister, cut back on her habitual visits to Herzogenaurach. 'Käthe had learned to stand up for herself, which didn't sit too well with the Dassler parents,' she said. 'There always seemed to be some argument going on out there'.

The rise of the Nazis caused deeper disagreements between the two brothers. The stranglehold which the Nazis established on all aspects of German life forced them to become more deeply involved with the movement. They signed off letters with the obligatory 'Heil Hitler!'. They held the same, swastika-stamped membership card of the National Socialist Drivers' Corps, the NSKK. The two brothers, however, didn't embrace the cause with equal warmth. While Rudolf vocally expressed his approval of the government's policies, Adi usually stuck to his ordinary, hard-working decency.

Hans Zenger was among the employees who benefited from Adolf Dassler's protection. After he misbehaved during a visit by a high-ranking Nazi dignitary in Herzogenaurach in 1937, he was barred from the Hitlerjugend. Adolf Dassler was then ordered to sack Zenger, but he consistently ignored the instruction. 'It was Adi Dassler who prevented my dismissal,' Zenger recalled. 'He knew that, if Gebrüder Dassler sacked me, I would likely end up at the Front.'

Such discussions increasingly raised questions about the company's leadership. Käthe's somewhat defiant attitude convinced Rudolf that she was a pushy, hostile intruder trying to undermine the Dassler brothers' previously close relationship. With the outbreak of the Second World War, the frictions that had built up between the two couples escalated to full-blown enmity.

3

Two Brothers at War

The war spelt trouble for Gebrüder Dassler. On the back of the Berlin Olympics, the company had benefited greatly from the Nazi enthusiasm for sports, and the sports craze had pushed annual sales up to about 200,000 pairs. But once the Nazi priorities shifted to the battlefield, the Dasslers' progress stopped dead in its tracks.

On 28 August 1939 Adolf Hitler imposed rationing for all essential goods, including footwear. Gebrüder Dassler was forced to rein in its output, and in September the government instructed the company to halve its staff and production.

As part of the Nazi economic reforms, German shoe production as a whole was supervised by the Reichswirtschaftsgruppe für Leder, the economic committee for leather. This was meant to keep a close eye on leather stocks and to make the country's shoe production more efficient by concentrating it in large plants. Although leather was clearly less vital to the war effort than steel or fuel, it was still regarded as a resource of strategic importance, needed to make boots for the Wehrmacht as well as gloves and other pieces of army equipment.

Sitting in their offices in Berlin, the men in charge of the unit drew up huge charts mapping out half-yearly instructions for shoe production throughout the country – with precise assignments for army boots and other military footwear. The leather owned by Jewish traders was seized immediately and the smaller plants were gradually closed. The problem with Gebrüder Dassler was that the meticulous Nazi charts failed to include sports shoes. The authorities apparently scratched their heads over their case for several months. Towards the end of 1939 they ordered the complete closure of Gebrüder Dassler for the following year, but soon afterwards the decision was reversed and the plant was authorized to turn out up to 6,000 pairs per month.

The war came closer to the Dassler family when Adi received a dreaded letter from the Wehrmacht on 7 August 1940. He was instructed to report for training as a radio technician at Intelligence Regiment 13 in Buchenbühl, near Nuremberg, from the beginning of December. Many other men from Herzogenaurach headed for their army barracks, among them the two sons Marie Körner had borne in the 1920s. But unlike his two nephews, who had barely reached adulthood, Adi was promptly relieved of his military duties. Ranked as an officer, he was declared *unabkömmlich* (exempt) on 28 February 1941, after three short months of military duty. For all the emphasis on the war effort, sport was still an integral part of the Nazi ethos. The authorities needed Gebrüder Dassler to fulfil the need for sports shoes, and Adolf Dassler apparently convinced them that the company required his technical expertise.

By then the shoe production had become strictly regulated and restricted to the disciplines that mattered most to the Nazis. In a letter to store owners, Adolf Dassler explained that his output had been regulated to 80 per cent gymnastics shoes, 15 per cent football boots and 5 per cent running spikes. Under the same diktat, shopkeepers had to place orders for the three categories of footwear in exactly those proportions. While the Dassler catalogue still featured Waitzer running shoes, the footballing range had been widened to include such names as 'Kampf' and 'Blitz', clearly evoking the war effort.

While German soldiers wreaked havoc throughout Europe, the small town of Herzogenaurach was relatively unperturbed. The Dasslers supplemented their diet from a vegetable patch in their garden; Käthe had turned the courtyard into a small farm, with chickens running round and a couple of pigs grunting nearby. With Adi back home, the family led an almost bucolic lifestyle on the banks of the Aurach. On Sundays they had long brunches with friends and organized picnics along the river.

Since his wedding to Käthe, Adi's branch of the family had grown by three. Käthe gave birth to their first child, a boy, in March 1936. Following Rudolf's lead with Armin, Adi affixed his brother's name to that of his firstborn, calling him Horst Rudolf. Inge followed in June 1938 and a second daughter, Karin, came along in the early days of the war, in April 1941. Rudolf and Friedl still lived just one floor up. Their son Armin, by then almost a teenager, had to share his toys with his new brother, Gerd, born in July 1939.

As the war progressed, the authorities continued their policy of closing down small factories and centralizing production in larger ones. Although of only middling size, Gebrüder Dassler escaped several rounds of closures. It remains unclear what was behind this decision: the most likely explanation is that few factories specialized in sports shoes, but the connections of the Dassler brothers may also have helped. While the bureaucrats in Berlin wiped hundreds of small businesses off their charts, Gebrüder Dassler's authorized monthly production limit was increased to 10,000 pairs. The relaxation was accompanied by a stern warning that this level was not to be exceeded, which must have raised a wry smile since the company found it hard enough to meet the requirement, let alone exceed it. The quality of raw materials was so poor that the shoes produced by the Dasslers during the war had little in common with the ones they had proudly sold a few years earlier. They even ran short of staff: to complete his assignments, in October 1942 Adolf Dassler requested five Russian prisoners of war.

Just like Gebrüder Dassler, the few other international sports-shoe manufacturers had been drawn into the war efforts of their respective countries. Converse, a company that shot to fame with the All Star basketball shoe, made flying boots that were worn by the entire US Army Air Corps. Gola, one of the oldest manufacturers of football boots in England, turned out marching boots for British soldiers. Their Finnish counterparts were equipped with boots from the Karhu plant.

Meanwhile the war had entered yet another deadly stage, as Allied bombs virtually erased entire towns from Germany's map. The people of Herzogenaurach shivered in their cellars for two nights in February 1943 as an incessant stream of bombers flew overhead to destroy large parts of neighbouring towns such as Nuremberg and Würzburg. Herzogenaurach itself escaped largely unscathed, with just five casualties due to stray bombs. Its absent sons were less fortunate, the opening of the eastern front resulting in the deaths of many more men from the town during the Nazis' ill-fated attack on the Soviet Union, launched in June 1941 as Operation Barbarossa, which saw some of the war's most brutal battles.

The heightened demands of the war began to take their toll on the Dassler family. Existing tensions were aggravated by proximity: with the Dassler elders, two bickering couples and five children behind one front door, the Villa seemed overcrowded.

While Adolf was clearly regarded as the linchpin of Gebrüder Dassler in the factory, his brother strove to impose himself as the company's leader. Marie had been devastated and Adolf apparently helpless when Rudolf had refused to employ her two sons at Gebrüder Dassler. If the

6. Nazi banners flew in Herzogenaurach during the Second World War.

Dasslers had insisted that the two boys were vital to the running of the company, they might not have been sent to war. 'Rudolf bluntly rejected his sister's pleas, saying that there were enough family problems at the company,' recalls Betti Strasser, Rudolf's sister-in-law. 'He could be incredibly harsh and mean.'

So could Fritz, the eldest brother, whose lederhosen company in the former family home on the Hirtengraben was now producing leather pouches for German soldiers. Adolf was particularly angry when Fritz picked Maria Ploner, a young employee who had previously worked at Gebrüder Dassler to be drafted as a *Flakhelferin*. These teenage girls were used as helpers for the army at the front, and very few of them returned unharmed. 'Adi thought Fritz was being unfair because my two brothers were already at the front,' she recalled. Adolf found space for her at Gebrüder Dassler, where she worked in safety until the end of the war alongside her father, Jakob Ploner, whose communist sympathies were widely known in Herzogenaurach.

Such brotherly disagreements were not uncommon. In the end, Fritz and Adolf were barely on speaking terms.

*

Adolf's early release from military duties caused further friction. The decision identified the younger Dassler as the indispensable half of the leadership duo, which deeply irked Rudolf and Friedl. They became convinced that, egged on by Käthe, Adi was plotting to oust them from Gebrüder Dassler. The tension that had been building up between the two couples boiled over into full-blown arguments, and Rudolf's suspicions took a paranoid turn.

One night, while Allied bombers were unleashing their deadly loads, Rudolf took refuge in the family shelter with Armin, Friedl and her sister Betti. They were soon joined by Käthe and Adi, who was in a foul mood. 'Here are the bloody bastards again,' Adi snapped as he entered the cellar. It was obvious to all that he was referring to the RAF – except Rudolf, who was convinced the comment had been directed at him. Suspicion turned into hateful resentment after January 1943, when Hitler called for the complete mobilization of the German people to put a quick end to the war. As part of this all-out effort, all men aged 16 to 65 and women aged 17 to 45 could be asked to defend the Reich. While Adolf Dassler was still regarded as exempt due to his duties at the factory, Rudolf was drafted to reinforce a regiment in Glauchau, Saxony.

From the beginning of April, Rudolf was moved to the customs department in the small town of Tuschin. On the eastern outskirts of the Reich, Tuschin was in the district of Litzmannstadt – the name given by the Nazis to the Polish city of Łódź with its infamous Jewish ghetto, after the German invasion of Poland in 1939. Because of alleged night blindness Rudolf was assigned to an office job. Compared with those of millions of other able-bodied German men, his position was comfortable but he still couldn't stand the thought that his brother had escaped the army. 'I will not hesitate to seek the closure of the factory,' Rudolf wrote to his brother in a spiteful letter from Tuschin, 'so that you will be forced to take up an occupation that will allow you to play the leader and, as a first-class sportsman, to carry a gun.'

Six months later, Rudolf seemed to have prevailed. A letter from Berlin informed Adolf that Gebrüder Dassler was to be closed down. The factory's run of luck was over as the ongoing war called for the requisitioning of yet more workers and machinery for weapons manufacturing. Josef Goebbels, the propaganda minister, had called for a *Totaler Krieg*, an all-out war, which ushered in an era of heightened terror for

German civilians. The country's last reserves were to be thrown into the war, requiring most remaining civilians and prisoners to work in armament factories for up to seventy hours per week. Sports shoes would no longer be needed since in *Totaler Krieg* there was no place for culture or sport. Gebrüder Dassler's equipment would be used to manufacture spare parts for Panzers and bazookas.

Rudolf, who happened to be on leave in Herzogenaurach when the decision was confirmed, rushed to the factory intending to seize stocks of leather and so paralyse shoe production at once. He was enraged to find out that his brother had been to the stockpile before him and put aside some supplies already. As the Dassler employees ignored Rudolf's angry outburst, he turned to some of his high-ranking Nazi friends in the Kreisleitung, the regional government. Adi was swiftly invited to their offices. 'My brother-in-law apparently had some high-placed contacts, because my husband was instructed to show up immediately and these gentlemen treated him in the most demeaning manner,' Käthe Dassler later wrote.

The dust settled in Herzogenaurach when Rudolf had to return to his desk in Tuschin. In his Polish outpost, he still plotted incessantly to regain control of the factory. Through his contacts at the Luftwaffe he persistently attempted to have Gebrüder Dassler's welding directive replaced with an order for parachuting boots, for which he personally held a patent. Rudolf calculated that, if such an assignment were made, he would be sent back to Herzogenaurach to take charge of it. The patent, like the plan, turned out to be flawed.

While Adolf tinkered with Panzer parts, Red Army tanks advanced towards his brother in Tuschin. By the beginning of 1945 they had come so close that Rudolf became jittery and decided he'd had enough. One of his declared reasons was that his unit had been integrated into the Schutzstaffel (SS), Heinrich Himmler's security police. 'My disapproval of Himmler's police rule, the proximity of the front and the fact that the war had long been lost, prompted me to refuse any further military duties,' he wrote later. Rudolf left for Herzogenaurach where, exhausted and dishevelled, he headed straight to a friendly physician who compliantly issued a medical certificate declaring Rudolf unfit for service due to a frozen foot.

Several weeks later he learned that his former unit in Tuschin had been disbanded – rolled over by the Soviet tanks which liberated Łódź on 19 January 1945. But the Third Reich still hadn't capitulated, so Rudolf's superiors at the SS ordered him to report to another of their branches: the Sicherheitsdienst (SD), its infamous intelligence service. One of the most reviled units of the Nazi regime, set up by Himmler and run at the time by Ernst Kaltenbrunner, the SD worked closely with the Gestapo to smash any potential opposition. Relying on thousands of informants, it provided the intelligence required by the Gestapo to perform its murderous tasks. Rudolf wrote that he was summoned to report to the Gottsmann cell of the SD in Fürstenwalde, near Berlin, but he refused to join the intelligence service and failed to show up as ordered.

Although the Allies were closing in fast, zealous Gestapo officials apparently deemed it useful to open a file on the suspected desertion of Rudolf Dassler. As he recalled, he reported to their offices in Nuremberg on 13 March 1945 and was told to remain at their disposal until they finished studying his case. In breach of these orders, Rudolf slipped out of the Gestapo offices and returned to Herzogenaurach on 29 March. The US Third Army, led by General Patton, had just crossed the Rhine at Oppenheim, and Rudolf had heard that his father lay dying. 'I expected that, given the turbulent situation at the time, my absence would not arouse any particular interest in Nuremberg,' he wrote.

The Dassler family was briefly reunited in Herzogenaurach on 4 April for the funeral of Christoph Dassler, the humble slipper-maker, who died of heart failure at the age of 80. The next day Betti Strasser, Rudolf's sister-in-law, felt uneasy as she headed down to the Dassler home. There seemed to be some agitation. When she pushed the door open she found her sister Friedl in shock, wailing that Rudolf had been arrested. The Gestapo had fetched him, she explained. He was held at the Bärenschanz prison in Nuremberg for several days, and he would not return home until after the Liberation.

Over the previous months only diehard supporters of the Nazi regime had failed to admit its defeat. The people of Herzogenaurach began to prepare for the arrival of the Allies by the end of March 1945, when US tanks crossed the Rhine. The Nazi authorities fulfilled their duty by calling for an insurrection to defend Herzogenaurach. However, the effort was less than half-hearted. On Saturday 14 April about sixty men left the town and headed west to confront the might of the US army. A few miles down the road half of the contingent had somehow vanished along the way. The others called it quits and turned round after less than one day. Their less than glorious retreat took a farcical turn when the would-be fighters met a group of women who had just plundered the nearby wine cellar of Joachim von Ribbentrop, the Nazi foreign minister. They walked away with buckets full of fine wine and generously shared it with the tired soldiers of Herzogenaurach.

The two bridges over the Aurach were blown up by the Nazis but when US troops entered Herzogenaurach in the early hours of Monday 16 April they didn't have much to fear from the local insurgents. Valentin Fröhlich, the conservative pre-war mayor, convinced the town's staunchest Nazis to avoid bloodshed by surrendering immediately. Again, the people of Herzogenaurach were spared from the atrocities that accompanied the fall of many German towns.

Apparently, some US tanks halted in front of the Dassler factory. They were pondering the destruction of the building, which was believed to harbour SS officers, when a young woman stepped out. The 28-year-old Käthe bravely walked towards the soldiers and pleaded with them to leave the factory intact. All that the people in there wanted was to make sports shoes, she explained. Käthe's charm probably helped, but the Americans had another motive to leave the Villa standing: it was clearly one of the most comfortable houses in town, and they needed a place to stay.

Chaos and uncertainty reigned in Herzogenaurach over the following weeks. Valentin Fröhlich was temporarily reinstated in the mayor's office while American troops rounded up the town's worst Nazis. Under the agreement sealed in the Ukrainian town of Yalta in February 1945, the former Reich was carved up into four occupied zones. The eastern quarter was placed under the rule of the Red Army, while the British took charge in the north and France was given two smaller chunks on the western side. But the southern part of the territory, from Bavaria to Frankfurt, was under the control of the Americans.

As part of their efforts to restore democracy, the military government set up so-called 'denazification committees'. Composed of representatives from several political parties, they examined the war records of thousands of suspects. Citizens were then classified into specific groups, indicating their level of involvement with the Nazi regime. The results of these investigations determined their rights to own a company or to take part in public life. Loyalties were put to the test as many attempted to minimize their guilt, often distorting the truth and shifting blame to others.

Among the occupying forces, the Americans and the British were most stringent about denazification. They closely observed social life, watching out for any signs of Nazi resurgence. To purge the conscience of German citizens, the US rulers bluntly confronted them with the unthinkable devastation caused by the Nazis, which many had refused to see and others failed to condemn. They instilled guilt and shame. The people of Herzogenaurach got their share when the Americans herded them into the local cinema and forced them to watch films that revealed the unspeakable horrors they discovered upon the liberation of Dachau concentration camp.

It was precisely this inferno that Rudolf Dassler claimed to have escaped when he returned to Herzogenaurach about two weeks after its liberation. Rudolf told his family, who last saw him being taken away by the Gestapo, that they had detained him for fourteen days. Then the local Gestapo chiefs rounded up some of the inmates and instructed guards to bring them to Dachau. The twenty-six men were to walk the two hundred miles down to the concentration camp in chains, shackled two by two.

On the way, Rudolf said, the driver who was supervising the march, Ludwig Müller, was instructed by a local officer of the Waffen-SS to shoot the prisoners. Müller ignored the command and led the prisoners further south, but they never reached Dachau. The convoy was halted by Americans near Pappenheim, and Müller gladly let the prisoners walk back to their homes.

When Rudolf Dassler returned to Herzogenaurach he was determined to regain his influence at Gebrüder Dassler, but at 5 p.m. on 25 July he was arrested again. This time he was in the hands of American soldiers. It was an 'automatic arrest', mandatory for anyone who had held a high-ranking position in the Nazi machine. In Rudolf Dassler's case, the arrest sheet stated that he was suspected of working for the SD, performing counter-espionage and censorship.

Like hundreds of thousands of other women in these chaotic days, Friedl Dassler desperately looked for her husband for several weeks, aided by her sister, Betti. When they finally located him in Hammelburg, a camp in the northern part of Franconia, Rudolf Dassler was fuming.

He had been told by the Americans that his arrest had been triggered by a denunciation, and he didn't have the slightest doubt about its source.

4

The Split

For Adolf Dassler it was back to scavenging. In the desolation that followed the Second World War, Gebrüder Dassler suffered from shortages of just about everything that was required to make sports shoes, from leather to glue and nails. As millions of Germans struggled through the debris, scraping for food and begging for shelter, sport was hardly a priority. The rescue came in the form of sports-crazy US soldiers, who were not prepared to sit around smalltown Bavaria without a weekly ballgame or two.

Having requisitioned the Villa, the American soldiers set about their task of helping to rebuild Germany and to restore its democracy. There was hardly any rubble to clear in Herzogenaurach, but many of its citizens suffered from hunger and squalid living conditions. Due to the inrush of millions of refugees from the eastern provinces of the former Reich, which had been annexed by Poland and the Soviet Union after the war, they often had to share their dwellings with strangers.

In principle the country was governed by a council comprising the supreme commanders of each zone, but the four Allies often failed to reach a unanimous decision and therefore went their own way. The Americans were particularly vocal in their opposition to punitive sanctions, believing that they would only undermine the return to peace. They deemed it smarter to alleviate the hardship of the Germans and turn the country into an efficient buffer against the increasingly menacing Soviets.

Food parcels and other forms of economic aid were vital if Germany were to get back on its feet, but the American occupying forces also regarded sport as an alternative means to lift the spirits of this utterly demoralized nation. Gripped by humiliation, grief and misery, the Germans could let off some steam on and around the football pitch. Barely six months after the end of the war, when others still deemed German sport and its exuberance indecent, the Americans approved the setting-up of an Association Football league for the south of the country. As for the soldiers themselves, their social life in Germany often revolved around sport. They needed sports shoes by the truckload.

For the American soldiers, the German shoes were something else. They had grown accustomed to the sneakers turned out by the likes of Converse, with rubber soles and canvas uppers. When the GIs discovered that Adolf Dassler had crafted the running shoes worn by Jesse Owens in Berlin, they made sure that the factory speedily obtained the approval of the military government. From the beginning of November 1945, Gebrüder Dassler was authorized to begin production for a consignment of shoes that would be used for basketball and baseball.

Eager to get their hands on Dassler shoes, American soldiers stationed in Herzogenaurach set aside any useful material they could find. One day they arrived with a truckload of discarded tents. They had to be cleaned up and brushed for hours, but eventually they were used to make lightweight running shoes.

The winter brought more orders for Gebrüder Dassler. For several months the machines kept busy producing thousands of ice hockey boots. The company was favoured for the order by the US army chiefs in Garmisch-Partenkirchen, in the Bavarian Alps, to cover the needs of many units. Adolf Dassler had another stroke of luck when he managed to get hold of a consignment of baseball gloves. He ripped them apart and used strips of their fine leather for the heels and eyelets of his running shoes, improving both the appearance and construction of the thick canvas uppers.

Such orders from the American Army Exchange meant that the Dasslers were relatively well-off. While others scraped for food, Adolf Dassler could barter shoes to obtain some extras for his wife and children. During the villa's occupation by the US army, the family had to move into the *Turm* (tower), a tall building adjacent to the factory, but their space was still relatively comfortable compared with many other families. At last peace broke out in the Dassler household as they worked doggedly to save Gebrüder Dassler. Then Rudolf came storming back.

For several months, the Hammelburg internment camp for German war prisoners consisted of little more than a bare field fenced off by barbed wire patrolled by heavily armed American soldiers. The sanitary conditions improved only slowly, as the barracks were not constructed until after the arrival of the prisoners. Internee 2597 Rudolf Dassler repeatedly wrote to the people in charge of the camp, desperate to make his voice heard and to return to Herzogenaurach, but Hammelburg was overflowing with hundreds of political prisoners, and in the immediate post-war months the Americans were intent on studying each case thoroughly.

While his file sat at the bottom of a huge stack, Rudolf Dassler prepared his defence. Imprisoned with him in Hammelburg was his cousin Valentin Zink, the Nazi propaganda chief in Herzogenaurach, and Markus Sehring, head of the NSDAP in Herzogenaurach since 1926. Many of the town's other leading Nazis were detained in the same camp. More importantly for Rudolf, the inmates included several men who agreed to act as witnesses in his favour. One of them was Friedrich Block, his immediate superior in Tuschin, who was arrested by the Americans as head of the intelligence service for the district. Another was Ludwig Müller, the man who supposedly escorted the convoy of twenty-six prisoners of the Gestapo, including Rudolf Dassler, from Nuremberg to Dachau.

The statement by Block appeared to confirm some of Rudolf Dassler's most paranoid suspicions about a plot to keep him away from Gebrüder Dassler. As his former superior in Tuschin wrote, Rudolf repeatedly asked for leave to take care of his shoe company. Block eventually agreed to release Dassler from his duties as soon as the local authorities gave their approval. However, Block continued, he then received an odd instruction from Nuremberg, marked 'secret', that 'Rudolf Dassler should not be allowed to take any leave for the purpose of checking on his factory'.

The investigation conducted by the Americans uncovered other things. They established that Rudolf joined the NSDAP in 1933 and had volunteered for the Wehrmacht in 1941. At the border police station in Tuschin, he worked on records of 'personal and smuggling cases', presumably helping to inculpate individuals accused of unauthorized trading or other illegal activities. The crux of the file, though, was Dassler's activities for the Gestapo in Nuremberg in March 1945: Rudolf Dassler contended that he merely reported to the office on a daily basis while they conducted investigations into his departure from Tuschin, but the Americans became convinced that he was lying.

As the US officer wrote in his report: 'According to his wife, interrogated [in] this office, he actually worked there. According to Adolf Dassler, subject's brother, also interrogated this office, Dassler actually worked there.' With a hint of irritation, the officer relayed Rudolf Dassler's claims that he was arrested by the Gestapo and sent to Dachau. 'Dassler continuously reminds the interrogator of this fact,' he noted. However, 'investigation of Dassler in Herzogenaurach reveals that all informants consider this as a mere cover by the Gestapo to protect him, considering his work in Poland in the Abwehr, his party affiliation and political Nazi ideals'.

The picture was less than flattering for Rudolf Dassler. The American investigator clearly felt that Dassler should not get away scot-free, but the chaos then reigning in the internment camps had forced the US authorities to alter their policies. They acknowledged that it would take decades to conscientiously clear up every single case. Just like Dassler's, hundreds of thousands of other files contained claims and counter-claims that were almost impossible to verify, due to obvious bad faith and the destruction of many documents. The delays were causing massive problems in the camps and frustration elsewhere, at a time when all agreed that efforts should concentrate on reconstruction. The Americans therefore decided to release all prisoners who were not considered a security threat. With several other men from Herzogenaurach, Rudolf Dassler was freed on 31 July 1946 – almost exactly one year after his arrest by the Americans.

His return caused ugly scenes, as the two brothers and their wives attempted to clear up what had happened during the war and its immediate aftermath. The rows were particularly explosive between Rudolf, who became obsessed with his brother's supposed betrayal, and Käthe, who staunchly defended her quiet husband. Rudolf was raging that he had been arrested on the back of 'a malicious denunciation', as he wrote to his US guards in Hammelburg. As he saw it, Käthe was a venomous hag who had wanted to oust him all along, and during the war she had used the most revolting means to push him out. Käthe vehemently denied any wrongdoing, and countered that Rudolf's resentment had driven him to some disgustingly disloyal deeds.

To make matters worse the two couples were still living under the same roof. By then Adolf's family had been enlarged again with the birth of a third daughter, Brigitte, in May 1946. The *Turm* was large enough for the Dasslers to erect partitions and organize separate homes for the two families, but the walls were too thin to protect the children's ears from the furious arguments that raged between their parents. Horst and Inge, the two eldest children of Adi and Käthe, were sent to boarding schools.

The situation finally became untenable when Adolf Dassler had to defend his own case before the local denazification committee in July 1946. Rudolf closely followed the deliberations, because they would have a decisive influence on the control of Gebrüder Dassler. From then on, the recriminations which the two couples hurled at each other in the *Turm* were thrown into the court proceedings. Rudolf's suspicions turned into vicious accusations.

Just two weeks before Rudolf's release, on 13 July 1946, Adolf was classified as a *Belasteter*, meaning that he had actively contributed to the Nazi regime and personally profited from it. The written ruling was devastating for Adolf, because it implied that he would be barred from the shoe factory and probably dispossessed. It was based on the *Fragebogen*, a form which each citizen had to fill out at the end of the war, indicating his or her party affiliations, as well as the opinions of several representatives of democratic society. Adolf Dassler could not deny his party membership, from 1933, and his involvement in the Hitlerjugend since 1935. On the other hand, he swiftly put together a thick file to protest the judgement of some local opposition leaders, who branded him '100% Nazi'. 'He was a proponent of the Nazi ideals and not liked in anti-fascist circles,' they wrote.

Adi did find some support from the mayor's office: 'In contrast with his brothers, D. is appreciated in the community and, contrary to his brothers, he was ready to help anyone,' was their official opinion. The pre-war mayor, Valentin Fröhlich, who was honoured by the Americans for his impeccable behaviour during hostilities and elected to the Land-rat, the regional council, emphasized the point in a personal letter: 'Anybody who knows Adolf Dassler would acknowledge that he is a man who is always prepared to help, regardless of status or political opinions,' he wrote. Fröhlich added that he had often expressed his disgust at Nazi policies in conversations with Adi Dassler and never felt it was unsafe to do so.

In his plea to the committee, Dassler added that only one of the sixty people who remained at the factory at the end of the war was a party member. He referred to Hans Zenger, whom Adolf refused to fire when he dropped out of the Hitlerjugend, and to Jakob Ploner, a known anti-fascist whom he continued to employ throughout the Nazi years. The five refugees and four prisoners whom Dassler had requested to work at the factory were treated as generously as the other employees: 'These nine people obtained extra rations of coffee from us every day, we often gave them extra bread and sometimes clothing,' said Adi.

On his ties with Nazi organizations, he argued that his membership of the NSDAP should be regarded as a sign of political ignorance. His activities in the Hitlerjugend were concerned exclusively with sport. He conscientiously stayed away from any political rallies. Before the war, Adolf Dassler had been a member of many sports clubs, some of them with conflicting political outlooks, from the liberal gymnastics club to Herzogenaurach's conservative FCH football club and even a workers' sports club called Union. 'The way I knew him, sports was the only kind of politics that counted for him. He didn't know political politics,' confirmed a longtime member of the local communist party, the KPD. Furthermore, Dassler wrote that he refused to be enrolled in the Volkssturm, the near-compulsory citizens' defence groups, and prevented others from joining by systematically arranging overtime work on the Sunday mornings when the Volkssturm met.

When it came to his relationship with Jews, the shoemaker's records confirmed that he continued to deal with Jewish leather traders long after this had become politically incorrect. But his most convincing piece of evidence in this respect was a letter from Hans Wormser, mayor of the adjoining village of Weisendorf, who described himself as a half-Jew. Wormser vividly recounted how Adolf Dassler warned him of his impending arrest by the Gestapo and sheltered the mayor in his property. 'A true supporter of Adolf Hitler would certainly not have done this, putting his existence and the well-being of his family on the line,' Wormser wrote.

Dealing with the accusation of profiteering, Dassler further contended that the increase of Gebrüder Dassler's sales was unrelated to any favours from the Nazi regime. True, the number of employees had roughly doubled to eighty between 1934 and 1938, but this was due to the fact that the demand for sports shoes had boomed after the Berlin Olympics. Since the ban on shoe production in October 1943 and the subsequent switch to weapons manufacturing, the company had lost about 100,000 Reichsmarks – a considerable sum.

None of this sufficed to clear his name completely. On 30 July, just as Rudolf was packing his few belongings in Hammelburg, Adi received another letter from the denazification committee, informing him that it had changed its verdict: Adolf Dassler was to be classified as a *Minderbelasteter*, which was less severe than the previous ruling but still meant that he was deemed guilty. He would have to pay a fine of 30,000 Reichsmarks, but most damagingly he would be on probation for two years. In other words, Gebrüder Dassler would be placed in the hands of a caretaker. For two years, Adolf Dassler would not be allowed to own or run his shoe factory. Somewhat panicked, Adi hired a lawyer who appealed the decision.

When the freshly liberated Rudolf Dassler was questioned about the wartime activities of Gebrüder Dassler, he leapt at the opportunity to implicate his brother. Rudolf apparently told the denazification committee that the weapons production had been organized solely by Adolf, that he knew nothing about such assignments and that he would have firmly opposed them.

This blatant lie infuriated Käthe Dassler. It was on this occasion that she wrote her own account of the wartime quarrels between the two brothers. Evidently exasperated, Käthe insisted that Adolf had consistently gone out of his way to help his brother, in spite of Rudolf's openly malevolent attitude. 'Rudolf Dassler further accuses my husband of having denounced him,' she wrote. 'I certify that this is untrue. My husband did everything that he could to exonerate his brother.' Käthe was equally livid that Rudolf accused her husband of holding political speeches at the Dassler factory. 'The speeches held inside and outside the factory should be attributed to Rudolf Dassler, as any factory employee could confirm,' she concluded.

Käthe's statement, written on 11 November 1946, was duly added to the denazification committee's files. Before the end of the month, it reversed its earlier verdict on Adolf Dassler, classifying him as a *Mitläufer* – one of the millions of Germans who became party members without actively contributing to the Nazi regime. For Adi Dassler, this was akin to a clearance. As a *Mitläufer* he was allowed to pursue his activities at Gebrüder Dassler, which was being solicited from all sides to step up production.

Cohabitation in the *Turm* was now impossible. After all the rows and mudslinging, the two brothers resolved to split. Rudolf Dassler gathered up his family and his belongings and moved across the Aurach. Convinced that Gebrüder Dassler would go bankrupt without him, Rudolf agreed to take control of the small shoe factory they owned on the Würzburgerstrasse, leaving the larger plant near the railway station to be run by his brother. Rudolf further agreed to leave the requisitioned Villa to Adolf and Käthe. The rest of their assets, from the equipment to the patents, was painstakingly divided between the two brothers.

Adolf and Rudolf let their employees pick the brother for whom they wanted to work. Predictably, most of the sales staff decamped to the Würzburgerstrasse while the technicians threw in their lot with Adolf. Their sister, Marie Körner, supported Adolf and Käthe. She could not forgive Rudolf for refusing to employ her two boys, who never returned from the war. The widowed Paulina opted to live with Rudolf and Friedl, who took gentle care of her until she died under dreadful conditions, from a skin disease that tormented her to distraction.

After many months of wrangles regarding the distribution of assets, the separation between the two brothers was finalized in April 1948. It paved the way for the registration of two separate companies over the following months. Adolf filed a registration for a company called Addas, but this was promptly turned down due to the objections of a German children's shoe company with a similar name, so he contracted his name and surname to form 'Adidas'. Rudolf did the same, registering 'Ruda' soon after the split. However, the name was deemed inelegant and plump. Rudolf then took on another suggestion and registered the much sleeker 'Puma'.

The rift between the two Dassler brothers tore apart their family, setting the scene for an ongoing feud over the coming decades. At the same time it deeply divided Herzogenaurach, with the Aurach river acting as a liquid partition between Rudolf's supporters on one bank and Adolf's on the other. It became known as the town where people always looked down, because they were careful to note which shoes someone was wearing before starting a conversation.

For the family and some close employees the feud was deadly serious, but in the conservative small town it gave rise to the wildest gossip. To this day, mischievous old men in Herzogenaurach whisper that the split was over catty women. One is convinced that Adolf showed Rudolf the door when he made a pass at Käthe. One of the latest rumours to have surfaced in Herzogenaurach is that Horst was fathered by Rudolf. Another spreads the story that the rows began when Rudolf was caught with his hands in the company kitty.

On either side of the Aurach, the split left the Dassler brothers half-stranded. Rudolf was joined by nearly all of Gebrüder Dassler's administrative and sales staff, but since most of the technical staff had stayed behind, Rudolf's men didn't have anything to sell. Conversely, Adolf quickly restarted production but he lacked any means of promotion. In his late forties, Adi Dassler had to crank up his business yet again.

To make up for Rudolf's abrupt departure, the rest of Adi's family was drawn into his company more intensely than intended. Käthe began to handle all sorts of small tasks, filling out orders and supervising dispatches. Her sister Marianne became another influential member of the Adidas family. The entire Martz family had been evacuated from Pirmasens at the beginning of 1939, like thousands of others who were unceremoniously driven out of the region by the construction of the Siegfried Line – a wall of bunkers and other concrete constructions erected by the Nazis ahead of the war along 630 kilometres of the country's western border. The Martz family was scattered far and wide, but they slowly congregated in Herzogenaurach, where Käthe found shelter for her relatives. Enamoured with a local man, Marianne decided to stay behind and help rebuild a sales force for Adidas.

Shortly after the separation, Adi called up the two women to inspect some samples. They watched curiously as several employees ran laps around the Dassler factory grounds. Their dark leather shoes were adorned with white strips of leather running down the sides, between two and six on each side.

Such strips had long been used by the Dasslers and other shoemakers to strengthen the sides of their shoes, but most of the time they weren't noticeable because they were made of the same leather as the rest of the upper, nearly always black or dark brown. Such uniformity made it hard for the Dasslers to back up their claims that some outstanding athletes had been wearing their spikes. On most pictures, even experts were unable to tell whose shoes the runners had on their feet. Advertising material and catalogues contained plenty of quotes from the athletes or their trainers extolling the virtues of Dassler shoes, but Adi Dassler figured that if the stripes were coloured white, they could be used to identify his spikes from afar.

The two-stripe design was rapidly discarded because it had been used by Gebrüder Dassler – they might as well avoid another bust-up with Rudolf – and four stripes looked somewhat confused. Three seemed an excellent compromise: a design that could easily be identified from a distance and would clearly distinguish Adidas from competing shoes. The trademark was registered in Germany in March 1949 at the same time as the company, the official title of which was 'Adolf Dassler adidas Schuhfabrik'. Adolf and Käthe Dassler designed an Adidas company letterhead with two long ascenders from the 'd's bridged by a three-striped spike to form a high-jump bar. The product was described by the lawyers as 'sports shoe with stripes running from the eyelets', but the company slogans referred to *Die Marke mit den drei Riemen* – the brand with the three stripes.

The Dasslers on the Adidas side were keenly aware of the advantages in terms of publicity. Shortly after the split with his brother Adi hired his own advertising manager, Wolfgang Krause. He was from Silesia, one of the millions of Germans who had fled the advances of the Red Army in the eastern provinces of the former Reich at the end of the war. A former grocer, Krause had become stranded in Herzogenaurach. He gladly took the meals which Adi and Käthe Dassler offered him, and later a job. While the word 'marketing' had still to be invented, Krause built on the reputation of Adidas by smartly exploiting its ties with athletes. Small ads placed in athletics magazines invariably featured a drawing of the distinctive three-striped shoe and a reference to a recent triumph.

On the other side of the Aurach, Rudolf Dassler quickly poached technicians from competing companies to run his share of Gebrüder Dassler's machines, often turning out shoes that looked intriguingly like his brother's designs. After all, there were still plenty of unemployed shoemakers in Herzogenaurach. Using the contact lists which Rudolf's aides had brought with them from Gebrüder Dassler, Puma sales rapidly took off.

The earliest form of the Puma logo was registered along with the brand name in October 1948, a square and rapacious-looking beast jumping through a 'D'. Just like his brother, Rudolf hit upon the thought of using white stripes on the side of his shoes, but his early version was just one thick stripe. This later evolved into the 'formstripe', a single stripe that started from the same place but then became thinner as it

7. *Rudolf Dassler* (with glasses) *endeared himself to many employees with a joyous and paternalistic touch.*

curved to the heel. The three stripes and the formstripe quickly became critical in the fight between Adidas and Puma, as the two companies became increasingly reliant on publicity to boost their sales.

For a few years after the end of the war, the Dassler brothers barely met any competition beyond Herzogenaurach. Germany was barred from international sport and in many countries it was deemed un-patriotic, if not prohibited outright, to buy German products. Therefore, the Dasslers' immediate rivals were other German shoemakers, some of whom also made headway in these years. The most prominent of these was Eugen Brütting, a specialist from Nuremberg who outfitted many German athletes with spikes called Meister Eugenio. But the Dasslers had long set their sights beyond Germany, and they eagerly waited for an opportunity to begin their international comeback.

This came in 1952 at the Helsinki Olympics. The first post-war Games had been held in London in 1948 but the Dassler brothers were then in the middle of their divorce and Germany was anyway not allowed to take part. But Adi Dassler had thoroughly prepared the ground for the Helsinki Games by establishing long-distance friendships with leading athletes. He had gone out of his way to meet the trainers of Olympic teams and convinced them to give Adidas spikes a try. Adi had made sure that, in spite of the restrictions on international trade, the Adidas name had still travelled well beyond Germany. He built on this reputation by making the journey to Finland.

Among the most spectacular athletes in Helsinki was Emil Zatopek, the Czech long-distance runner, shod in Adidas as he came panting down the finishing straight with his nose running and his tongue hanging out. As Zatopek explained, he was 'not talented enough to run and smile at the same time'. He went on to take an astonishing three medals for the 5,000 metres, the 10,000 metres and the marathon, although he had never run the longer distance before. The crowd chanted his name as he entered the stadium way ahead of the next contestant. Zatopek was already signing autographs by the time the silver medallist arrived.

Unfortunately for Adidas, Zatopek's shoes had only two stripes. The Czech runner, whom Adi Dassler had contacted after his notable performance at the 1948 Olympics, gladly wore three-striped spikes for training and his wife, Dana, a Czech javelin champion and gold medallist in Helsinki, received separate batches of three-striped shoes. But for the Helsinki Olympics Zatopek asked Adi to remove one of the stripes. As he explained, he didn't want to aggravate his country's communist rulers by conspicuously wearing the product of a capitalist economy. (He abandoned his caution in later years by supporting the Czech uprising, which cost him several years of hard labour.)

Stripes were the cause of yet more headaches for Adi when he discovered that Karhu, the leading Finnish company, was using three of them as well. Karhu spikes had for years been fitted with anything between two and six stripes for reinforcement, but the Finns apparently failed to grasp their publicity potential.

In Helsinki, Karhu had a field day. Many of the athletes who turned up for the Olympics seized the opportunity to visit Karhu's factories and pick up a pair of the famous Finnish spikes. As he carried the Olympic torch to the stadium, Paavo Nurmi, the Finn who dominated long-distance running in the twenties, was wearing Karhu shoes. Fourteen of the gold medals handed out in Helsinki had Karhu-clad feet. Even for the Adidas technicians it was tricky to make out from a distance if the three-striped shoes on the track were Adidas or Karhu. This was fine so long as Karhu were winning, but Adi didn't plan to stay behind them for long.

8. *Emil Zatopek leads in Helsinki.*

Since trademark legislation was rather sketchy at the time, Dassler decided to approach the matter amicably. Shortly after the Olympics, he invited some of the Karhu managers to an international sports fair in Frankfurt. The Finns were so naive that they agreed to relinquish their three stripes in exchange for a relatively small sum and two bottles of schnapps.

On the other side of the Aurach, Puma made much of the tears of Josy Barthel, a tiny runner from Luxembourg. He was unable to contain his emotions after he unexpectedly won the 1,500 metres, beating Roger Bannister and wearing Puma spikes. However, this would not have the same repercussions as the much wider publicity achieved by Adi's three stripes. The Helsinki Olympics kick-started the international business of Adidas, which began to export its three-striped shoes to nearly thirty countries.

When it came to football, Rudolf Dassler held some of the best cards. With their rounded ankle cut, Puma's football boots looked remarkably sleek compared with the clunky, steel toe-capped versions worn by most players at the time. By building quietly on his assets, Rudolf might well have seized the leadership in the largest chunk of the sports market. But unfortunately for Puma, he instead picked a fight with the wrong man.

5

Screw Them On!

The seating arrangements were always the same: when the players on the German football team boarded their bus, they made sure to leave the first row empty. On the right-hand side of the aisle, the front seat would be occupied by Sepp Herberger, their trainer. The seat on the left was reserved for Adi Dassler.

A short man with a crumpled face, Herberger had long worked with the Dassler brothers. The relationship had initially been built up by Rudolf Dassler, but the elder brother blew it. 'You're a small king,' Rudolf reportedly told Herberger. 'And if you don't suit us, we'll just pick another guy.' It remains unclear what provoked this tirade – Rudolf's friends argued that the trainer had demanded payment if the players wore Puma and his enemies asserted that he had simply flown off the handle again – but in any event it turned out to be one of his most damaging outbursts.

For several years, Sepp Herberger had struggled to give any substance to his position. Hitler famously took little interest in football, and his lack of enthusiasm was made worse by the poor performance of the German team during the Nazi era. Albert Forster, the Nazi leader of Danzig, once persuaded Hitler to attend a football match during the Berlin Olympics in 1936, assuring him that the team stood to win. Josef Goebbels, who was watching the game with them, nearly suffered a nervous breakdown. 'The Führer is very excited, I can barely contain myself. A real bath of nerves,' he wrote. As things turned out, Hitler witnessed a humiliating defeat to Norway. The debacle led to the dismissal of Otto Nerz, then national coach. He was swiftly succeeded by his assistant, Josef 'Sepp' Herberger.

A former banking clerk, Herberger went to amazing lengths to piece together a decent German team. Walking around with a thick, green notebook, he assiduously attended dreary league games. His patience paid off in 1938 when he spotted Fritz Walter, then an 18-year-old player in Kaiserslautern, a town in the west of Germany with a strong football club. The *Reichstrainer* began to fill entire pages with notes on 'FW' and he spent much of the following years grooming his favourite player for the leadership of a national side.

In spite of Hitler's distaste for football, the sport continued to be stimulated by the Nazis. The team took part in several international encounters in the late thirties – causing one of the most disgraceful scenes in English football history when, before a friendly in Berlin in May 1938, the entire England team gave the Nazi salute. Even as the war raged, propaganda minister Josef Goebbels was convinced that the Nazis should keep investing in their football team. As he remarked in his diaries, a football victory seemed to matter more to Germans than any eastern conquest. It was not until the last years of the war that the football programme was suspended entirely.

Throughout the war Herberger's efforts were thwarted by the armed conflict, which did not spare his men. It took a lot of persistence and cunning to get eleven able-bodied players on the same pitch. On several occasions, he made up military distinctions for his players to prove that they had contributed to the war effort, and he had several players transferred to a Luftwaffe division. In the case of Fritz Walter this raised some eyebrows, since the young soldier admitted on arrival that he had never seen the inside of an aircraft. The point was that the air-force unit was run by a footballing friend and well-known fighter pilot, Hermann Graf, who would protect Walter and make sure he'd get plenty of practice.

After some kow-towing to the denazification committee, Herberger was reinstated as German coach after the war. His opponents pointed to the fact that he had knowingly served the purposes of the Nazis and contributed to their propaganda machine and nowhere in his hundreds of pages of notes is there a hint of soul-searching on the wider implications of his role, yet those in charge of the trainer's selection had to admit that they could never hope to find a more qualified candidate.

Herberger then redoubled his efforts to find both surviving players and proper equipment for them. When Germany was quartered in the aftermath of the war, each of the victorious powers held its own views on football, impeding the launch of a national league, but this was almost incidental compared with the problems caused by Germany's post-war shortages. As millions of people with bombed-out homes

scraped a living, football could hardly be regarded as a priority anywhere. Most of the authorized clubs and players had to find their own
equipment – sometimes using discarded Nazi banners, the swastikas
carefully removed, to make shirts and corner flags.

All these troubles failed to diminish public enthusiasm for football,
the popularity of which had spread throughout Europe. There was no
other sport that unleashed such mass fervour all across the continent,
drawing hundreds of thousands of players and spectators every week at
all levels. The Dassler brothers easily identified football as a sport offering the most stupendous prospects in terms of sales, and a prominent
platform on which to build their reputation.

Unlike their counterparts in several other European countries, German
football players long remained amateur, supposed to hold down a regular job and to refuse any compensation for their football talents. The
rules were often bent by club owners, mostly industrial chieftains who
bought a football club to enhance their local standing. The strongest
players received under-the-table payments or other incentives to stay
with their clubs. However, there still wasn't much money to be earned
from equipment, which was regarded as purely functional. The teams
just used whatever they could lay their hands upon, and it certainly
would not have occurred to any of them to ask for payment to print a
company's name on their shirts or to wear specific football boots. The
same went for the players picked by Sepp Herberger: when they were
told that they would be wearing Adidas at the next World Cup in 1954,
none of them thought of asking for an endorsement fee.

Since Rudolf's rebuff, the German trainer had cultivated a close
relationship with Adi. Both men of few words, they formed a quiet
couple, understanding each other with a short sentence and a nod.
Herberger appreciated the bootmaker's devotion to detail. Adi became
a familiar sight in the small entourage of the national team – the little
man who sat next to Herberger with a modest grin and a tool-box,
always at the ready to get the boots precisely right for each of the players,
tightening a screw here and adjusting some padding there.

Until the end of the war, the German boots were inspired by their
ancestors in Britain. With a high ankle-cut, a thick leather sole and
heavy toe caps, they would have gone unnoticed on a building site.
To some extent, the British clodhoppers were right for the playing
conditions of the day: still made of permeable leather, balls could become

painfully heavy if the pitch was wet. The sometimes brutal British style of a 'kick and rush' play was another explanation for the heavy protection. Some British boots were even designed purposely for 'hacking', whereby a player is kicked on the shin while running with the ball.

Both Dassler brothers envisaged a much slicker and lighter boot. Before their split Adi had been working on all sorts of adjustments to reduce the weight of the boots. Football players spent most of their time on the pitch running, and over the ninety minutes of a game they covered a good few miles. If just a little weight could be removed from the boots, the Dasslers figured, a great deal of energy could be conserved.

Puma came up with some of the sleekest football boots yet seen, praised by the coaches of many German clubs. They distinguished themselves as the lightest in the market, their weight roughly half that of their British equivalents. Puma's innovations were manifold during these years, and ranged from new lacing patterns to improved leather cleats.

But before the 1954 World Cup (Germany had not entered the competition in 1950), Adi Dassler began to experiment with an unprecedented concept: a construction that was intended to make Adidas boots flexible and to refine the players' contact with the ball. They would have no toe caps and they would match Puma in terms of weight. In the four years that preceded the tournament in Switzerland, the German players were sent several batches of light Dassler boots. Some of them expressed their disapproval, complaining of injury to their toes and ankles, but the Dassler boot was perfectly suited for more refined players such as Fritz Walter, who relied on their skilful touch.

As things stood at the time, Herberger needed all the help he could get from his friend in Herzogenaurach. The German team had resumed playing international fixtures four years earlier but its prospects seemed uncertain, in line with the mood that prevailed in the country at the time. The three Western-occupied zones had merged to form the Bundesrepublik Deutschland, the Federal Republic of Germany, with Konrad Adenauer at its head. At the same time, the Germans had lost a large chunk of their country to the German Democratic Republic, which was fast turning into a Soviet satellite. West Germany had the Deutschmark, its own constitution and an economy that was recovering at staggering pace, yet all of this failed to lift the veil of humiliation and grief that still shrouded the country. Unable to shake off their overwhelming guilt, many Germans were mired in soul-searching and confusion.

The (West) German side was built around Fritz Walter, with whom the childless Herberger had developed an almost filial relationship. The coach added Ottmar Walter, Fritz's younger brother, who narrowly escaped death during the war when his ship was ambushed in the Channel. One of the trainer's wildest bets was Helmut Rahn, an impetuous striker from Essen with a penchant for beer and various forms of unruliness. Sepp Herberger described him as a 'genius at positive improvisation, who never ceases to surprise us'.

As for Herberger himself, the pundits didn't quite know what to make of him. He showed unwavering confidence, delighting reporters with profound comments that qualified him as the inventor of football philosophy: 'The game lasts ninety minutes', 'After the game is before the game' and, most famously, 'The ball is round'.

The competition in Switzerland proved to be unpredictable. The hopeful England team of Stanley Matthews was a disappointment, as were the Champions Uruguay and the fancied Austrians. After some roller-coaster progress Herberger's squad made it to the final, which would pit them against the Hungarians. Led by Ferenc Puskás, the heroic Hungarian striker, the Mighty Magyars had not conceded a single international defeat in more than four and a half years. This time the prognosis for the game, scheduled for 4 July at Berne's Wankdorf Stadium, was near-unanimous: the Germans, who had already been battered 8–3 by Puskás and his team-mates in the group stage, didn't stand a chance.

On that fateful day, Dassler and Herberger scanned the skies that hung over their balcony at the Belvedere Hotel, overlooking Lake Thun. They were hoping for some rain, because Fritz Walter was known to favour heavy pitches. There was not a cloud in sight that morning, but by the time the players departed for the stadium they were delighted to feel the first drops of a steady downpour.

The time had come for Adi Dassler to do his trick. As he revealed to his friend Herberger before the start of the World Cup, the bootmaker had just come up with a technical invention that became known as adjustable studs – to be screwed in or out, in several lengths, depending on the state of the pitch. If it was dry, the players could keep short studs to give them traction. But if the grass turned to mud, the studs could easily be lengthened to increase the grip of the boots on the slippery surface. 'Adi, screw them on!' Sepp Herberger instructed when it became clear that the Wankdorf Stadium would soon be soaked.

The German boots could not prevent Ferenc Puskás from hammering in his first goal just minutes into the game. After a sloppy defensive move, the Germans were two goals down in the eighth minute and their fears of a humiliation seemed more justified than ever. Still, Herberger's men fought back tooth and nail. By half-time they looked at each other in disbelief. They had levelled with the mighty Hungarians.

The dénouement came just six minutes before the end of the game. Supposed to provide a calm, matter-of-fact description to the millions of people glued to their radios, a German reporter flipped. 'Schäfer delivers a cross into the box. Header, cleared,' commented Herbert Zimmermann, still calmly. But then he saw the ball landing on Helmut Rahn's feet. 'Rahn should take a deep shot, Rahn shoots. Goal, goal, goal!' he shrieked. After a moment of stunned silence he tried to capture the madness of it all. 'Germany lead three to two, five minutes before full-time! Call me mad, call me crazy!'

Zimmermann's voice betrayed his nerves over the next few minutes, willing the whistle to blow. Hundreds of jubilant fans then ran onto the field and scenes of boisterous elation erupted all across Germany. The exhausted players lifted Herberger onto their shoulders. He tugged at Adi Dassler, insisting that the bootmaker should be included in the victory snapshot.

The unlikely triumph would be celebrated as the unofficial rebirth of German democracy – a founding moment for the Bundesrepublik. On paper, the country had regained its economic standing and earned its democratic credentials. Yet for millions of people, it was Helmut Rahn's shot that ended the dark years of shame and shortages suffered by many Germans after the defeat of the Nazi regime. For the first time in many years, they could innocently rejoice together and affirm their pride in something German. It created a reassuring sense of togetherness, as millions of Germans identified with the triumph. The euphoria was captured in an unequivocal phrase: 'Germany is somebody again!'

Due to the amazing outcome of the game, as well as its repercussions, the 1954 final was heralded as *das Wunder von Bern*: the miracle of Berne. Along with the tired football heroes and their deadpan coach, Adi Dassler was widely acclaimed as an instrument of the triumph. German newspapers tagged him 'Shoemaker of the nation', while others marvelled at the ingenuity of Dassler boots and their screw-in studs.

9. Adi Dassler with Sepp
Herberger on the pitch of the
Wankdorf Stadium, Berne,
after the team's unexpected
victory in the 1954 World
Cup.

'What a Dassler!' ran an English newspaper headline. It pointed out that
the Adidas boot was 'only half the weight of the orthodox English
football boot'.

On the other side of the Aurach, the compliments stung badly. Rudolf
Dassler was entirely sidelined in Switzerland, crushed by his younger
brother. The technicians at Puma angrily claimed that they had introduced light boots with screw-in studs several months before the Berne
game. The protests were drowned in the euphoria of the Berne triumph.
Yet there is no denying that Adidas adroitly milked the Swiss miracle.

The victory inspired a slogan which Adidas printed on all its stationery
and packaging: 'Adidas, der Sportschuh der Weltbesten!' ('Adidas, the
sports shoe of the world champions!'). In advertising inserts the company
proudly depicted itself as the inventor of the screw-in stud and, by
extension, the brand that was at the forefront of the football business.

The truth of the matter was that, on both sides of the Aurach, the
Dasslers had begun to fiddle with studs long before the match against
the Hungarians. More than two years earlier, a football club in Bremen
warmly thanked Adidas for its delivery of Matador boots with screw-in

studs. As for Puma, it proudly advertised its own studs in German newspapers in May 1954, boasting that its boots could be fitted 'with the well-tried and approved *Schraubstollen*'.

What the bickering brothers altogether failed to acknowledge was that the light boots they came to regard as their trademark had long been used in other parts of the footballing world. They had been spotted by Stanley Matthews, a remarkably talented England player, when he travelled to Brazil to play in the 1950 World Cup. They were so light that the Brazilians appeared to be flying over the pitch, and Matthews observed that the absence of toe protection enabled them to bend balls with incredible precision. Awe-struck by the deftness of the South American players, he brought a pair back with him from Rio.

Upon his return from Brazil Matthews turned to the Cooperative Wholesale Society (CWS) shoe factory in Heckmondwike in Yorkshire. They pulled the Brazilian sample apart and agreed to make boots along the same lines for the player. By English standards, their lightness was unprecedented: entirely hand-made using kangaroo leather, they weighed just two ounces. Matthews boasted that he could fold them up and put them in his pocket. 'They kept him going when he was getting old and no longer wanted to drag heavy boots around the pitch,' said Donald Ward, the engineer who crafted the boots Matthews wore. 'The problem was that they were not very resistant, so I had to make a new pair for almost every game.'

On the back of this arrangement the CWS went on to make a less sophisticated range of boots bearing the Stanley Matthews name – apparently the first ever deal of this kind. The endorsement earned the player sixpence a pair, and CWS sold more than half a million of them. Intriguingly, they had three stripes running down the sides, closely resembling the Adidas emblem, which was still hard to protect under existing trademark rules, especially when other shoemakers argued that the stripes were used merely as reinforcement or decoration.

But by then, the Dassler boots had travelled much further. While the Stanley Matthews boot was being sold to a largely British clientele, the Dasslers had fully grasped the concept of international marketing. The Berne boots were given such exposure that Adidas was suddenly bombarded with requests from abroad. One of the most interesting queries came in the form of a letter from Ray Schiele, a German who had moved to Canada in the early fifties and taken on all sorts of sales assignments, peddling anything from marmalade to locomotives. A football enthusiast, he pleaded with Käthe Dassler to send him some Adidas football boots. The three pairs which he received didn't suffice to build up a business, but Schiele persisted and he broke through when he obtained the endorsement of the Edmonton Eskimos, the local football team.

Ray Schiele was later placed at the head of the company's first foreign subsidiary. While the Dasslers fully controlled all of their operations, they built up such a close relationship with Schiele that they gave him a large chunk of Adidas Canada. Over the next five years the Canadian business grew so rapidly that it had to move three times. As scores of other traders began to hawk Adidas in the fifties, the three stripes established an international advance with which others would never manage to catch up.

Although Adolf Dassler was reluctant to leave his workshop in Herzogenaurach, Käthe steered the setting-up of an export department, from which she dispatched three-striped football boots all around Europe. The Dasslers pumped up their production volumes to roughly 2,000 pairs per day, but they were still unable to meet the exploding demand. They began to consider building more factories, beginning with a second German plant in Scheinfeld, about thirty kilometres to the north of Herzogenaurach.

With no competition from his bullying brother, Adolf imposed himself as *der Chef* at Adidas. Quiet and withdrawn, he gladly entrusted business relationships to his wife, and he was still most at ease behind his desk, poring over technical drawings, but his employees on the shop floor appreciated the little man's down-to-earth attitude and deadpan humour. Two things that Adi did not tolerate, however, were sloppiness and ignorance. 'If Adi felt that somebody was not completely up to scratch, just because he held up a shoe in the wrong way, the poor guy was out,' recalled Horst Widmann, long-time personal assistant. 'The same went for anybody who spoke up at meetings for the sake of it. Adi just didn't have time for these kinds of people.'

Dassler's own office was littered with strips of leather, rubber samples and scores of little notes. 'He was particularly prolific at night,' said Heinrich Schwegler, one of his early assistants. 'In the morning he would do the rounds with his scribblings and hand them out. That was the way he organized his business.' The heavy machinery sometimes filled Adi with fear, however, and with good reason: some years earlier he had been using the sharp leather punch and forgot that it often recoiled. The machine cleanly severed the index finger of his left hand.

His experiments concentrated on weight and materials. Adidas technicians tried everything from dog to pig to ostrich leather until, like CWS before them, they discovered kangaroo and established it as a norm for leather football boots. The advantage was that, unlike other sorts of leather, kangaroo just stretched on one side. If it was used the right way, it would allow the boot to adjust to the width of the player's foot without loosening at the toes and ankles.

Fresh techniques to process rubber and plastic, devised by the chemical industry, provided Adi Dassler with plenty more scope to potter about. They revolutionized the manufacture of many consumer goods, notably Tupperware, and they entirely changed the look of sports shoes, which could now be made with much more versatile plastic soles.

The informal relationship which Adi Dassler cultivated with Sepp Herberger and his players yielded many improvements. Uwe Seeler, a chubby teenager from Hamburg, was among the players who provided Dassler with invaluable comments on his boots. The two had known each other since Seeler joined the national youth squad in the early fifties. Like many German boys at the time, Uwe regarded any kind of shoes as a prized possession – never mind football boots. He was thrilled when Adi Dassler lent him a pair. Ever the polite lad, Seeler insisted that he wanted to brush off the mud on his boots before he handed them back after training, but Dassler wouldn't hear of it: the point was that he wanted to study exactly where the mud had stuck to the cleats.

Over the years, Uwe Seeler became a regular guest at the Dassler home, now formally known as the Villa. Dassler would then haul him to his workshop and excitedly display all the samples he was working on. 'He was completely obsessed. He harangued me all day, starting from breakfast, about all the things that popped up in his mind,' Seeler recalled. 'He never gave it a rest.'

On the other side of the Aurach, Rudolf ruled over his company more brazenly. He burst into meetings with resounding laughter, brimming with enthusiasm. Prone to paternalistic chats with the workers, Rudolf wouldn't hesitate to sit down and share a packed lunch with them. He inspired much loyalty at the company, where most employees regarded their chief as a good-humoured patriarch. When his mood swung, which occurred quickly and recurrently, the employees soon became aware of it, too. Rudolf made his presence felt loudly under any circumstances, cheering away one minute and booming with anger the next. But many who worked with him were still charmed by his wit and his ebullient manner.

The problem was that, for all his impulsiveness, Rudolf often had the reflexes of a small-time family businessman, 'tight and generous at the same time'. 'Sometimes we made mistakes because Rudolf didn't have a real entrepreneurial attitude,' said Peter Janssen, a former production manager. 'He was often exceedingly thrifty and even more risk-averse. For me it was always a struggle to convince him when we needed to buy upgraded machines.'

In the tug-of-war between the Dassler brothers, the women had to pull their weight. They were meant to support their husbands, to lend a hand here and there and to contribute to the family atmosphere at the company. They were always at the ready to welcome guests, athletes and retailers who just dropped by to pick up some spikes and to have a chat with the Dasslers. Forging such friendly relationships was critical at a time when money hardly played a role in sports: athletes just picked the shoes that fitted best or the ones that were recommended by their trainer, but a friendly touch could still make all the difference.

Käthe was one of Adolf's most precious weapons. With her forceful personality and diplomatic charm, she more than made up for her husband's withdrawn attitude. She became known among German employees as *die Cheffin*, and some even referred to her as 'Catherine the Great'. Aided by an inventive housemaid, Käthe turned the Villa into a byword for hospitality in the sports world. Entire football teams crashed into the kitchen before their games in Nuremberg. Since the departure of Rudolf and the Dassler parents, six rooms had been refurbished for the many guests who turned up in Herzogenaurach. With Käthe, retailers and athletes instantly felt at ease. As many recalled, the Dasslers treated them almost as members of the family. There were always some spare boots for footballers who dropped by at the weekend. Athletes were ushered into the kitchen without further ado, a hot meal shoved under their nose.

On the other side of the Aurach, Friedl Dassler was similarly support-ive of Rudolf. Her gentle attentions were appreciated by the employees,

10. Rudi's big signing was Ferenc Puskás, the illustrious Hungarian striker.

who called her *die Puma-Mutter*, the Puma mother. She managed to put up with the mood swings of her husband, who was becoming increasingly gruff, but Friedl still couldn't compete with Käthe's ebullient, spontaneous charm.

The diminutive general manager of Sporthaus Löhr, a specialist retailer in Duisburg, vividly experienced the contrast. The little man was exhausted and rain-soaked when he arrived in Herzogenaurach, late on a Sunday afternoon after a long bike ride. Before the dissolution the retailer had dealt with both brothers, though primarily Rudolf, and hoped to gain appointments with both for the next morning. On the Puma side of the Aurach Friedl, peering out at the rain, politely told the retailer that Rudolf would speak to him on Monday and sent him on his way, but when he rang Käthe's doorbell she immediately pulled the apologetic and dripping retailer inside. A few minutes later, freshly showered and wearing some of Adi's clothes, he was devouring a warming dinner at the Dasslers' kitchen table. The next morning, he didn't bother to attend the Puma meeting.

West Germany's World Cup triumph reinforced Adi Dassler's edge, but Puma continued to expand alongside. The Adidas camp attributed this chiefly to the cheek of the Puma technicians, accused of blatantly copying Adidas innovations. 'If there had been a hole left in Rudolf every time I had to poke at him and say, "Heh, that was my invention", he would look today like a piece of Gruyère,' Adolf grumbled. The suspicions led to a volley of lawsuits.

One of the most bizarre *Dassler* v. *Dassler* disputes erupted in 1958, after the World Cup in Sweden. Featuring some of the 1954 veterans, along with the hard-grafting Uwe Seeler, Herberger's squad lost a turbulent semi-final to Sweden, but there was nothing the host nation could do in the final to defeat the supreme Brazilians. Rudolf Dassler seized the opportunity to sue Adidas for the slogan which proclaimed that it was outfitting the world champions. Rudolf Dassler argued that the line had become untruthful, since some of the Brazilian football players had been wearing Puma.

Wolfgang Krause, then in charge of advertising at Adidas, ignored the warning. Rudolf Dassler filed a legal complaint, demanding that the slogan should be removed immediately. 'Puma attempted to paralyse us completely,' Krause recalled. The court ruled in Puma's favour, but it still gave Adidas several weeks to change all of its letterheads, order sheets and shoe boxes.

Adidas took revenge through a fishmonger who lived opposite the Puma building on the Würzburgerstrasse. Before the court case he had acquired an old van that once belonged to Adidas. The brand's tag-line, *Der Sportschuh der Weltbesten!*, was still brightly painted on the side of the van. There was nothing the enraged Puma people could do to prevent the fishmonger from parking the offending vehicle right under their office window until it was eaten away by rust.

The two brothers invested considerably in their legal shenanigans. While Rudolf Dassler's complaints were mostly targeted at Adidas, he once filed a suit against Möbus, another German sports-shoe company – arguing that the stripes on the Möbus spikes too closely resembled the 'formstripe' used by Puma. Frieda Möbus, the company's general manager, obtained unexpected support to fight off Puma. Rudolf Dassler was defeated by Möbus 'with active support from Adi Dassler and the patent lawyers at Adidas', as the company's owners observed gratefully.

By the end of the fifties, the feuding Dassler brothers both ruled over respected sports companies. Puma was most firmly established in

German club football. Adidas had achieved much stronger recognition on the international scene and it would remain unrivalled as the national team's footwear of choice as long as Herberger remained at its helm. Nearing retirement age, the two brothers weren't yet prepared to relinquish the leadership of their companies, but they could each rest assured that, when the time came, their sons would drive Adidas and Puma with equal obstinacy.

6

Olympic Handouts

Horst Dassler was in London in 1956 to brush up on his English when his parents rang. Adi and Käthe insisted that their son should depart at once. He would have to pack his bags quickly and hop on the next plane to the other end of the world.

Barely twenty years old, Horst Dassler was to peddle Adidas spikes at the Melbourne Olympics. There wasn't any other reliable person at the company who spoke English, and Adidas could not afford to stay away from Australia. To be filmed for television around the world, the 1956 Games could be a prodigious stage for the three stripes.

To some extent, Horst Dassler had been groomed for this assignment from the moment he began to walk. On both sides of the Dassler family, Adolf and Rudolf's children were all drawn into the business, starting with menial tasks during their school and university holidays and graduating to full-time positions in adulthood. But for Horst Dassler, the Melbourne Olympics represented much more than a student job: it marked the onset of a career that would reshape the sporting world.

Horst was the eldest of Adolf and Käthe's children, and he remained their only son. He spent much of his childhood in the Villa together with his four sisters – Käthe had given birth to a fourth daughter, Sigrid, in 1953 – and his cousins Armin and Gerd. In spite of the war's deprivations, the Dassler children were among the most privileged in Herzogenaurach. When the delivery boys arrived with bread and vegetables from their garden patches, they marvelled at the toys in the Dasslers' living room.

Yet the childhood of the older children was deeply affected by the war and the rift between their parents. None of the boys dared to enquire about the motives behind the split. Once their fathers had settled on opposite sides of the Aurach, their offspring barely needed telling that they should not mingle with their cousins. Like the rest of the village they had to stick to their own side – at a safe distance from the relatives and playmates with whom they had shared a house since birth.

At the weekends Horst was often dragged along for lengthy runs in the forest with his father. They spent hours running together, pausing occasionally to learn throwing and jumping techniques. Horst's average school grades probably didn't mean as much to Adi Dassler as his son's deftness with the javelin – a discipline at which Adi excelled, partly owing to the expert advice he had received from Jo Waitzer. In turn, Horst's prowess was rewarded with a distinction as Germany's junior javelin champion.

The young man relished the shared sporting activities which gave him time to forge bonds with his father, albeit silent ones. 'My father wasn't exactly bubbly in terms of conversation. His words tended to be pragmatic,' Horst told a German reporter much later. Between sprints, Adolf often consulted his son about the business. When it came to his mother, Horst Dassler's biographer noted that 'he respected her highly and, to some extent even appreciated her', but 'he didn't have such a close relationship to his mother'.

On the Puma side, Armin Dassler was bullied into the company. Rudolf and Friedl's eldest son pleaded with his parents to let him study electronics, but they wouldn't hear of it. Rudolf wanted him to learn the tricks of the shoe business as soon as he left college. Armin Dassler long endured the displeasure of his father, who made it cruelly clear that he held high ambitions for his son, and that he had been disappointed. 'Rudolf wanted a child with athletic gifts and supreme intelligence,' recalled Betti Strasser, Armin's aunt. 'He constantly belittled Armin, often in public.'

This was all the more appalling since Rudolf displayed apparently unjustified indulgence towards his second son, Gerd, ten years Armin's junior. Although Rudolf himself sometimes regretted the rift with his younger brother, he did little to prevent a repeat on his side of the family. By openly favouring Gerd, he stimulated aggressive and sometimes unhealthy competition between his two sons.

The problems also appeared at work, where the tension between

Rudolf and Armin caused embarrassing scenes. 'The relationship was not easy,' said Peter Janssen, one of Armin's former schoolmates and later a Puma board member. 'Young Armin was eager to climb the ladder, but his father consistently pushed him down.' Although Armin showed genuine respect for his father, it was never reciprocated.

The disputes between her sons crushed Friedl. She often begged her husband to put an end to this injustice, but he consistently brushed her pleas aside. Once a joyous and courageous woman, Friedl crumbled under the relationship with her despotic husband.

On the other side of the Aurach, Horst Dassler was brought up in a more harmonious setting. During the war he spent four years at the Bavarian monastery of Ettal, where he was less likely to encounter the terrors of the day. Thereafter he returned to attend the Fridericianum college in Erlangen, where he received a general education with a humanist slant. A quiet and unpretentious teenager, Horst commuted to Erlangen on the little train that halted nearly in front of the family's door. Then, after two years in a Nuremberg school of commerce and a stay in Barcelona to learn Spanish, Horst followed his father's footsteps to Pirmasens. Staying with his mother's family, he took a two-year course at the town's respected *Schuhfachschule*. Adi Dassler deemed that for his son to understand the craft was vital preparation to one day run the company and hold credible discussions with athletes.

But in Melbourne in 1956 the young Dassler heir demonstrated skills that could not be acquired anywhere.

A lean 20-year-old with intense eyes and a hawkish nose, Horst Dassler made the trip to Australia with a couple of summer suits and the address of an Adidas retailer in Melbourne. But when he landed, after a harrowing three-day journey, the Adidas spikes sent over by his parents were still blocked in the docks, awaiting clearance along with the Puma consignment.

Horst tackled the problem with characteristic shrewdness. Although the Olympics were a tall order for someone so untested, he knew exactly what was expected of him. He pleaded with well-known athletes to write to the customs officials, arguing that they needed Adidas shoes for the Olympics. There were also rumours – never substantiated – that money found its way into the pockets of a few customs men somewhere along the line. Whatever the truth, the outcome was that Horst's crates were released while the Puma consignment remained locked in the docks.

Melbourne was cheerfully dressed up for the occasion, with floral displays and fluttering flags all across the town. The exuberant atmosphere was marred only by the political upheavals that rumbled elsewhere: just two weeks before the opening of the competition, in November, Soviet tanks had brutally put down the Hungarian uprising. Spain, Switzerland and the Netherlands abruptly decided to protest by boycotting the Games. Some of the Dutch athletes were already warming up in Melbourne when they were told that they would not be competing.

Earlier, Egypt, Lebanon and Iraq had declared that they would stay away to express their disapproval of the Franco-British expedition to the Suez Canal. Meant to back up Israel's invasion of the Sinai Peninsula, the ensuing conflict would reinforce the standing of the United States and the Soviet Union as the two supreme leaders of the world. On the plus side, the Germans had miraculously agreed to field a united team.

Amid the excitement of the preparations, Horst Dassler drove to the Melbourne Sports Depot, a sports retail outlet that had just begun to stock Adidas spikes. Once he met up with its owner, Frank Hartley, Horst unveiled a startling project: instead of selling Adidas shoes, he would hand them out for free. At a time when money was still a dirty word in international athletics, this was a completely novel proposal. Athletes had always had to buy their own spikes; in some of the wealthiest countries they might be given a pair by their federation, but in most cases they had to find the money themselves.

The Olympics were strictly for amateurs. Athletes were barred from accepting payment in cash or kind for their sporting achievements. Likewise, equipment manufacturers were not supposed to exploit the commercial worth of their clients: when advertising they were forced to disguise the identity of any athletes pictured by blurring their faces or placing a black band across their eyes.

These rules were applied with particular zeal in the United States. Avery Brundage watched over them with near-fanatical devotion. In 1935 'Slavery Avery', then chairman of the American Athletics Union, insisted that Jesse Owens should hand over the $159 he earned from a job as an elevator boy when it emerged that the athlete hadn't actually pressed the elevator button but merely obtained a fictitious job and the small salary that went with it as a means of financial support. After Brundage was elected as chairman of the International Olympic

Committee (IOC) in 1952, there was little chance that the rules would be relaxed.

The same regulations would have applied for clothing, had clothing been on the agenda. No leading sports-goods producer had yet thought of adding clothing to its range, and of course it would have been unthinkable for any firm to advertise on the chest of an Olympic athlete. The plain shirts worn by most were provided by the national federation and featured only their country's emblem.

Despite all this proscription, Horst Dassler was confident that he would not be reprimanded for offering spikes, because spikes could be regarded as technical equipment, indispensable to runners at a time when races were still held on cinder tracks and athletes dug out their own starting blocks with a little shovel. Good spikes weren't cheap, and runners repaired and cared for them until they fell apart, often literally.

When Horst Dassler explained that he wanted to hand out shoes, Frank Hartley at the Melbourne Sports Depot was not impressed. He saw the Olympics as a splendid sales opportunity, but there was little hope of a bonanza while the owner's son was giving them away. Still, Horst convinced Hartley to take the long view: there could be no better publicity for his business than a throng of athletes hitting the tape in three-striped shoes. The retailer let Horst fill his store with boxes of spikes, designed for the Olympics. The newly designed Melbourne shoe bore three green stripes and a cross on the heel. Entire delegations were invited to take their pick.

Most of the British athletes had brought along their spikes from Foster's and G. T. Law, a small store in Wimbledon. While Adidas spikes had as yet failed to conquer British tracks, the outing to Law's small store had turned into a ritual for well-heeled athletes from Oxford and Cambridge. There, they had their feet measured by experts who produced hand-crafted shoes. For the Melbourne Olympics, some of them were fitted with titanium spikes recycled from a Rolls-Royce engine. 'They were relatively expensive and they wouldn't last very long, but they were remarkably lightweight,' said Chris Chataway, a British middle-distance runner who would later be one of the two pacesetters during Roger Bannister's historic first sub-four-minute mile.

For athletes with smaller budgets, however, such spikes remained inaccessible. Derek Ibbotson, the first British runner to cover the mile in precisely four minutes, was among those who eagerly took up Horst

Dassler's offer. 'We all trailed over to this store in Melbourne, chuffed as hell,' he recalled. Ibbotson returned to Yorkshire with his green-striped Adidas and a bronze medal for the 5,000 metres.

Al Oerter, an American discus thrower, had worn Adidas since the early fifties when his father, a plumber, found a pair for him at the back of a store selling electrical appliances in New York. 'None of the American companies made a size-fourteen shoe for throwing,' Oerter explained. After a record-breaking throw in Melbourne he went on to reap another three gold medals, all in Adidas.

American track and field coaches got to know the German brand through the Severn brothers in California. The six brothers, longtime importers of cricket equipment, had heard about Adidas spikes and begged the Dasslers to send them a consignment, which they did in 1953. They excitedly stored the boxes in their North Hollywood lock-up, but soon realized that selling them would be an uphill struggle. After the war California had adopted a 'buy American' policy, which meant that retailers were reluctant to take Adidas and the brand could not be sold to high schools. The only thing the Severns could do was to drive from one university campus to the other and painstakingly build the reputation of Adidas among upcoming athletes.

Clifford Severn had a head start here, since he once ran on the athletics team at the University of California at Los Angeles (UCLA). He badgered coaches until they agreed to blow their whistle and gather the athletes in the bleachers. Yet many of them were still reluctant to try Adidas, because they looked so different from the spikes worn ordinarily by US athletes. 'It was a blessing and a problem,' said Chris Severn. 'The athletes had always worn black spikes, and here we were with blue kangaroo leather and three white stripes.'

It took a lot of persistence to build up individual orders. In the process, the Severns became friendly with such coaches as Oliver Jackson, who headed the track team at Abilene Christian in Texas. Their star sprinter was Bobby Morrow, a farmer's son who became known as the San Benito Bullet. Some of the other coaches who watched Morrow run described him as the greatest sprinter they ever saw. With his relaxed and graceful style, they said, he could have run with a beer float on his head and never spilled a drop. Once the phenomenal sprinter had tried Adidas, he would not return to anything else. 'They were just the only good spikes around at the time,' said Morrow, and many others thought as much. While the American track and field federation supplied its Olympic athletes with Wilson shoes, many refused to wear them and ordered Adidas instead.

While such athletes as these rallied to the Adidas cause, Horst Dassler relentlessly pursued his quest to convince more of the others, and the friendly Adidas man toting his large holdall became a familiar sight at the Melbourne Olympic village. Armin Dassler, however, was nowhere to be seen.

Among Horst's unfamiliar rivals was a brand called Onitsuka Tiger. It had been established by a man who started life as Kihachiro Sakaguchi but changed his name after he was adopted by the Onitsuka family of Kobe just after the war. The company's mission was to keep Japan's youth off the streets by encouraging their participation in sport.

With raw materials in plentiful supply from Kobe's huge rubber factories, he set up his own plant and began to turn out basketball shoes that looked suspiciously like Converse All Stars. His breakthrough came in long-distance running shoes, however, with both Japanese and other marathon runners opting for the Tiger brand. Tiger shoes made their first high-profile appearance in international sport on the feet of Japanese athletes at the opening ceremony of the Melbourne Games.

With his persistent presence and affable manner, Horst befriended scores of confirmed medal prospects as well as unknown athletes. Some of them smirked about the names of his shoes, with one model ineptly called 'As' ('ace' in German). But they were flabbergasted by the lightness of the German spikes and the generosity of their representative. They had never experienced anything like this before.

Horst was shrewdly betting that, once they obtained a pair of Adidas, many athletes would gladly wear them during the competition. After all, they were an undeniable asset and there was no economic incentive for the athletes to stick to any other brand. Since payment remained strictly forbidden, loyalty could be fostered only through quality and personal relationship. The rewards to manufacturers could be huge and the cost of the handouts was peanuts compared with the benefits accruing from a snapshot of a gold medallist in three stripes. It seemed that the Melbourne shoe had been made to be particularly photogenic: against a white leather upper, the three green stripes seemed to be the focus of the entire picture.

When the medals were counted, Horst Dassler proudly informed his parents that more than seventy of them had been won in three-striped shoes. The athletes had taken to their free Adidas spikes with such eagerness that the brand seemed ubiquitous. The newspaper photos of many a close finish were dotted with Melbourne spikes, yielding unbeatable publicity for Adidas. Among the winners, Bobby Morrow lived up to expectations by taking two gold medals for the 100 and 200 metres, then another one for the 4 × 100 metres relay. The Severns could not believe their luck. 'There he was on the cover of *Life* magazine with his three-striped spikes,' smiled Chris Severn. 'It caused quite a stir, and all of a sudden retailers became interested.' Orders picked up so rapidly that the Severns no longer had enough storage space in their lock-up.

For Horst Dassler, the Melbourne Olympics would have much deeper personal repercussions. While networking in Melbourne, the young man established a reputation in the sports business. Many of the athletes who competed in Australia remained involved in international sports, and some of them went on to become high-profile executives in sports-related organizations. Horst Dassler made sure that they would remember him as the uncomplicated young man who gave them Adidas spikes.

One of the most endearing of these was Ron Clarke, an Australian middle-distance runner who set many world records but suffered an incredible run of misfortune at the Olympics. This started in Melbourne, where Clarke was honoured to carry the Olympic torch into the Melbourne Cricket Ground for the opening ceremony only to get his arm badly burned. Clarke would not meet Horst in Melbourne, but he heard all the stories and gladly teamed up with Adidas a few years later, his company replacing Melbourne Sports Depot as an Australian partner.

Another Australian friend was Kevan Gosper, who took a silver medal in Melbourne as part of the 4 × 400 metres relay team. When Horst Dassler handed the young runner a pair of spikes, he could not have guessed that Gosper would build his career to become chief executive of Shell in Australia, and that he would climb the sporting political ladder to be appointed vice-president of the International Olympic Committee.

When it came to Horst Dassler's contacts, the absence from the Games of the European protesters was more than compensated by the presence of emerging sports nations. The Melbourne Games were the first ones to include large contingents from several East European countries. As he whiled away time at the stadium, Horst forged friendly relationships

11. American sprinter Bobby Morrow, who ran in three stripes thanks to Horst.

with scores of apparently insignificant representatives from these countries, who were grateful for all the support they could get. Melbourne provided him with an unbeatable array of favours he could one day call in.

At the next Olympics, in Rome, athletes scoured the track in search of the nice German with the large holdall, but he was no longer the only benefactor in town. The Puma Dasslers had cottoned on, cultivating contacts with leading athletes and giving away their own spikes. The problem for Puma was that Adidas undeniably had market position: they had been there earlier and they offered the best spikes on the circuit. Puma therefore had to give something more.

Armin Hary, a controversial German sprinter, was the first athlete blatantly to exploit the rivalry. Several months ahead of the Rome Olympics, Hary had repeatedly demonstrated that he was the fastest man in the world. He was widely tipped to became the first man ever to run the 100 metres in precisely ten seconds. In fact he had done so, in Friedrichshafen, wearing white Adidas spikes with green stripes, but the time was disallowed because Hary was thought to have jumped the gun.

In June 1960, in Zurich, Hary was in the starting blocks again. Once again the German broke the world record and once again his time was disallowed due to a false start. However, Hary convinced the judges to agree to a restart, and this time there was no doubt whatsoever that the coal miner's son from the Saarland had lived up to his promise: he could and had run the 100 metres in ten seconds flat.

Adolf Dassler was elated. Armin Hary had been a regular guest in Herzogenaurach. Adi had eagerly followed his progress and appreciated the feedback given by the tall runner. He had spent many hours crafting Hary's spikes. If he stayed in shape, Adidas looked certain to feature prominently on the podium of the 100 metres at the forthcoming Olympics.

As Dassler observed, Hary's performance had improved substantially since he'd spent some time in the United States. However, along with the latest techniques on fitness training, he had learned that the best performers deserved to be rewarded. While such an idea remained anathema to the IOC, Hary appreciated this part of the American dream and firmly intended to apply it.

The sprinter apparently turned to Alf Bente, the man who had married Adi Dassler's eldest daughter, Inge. Alf had been fully adopted both by the Dasslers and by Adidas, and the couple oversaw much of the company's German business from their home in the Adidas compound. Handling production, Alf gradually imposed himself as the second-in-command in Herzogenaurach, while Inge was in charge of sales promotion. From then on, athletes who previously sat in Käthe Dassler's kitchen were often led to the Bentes' cellar, where guests were entertained until the early hours.

During one visit, Hary bluntly asked Alf what Adidas would be prepared to offer for his endorsement. Flabbergasted by this highly unusual request, Bente flatly refused to hand over cash, but he did agree to ask Adi Dassler to consider Hary's alternative proposal: that Adidas would appoint him as a distributor in the United States, with 10,000 pairs of shoes on credit for his start-up stock. As Bente had expected, Dassler angrily refused.

By then, Armin Hary had made some friends on the other side of the Aurach. The groundwork had been done by Werner von Moltke, a German and later European decathlon champion who began wearing

Puma in 1958. Von Moltke took some free shoes and he agreed to act as an intermediary for the brand at international track meetings. With Armin Hary it was easy: they were team-mates. 'I gave him shoes from Puma and we had a little bit of money so I could invite him for lunch,' von Moltke recalled. Over the months the relationship deepened and Hary soon commuted between the two banks of the Aurach.

When he took his seat in the Stadio Olimpico for the final of the 100 metres, Adolf Dassler was still convinced that Armin Hary would have forgotten about the money nonsense and that he would turn up in his Adidas spikes. He was utterly dismayed when the German sprinter emerged from the tunnel in a pair of Pumas. Although the other four contestants all had three Adidas stripes, Hary's Puma formstripe was clearly visible from the stands.

The Puma clan beamed as Armin Hary raced to his gold medal in 10.2 seconds. As von Moltke admitted, the sprinter's choice was at least partly motivated by a thick brown envelope. He was offered a bonus of an estimated 10,000 marks for gold, a substantial sum at the time. A few minutes later, however, the faces dropped on the Puma side. They watched in consternation as Hary mounted the winner's podium wearing Adidas shoes. 'It was truly hurtful for Rudolf and Friedl Dassler, who had welcomed him with open arms,' sighed Werner von Moltke. Hary was apparently trying to get paid by both sides, but Adi Dassler was so disgusted that he barred Hary from his factory. The German sprinter continued to collaborate with Puma, but the company's managers could not forget the Rome incident and consistently referred to Hary as 'a chap who eats on both sides'.

After the Rome Olympics it was clear that athletics, and the shoe business that fed off it, would never be the same again. The Hary precedent would inevitably be followed by others seeking to exploit the rivalry between Adidas and Puma. The Dasslers would have to adjust their strategy. The time had come for Horst and Armin to take over.

7

The Alsatian Plot

In the middle of the night, a group of young men sat huddled round a large table in a cosy Alsatian restaurant. Sipping vintage cognac, the excited managers were fomenting bold and elaborate plans. They were plotting to take over the sports business.

The group went into conclave almost every day at the Auberge du Kochersberg, a former hunting lodge that had been converted by Adidas France at considerable expense into a plush hotel with a gourmet restaurant and a formidable wine cellar. Guests were entertained there until late in the evening, when the French managers would gather around their youthful chief, Horst Dassler.

Horst had been in the Alsace since 1959. After the Melbourne Olympics, he had become restless. He had inherited both the drive of his father and his mother's persistence and hard-headedness. He badgered his parents for more leeway and influence in the company, but his pleas were met with his mother's insistence that all her children should be given an equal chance to succeed in the company. The discussions ended in increasingly acrimonious run-ins between Horst and Käthe.

The friction was further aggravated by the presence of Horst's girlfriend, Monika Schäfer. Horst saw her as a charming young woman with whom he would consider sharing his life but his parents, who had set their sights on the daughter of a well-established family, were not impressed. The older Dasslers cringed when they heard that Monika, a talented gymnast, was once part of a trapeze act in a local circus. To make matters worse she was a Protestant, while the Dasslers were raised as Catholics.

Adolf and Käthe decided that they would be better off sending their impetuous son away from Herzogenaurach, but they also realized that it would be foolish to deprive the family business of such a talented heir. The solution was to place Horst in charge of a separate plant. The move would have the dual benefits of putting some distance between Horst and his parents while also helping Adidas to cope with growing demand.

The Dasslers plumped for the Alsace. Just across the border with France, the region was sufficiently distant at more than four hours' drive from Herzogenaurach. Its shoe industry was in trouble, with scores of plant owners desperately looking for buyers. During the war the Alsace had been informally annexed by the Germans, forcing its shoemakers to contribute to the war effort. When the conflict came to an end the territory came back under French control but Alsatian companies were still hit with hefty war penalties.

To make matters worse, the Alsatian shoe business had been partly built on supplies of heavy boots to the miners of the Saarland, just south of the region, but after a referendum in 1955 the Saarland decided to become part of Germany, depriving the Alsatian shoemakers of their main market. By the late fifties, many factories had closed down and others were up for grabs. The Dasslers' eagle eyes spotted Vogel, an ailing company in the small village of Dettwiller.

Georges-Philippe Gerst watched with curiosity as a black Mercedes with German plates drove into the courtyard of his parents' decrepit plant in July 1959. It contained an entire family: Adi and Käthe in front and their four grown-up children crammed in the back. Adi Dassler explained matter-of-factly that he needed Alsatian partners to turn out roughly 500 pairs of football boots per day, starting as quickly as possible. 'For our company, which scraped to make ends meet on orders of fifty pairs, the figures were mind-boggling,' said Gerst. 'The black Mercedes seemed like a godsend.'

It was followed a few days later by a blue, three-striped Volkswagen bus containing a German technician and cases full of equipment to make Adidas boots. The entire Dassler family returned to clean up the decaying plant, just opposite Dettwiller's train station. Father, mother, aunt and children all rolled up their sleeves to scrub the walls and machines, which were in a deplorable state. Then the Dassler parents gave their son FFr350,000 of start-up capital and returned to Herzogenaurach.

Enjoying his independence, Horst gladly settled in the Alsace. By the beginning of December 1959 the Dasslers were convinced that Dettwiller was a shrewd investment, and that Horst had all that it took to manage the Vogel plant smoothly. They convened with the Gerst family in Pirmasens, Käthe's home town, just across the German border. For another 17.5 million francs, the Dasslers took complete control of the Alsatian plant.

Horst, who had been living in a small room in the Gerst home, moved into an apartment above the factory. Much to his parents' chagrin, this drab setting did not deter Monika Schäfer from joining her beloved. A celebration was held for their quiet wedding at the Auberge du Haut-Barr in Saverne. The Alsace would be Horst's home as well as the base for a sports empire of unparalleled scope.

Once he had spotted the cosy Auberge du Kochersberg, in the desolate village of Landersheim, Horst resolved to build his business around it. A block of offices was erected behind the former hunting lodge, with some tennis courts and a football pitch, to be inaugurated in 1967. Less than ten years after his Alsatian exile, Horst Dassler was at the helm of a full-fledged operation. From the small plant in Dettwiller, he had constructed a separate Adidas business. On paper it was just a subsidiary which had to take its instructions from Herzogenaurach, but Adidas France was run almost independently from the German company, with its own ranges and suppliers. Between the newly built offices and the Auberge, Landersheim became the nerve-centre of Adidas.

Whenever Horst spotted an opening he bulldozed ahead, ignoring any obstacle in his path. Alain Ronc, one of Horst's most intrepid managers, was among the trusted aides whom Dassler sent out with hairy instructions: 'He just didn't care about consultation, weighing problems and costs. He took bold decisions, then it was up to us to find the means to implement them,' said Ronc, who joined the company as an assistant in the export department. 'He was racing at two hundred miles an hour, and we were puffing behind, struggling to keep up.'

Horst made his employees sweat. Most of them worked indecent hours and gave up most of their private life to follow him. They started early in the morning and usually ended late at night, after a long dinner meeting at the Auberge followed by a nightcap with Horst. Although contracts didn't stipulate that employees should turn up on Saturdays, the offices were usually full. On Sundays the discussions often took place in more comfortable settings, at the Auberge and at Dassler's house in Eckartswiller.

'Le Patron', as Horst was known in the Alsace, worked hardest of all. A workaholic by any standards, he always looked for ways to exploit his time as efficiently as possible. One of his most bizarre ploys was known as the revolving dinner. 'Three groups of people would be set up in three separate rooms, with one leading executive at each table,' as one witness recalled. 'Horst would have drinks with one group. Sit at the table. Then, as planned, he would be called away for an urgent meeting. He would then move on to the next group, eat an appetizer, then be called away. And on to the next group for dessert. At the end of the evening all of those guests would feel they had dined with Horst Dassler.'

The worst part for his employees was that their boss barely needed sleep. Those who worked closely with Horst routinely received phone calls in the middle of the night. Fully awake, Horst had just been hit by another brainwave which he urgently wanted to discuss. The American girlfriend of one employee became so annoyed by the nightly intruder that she once picked up the phone herself. 'Horst, you are interfering with my sex life,' she told him angrily. For the next weeks her hapless husband was asked daily about the state of his intimate affairs.

The insomnia was worse for those who travelled with Horst. With Dassler, meetings would usually last until the small hours of the morning, but that still didn't prevent him from calling a few hours later. 'You weren't sleeping, were you?' Dassler would tease. At breakfast he casually asked his co-travellers what they thought of the bobsleigh competition that had been broadcast during the night.

Horst and Monika's marriage had quickly produced two children, Adi and Suzanne, but Horst rarely saw them and he didn't expect his employees to feel much need for a family life, either. Alain Ronc was confronted with a tough dilemma when Horst asked him to take part in a conference in Malta. Ronc explained that he couldn't attend because he was getting married on that day, but that didn't seem to bother Horst very much. 'He asked if my prospective wife had ever been to Malta,' said Ronc. 'When I replied that she hadn't he suggested that I could take her along. I would then spend three days at the conference and three days with her. That's how our honeymoon turned into a business trip.'

In return for such selfless commitment, Horst Dassler treated his employees with the same consideration he showed to his guests at the Auberge. Although he rarely discussed private matters with other Adidas executives, he was always prepared to lend a hand. At least two employees felt indebted to Horst because he got them out of police custody when they were caught drink-driving. Another acknowledged, with a mixture of embarrassment and affection, that Horst had helped to extract one of his family members from a dire financial situation. Yet another was visited by Horst in hospital, where he was recovering from a minor injury. The small gesture ensured his loyalty for years afterwards. 'Of course, there was a manipulative touch to it,' as one of them later admitted.

But most of the youthful Adidas managers were simply entranced by Horst: they were in awe of his drive, mesmerized by his stamina, his persuasive powers and the incessant activity of his mind. Horst was a shy person, a weak orator who avoided the limelight, yet he oozed a quiet charm that captivated most of the people he met. His followers felt that Horst had embarked on an extraordinary adventure, and they would have done almost anything to stay on board. 'It was exhilarating,' said Johan van den Bossche, company lawyer at the time. 'We all wanted to be a part of it, even if that meant that we had to run like hell.'

Owing to his technical studies in Pirmasens, Horst could deftly supervise operations in Dettwiller. His father, who turned up to advise the Alsatians from time to time, had to admit that their boots were worthy bearers of the three stripes. As demand continued to swell, Horst Dassler quickly acquired several other decaying plants in the Alsace. Yet the hungry young man hardly regarded himself as a production manager.

For the first couple of years, most production from the Alsatian plants was sent straight to Herzogenaurach, to be sold in Germany and to some foreign distributors. Then Horst launched an onslaught on the French market, turning Adidas France into a full-fledged subsidiary, surrounding himself with equally youthful sidekicks who relentlessly peddled French-made Adidas wares around the country.

At first they received only piecemeal orders from French clubs and individual athletes. The company competed chiefly against two others: Hungaria and Raymond Kopa, a company set up by one of France's most revered football players of the fifties. Kopa could open many doors in French football, but Horst Dassler had picked a resourceful team – the kind who would scour the country on match days to hand out Adidas boots and spend many more hours cultivating friendships at the club bar. Extra rounds were bought for photographers if they promised to shoot close-ups of Adidas boots.

Unlike athletes, football players were perfectly entitled to rake in some extra earnings by selling sports gear while they were still playing. Once they retired, Horst sometimes hired them as ambassadors. They provided prestige and precious contacts, but Dassler could also be certain that they would have the required drive and persistence. Surely it was easier to teach an ex-footballer the ropes of the sports trade than to teach a business graduate about perseverence and willpower.

Among the Adidas crew was Just Fontaine, a French player who scored a record thirteen goals in six games at the 1958 World Cup in Sweden. Four years later his career was ended by injury and he joined Adidas France as a sales representative, selling boots under his own name. It was an enticing deal for Fontaine, at a time when even the players of his calibre could not expect to earn much during their short playing career and often found themselves empty-handed when it was over.

In the early days Fontaine suffered many rejections, often accompanied by crude remarks about Germans. The chubby player further noticed that Adidas was at a disadvantage against some other French brands because it did not manufacture footballs. He often lost orders to Hungaria, a small company that sold both boots and balls. Their sales people were greeted heartily in almost any sports store just because they made 'le scaphandre', the brown leather ball that was used by every self-respecting French football club at the time. 'They pressured the retailers, telling them that they couldn't get the ball if they refused to order Hungaria boots,' Fontaine explained. 'Therefore I advised Horst that Adidas should have its own balls. It was an instant hit because he took up my suggestion to make Adidas balls with black and white sections, which easily distinguished them from the others. When you spotted it on the pitch you instantly knew what it was.'

Horst bought a processing plant in La Walck, another Alsatian village, where the leather sections were prepared, but he had the balls stitched by men and women imprisoned in Franco's Spain. Peter Lewin, the company's Spanish distributor, eyed Horst incredulously when he heard of the arrangement during a dinner party, but Dassler simply laughed and told him, 'Just cut one of the balls open.' When Lewin did so he found a scrap of paper bearing a handwritten name and cell number neatly folded inside. The prisoners had been instructed to insert these before they finished sewing, in order to prevent sloppy work. A van full of leather hexagons made the trip from La Walck to Fabara prison each week, returning with a load of Adidas balls.

Hungaria balls were promptly squeezed out of the market. François Remetter, the national team's goalkeeper, was well known for sneaking into the changing rooms and placing Adidas balls in the referee's locker. 'Otherwise he asked befriended players who were on the pitch that day to kick the ball above the bleachers,' recalled Jean-Claude Schupp, in charge of promotion at the time. 'François would stand there at the side of the pitch and casually roll an Adidas ball towards the players.'

While endorsement deals were still meaningless, Horst Dassler taught his employees to hook sportspeople by weaving personal relationships. One of the crew was gruffly rebuked when he lamented to Horst Dassler that some of the players on a team contracted by Adidas had trotted onto the pitch wearing a rival's boots. 'Were you in the locker rooms with them?' Dassler snapped. 'Do you know the names of their wives? Did you have lunch with them beforehand? Well then, what do you expect?'

Back in Herzogenaurach, Horst Dassler had closely observed how Adidas benefited from the personal touch developed by his parents. When athletes travelled to the factory, they knew that they would be treated to a hearty welcome. They could be certain that Adi Dassler would listen to them intently, and that he would do his utmost to get their shoes exactly right. All things being equal, they would rather wear Adidas shoes. All things not being equal, in many cases they would still opt for Adidas.

The art of making friends was particularly relevant in the sports business at a time when there still wasn't enough money around to buy loyalty. Even in football many deals were sealed informally and there wasn't much that Adidas could do if a player suddenly decided to switch to another brand. The best way to prevent such setbacks, Horst figured, was to make sure that the service was beyond reproach, and that the players were permanently pampered.

Horst himself excelled at this discipline. His phenomenal memory stored the names and faces of countless athletes and officials. Le Patron would never close a conversation without enquiring about the welfare of the other person's family. The interest was flattering enough, but it often turned out that Horst genuinely listened to the reply, too. One business contact who mentioned in passing his son's enthusiasm for a football team was stunned to receive, shortly afterwards, a package for his son with shirts autographed by several players. Such attention was perfectly in line with Horst Dassler's maxim that 'business is about relationships'.

12. The Auberge du Kochersberg. A former hunting lodge in the Alsatian village of Landersheim, it turned into a favoured haunt for international sports supremos.

To cement them, the ultimate tool was the Auberge du Kochersberg. Horst Dassler set his sights on it while seeking suitably picturesque venues for his guests and spent a fortune on the renovation. When they arrived in Landersheim to discuss their contracts, football coaches and players could spend several days at the Auberge. They were wined and dined at length before the Adidas men began to discuss business.

With his indefatigable team and his personal brand of hospitality, Horst Dassler cultivated a style of his own in the sports business. This required heavy personal investment, but Horst Dassler was certain that it would pay off.

Back in Herzogenaurach, Horst's older cousin still had to find his place at his father's company. In fact, Armin Dassler had left Herzogenaurach in a huff after yet another row with Rudolf, his irascible father. While Horst settled in France, Armin angrily packed his bags for Austria.

The relationship between Armin and Rudolf had always been strained. It deteriorated further when Armin became more self-assured and began to question the conservative methods of his father. Watching Horst, Armin acknowledged that the sports world was undergoing rapid changes, and unless he was allowed to steer Puma in the right direction, the company would be bypassed entirely.

At the time, Armin had just separated from Gilberte, the mother of his two children, Frank and Jörg. When he stormed out of Herzogen-aurach in 1961, he took with him Irene Braun, a former employee in the Puma export department. They settled in Salzburg with Jörg, the younger of the two boys, while Frank stayed with his mother.

Under a hasty agreement made with his father, Armin obtained the funds to buy up a plant in Salzburg and to cover the Austrian market. From there on, however, Armin was entirely on his own. His father stubbornly refused to provide any guarantees for Austrian bankers or any other form of support. 'The old man sure made things difficult for us,' as Irene recalled. To make matters worse, the couple soon discovered that the Austrian sports market was highly seasonal. From the beginning of November, the Austrians spent most of their weekends on the ski slopes. For nearly six months after that, there was no point in trying to sell trainers. Puma Austria quickly ran into financial troubles, and it certainly couldn't rely on the parent company to lend a hand.

Armin then resolved to complement his Puma business with a hidden operation. Although his father had strictly forbidden him to sell the Austrian products in any other market, Armin made secret deals with large distributors in the United States, exporting Austrian-made football boots under the name Dassler which bore a striking resemblance to the Puma brand, albeit with a slightly altered logo.

The move went blatantly against Rudolf's instructions, but Armin needed the extra orders to keep the Salzburg operation going. He had built up personal relationships in the United States, where his father had sent him on a reconnaissance mission in the early fifties, and Irene had contacts of her own. From their side, the distributors acknowledged that, with Rudolf nearing retirement age, they might as well lend a hand to his heir. It helped that they were an ocean away from Herzogenaurach and that, unless somebody picked up the phone to call Rudolf Dassler, he probably wouldn't find out.

The relationship between Rudolf and his son remained so distant that the old man turned down an invitation to attend his son's second wedding. The celebration was scheduled for September 1964, at the same time as Rudolf's annual break to Bad-Wörishofen. 'We offered to have him chauffeured back and forth for the day,' said Irene. 'But he replied with a letter saying that he would not interrupt his break for our wedding.' Unlike Horst, however, Armin was soon drawn back to Herzogenaurach. Three years after his Austrian exile, Rudolf Dassler sheepishly asked his son to return. Well into his sixties, he no longer had the stamina to drive Puma forward, and he needed Armin to reaffirm the family's grip on the parent company.

Too young to take up that role, Gerd Dassler, Rudolf's second son, then in his early thirties, was sent to establish a subsidiary for Puma in France. As if the Dasslers consciously chased each other, this operation was established in Soufflenheim, just a few miles away from Horst's Landersheim base. With Armin at the helm in Herzo, Puma regained its impetus, but the Puma heir quickly acknowledged that his rivals were no longer across the Aurach but across the border: Horst in France had become the driving force behind Adidas. However, it was in England that Armin Dassler would discover exactly what he was up against.

8

England Scores, Germany Wins

In June 1966 Horst Dassler unpacked his bags for a lengthy stay at the Coburg hotel, a convivial establishment on Queensway in Bayswater. For nearly a month this would be the headquarters of a hard-hitting Adidas contingent: their mission was to ensure that the upcoming World Cup would be entirely covered in three stripes.

Previous England teams had consistently failed to shine at international level, but on home turf the English were uncharacteristically upbeat about their prospects. After a strong run in friendly games, English newspapers were boisterously endorsing the national side. The England manager, Alf Ramsey, added to the expectations by boldly declaring that his side was favourite to snatch the trophy – and to reaffirm England's supremacy at the game that it invented. The excitement was palpable all over the country as the English braced themselves for some thrilling contests. Most of the venues were fully booked, and thousands had acquired television sets to watch the games.

For Horst Dassler, the opportunity was just as momentous. The three stripes had begun to spread on English pitches, but if he played his cards right over the next weeks he would achieve invaluable exposure among the players and supporters who still wielded the strongest influence in the game. A full Adidas squad joined Horst for the occasion, including Käthe, who flew over with Inge, his eldest sister. Several other rooms were booked at the Coburg for the company's international managers, as well as the efficient partners who had zealously promoted Adidas among English football players over the previous years.

Until the late fifties, English footballers were reluctant to let go of their heavy clodhoppers. The country's preference continued to be for English brands which prided themselves on sturdiness rather than style, with bulbous toe caps and ankle protection, and which could last several years. Among the best-selling makes were the Villain and the Hotspur, both manufactured by the Manfield factory in Stockport.

Barney Goodman, a sports retailer in Southgate, was stunned by the much sleeker Adidas boots when he was given a pair in the fifties. He knew that more skilful players would appreciate their lightness, and so asked Manfield if they could make boots along the same lines. The response bordered on sarcasm: the light boots were just a fad, Manfield replied, and they weren't in the least bit interested.

Jimmy Gabriel was a teenage player at Dundee United at the time. He distinctly recalled the day when his coach pulled him aside, explaining that he had received some weird German boots and would like Gabriel to try them on. 'They didn't look like anything I had ever seen before,' he said. 'We had always worn these brown and thick boots, but all of a sudden here were these slick black boots with white stripes that really looked more like shoes than boots.'

As he strutted onto the pitch, Gabriel was ridiculed by supporters and team-mates alike. The low cut looked effeminate, they told him less politely, and he couldn't possibly play football in shoes. 'I ignored the jibes because the boots felt unbelievable,' said Gabriel. 'It would take two years to break in the English boots and to get any control over the ball, but the Adidas felt comfortable from the start and I could feel the ball right away.' Watching his precision improve, Gabriel's colleagues soon cut out the snide remarks and asked him where they could get a pair.

The same happened to Roy Gratrix, a centre-half at Blackpool. He had been travelling to Europe and returned with a pair of Adidas. Gratrix immediately adopted them and extolled their virtues in the dressing room, but his manager was not impressed. There was no way he would let Gratrix play in these things that didn't even have ankle protection. They looked like carpet slippers!

But Adi and Käthe Dassler had picked a partner with unparalleled contacts in British football. Umbro, established near Manchester, had become a leading contender in the football-shirt business. The Dasslers reckoned that, distributed by such a prominent partner, the three stripes would quickly gain ground in England. Since Adidas sold only boots and Umbro only clothing, it seemed to be a judicious arrangement for both parties.

Umbro had been set up in the twenties by Harold and Wallace Humphreys, who ran a small workshop in Wilmslow, Cheshire. While their parents ran the Bull's Head pub in Mobberley, Harold and Wallace specialized in clothing for golf, cricket and football. They even had their own brand, Umbro, short for 'Humphreys brothers'. The name was registered in 1924 and adopted an emblem that became known as the double diamond.

Just like the Dasslers on the opposite side of the conflict, the Humphreys had to adjust their production during the war to make shirts for the British armed forces, and they returned with equal drive a few years later as 'the choice of champions'. The leading English supplier of football shirts at the time was Bukta, but in the fifties Umbro began to snatch some of their most coveted deals. Among their prestigious endorsees was Manchester United, which allowed them to sell 'sportswear styled by Matt Busby for Umbro'. It certainly helped that the Humphreys lived next door to Louis Edwards, the club's former owner.

Selling football shirts was still a somewhat thankless business back then, because the manufacturers were not allowed to place their logo on the strip. This meant that Umbro's shirts could not be identified by the public and they still had to invest in advertising to make it known that they had been chosen by well-known teams.

To complicate matters further, it had been agreed that the clubs would place their shirt orders through retailers. By far the most established outlet in the football trade was Barney Goodman's in Southgate. Taken over by his son Ronnie in the late fifties, it had nearly the entire Football League on its books, including Arsenal, Chelsea, Manchester United and Tottenham Hotspur.

By the early sixties Umbro was jointly run by Harold's two sons, John and Stuart Humphreys – although in practice, most of the business dealings were entrusted to John. An inveterate golfer with public school manners, the older of the two brothers was widely respected as a shrewd and courteous manager. As a director and shareholder of Manchester City football club, John Humphreys strongly contributed to the club's revived fortunes in the sixties. On the other hand, Stuart seemed more erratic and his extravagant behaviour regularly landed him in thorny situations.

Yet the company's most dedicated door-opener was Jim Terris, a stocky and avuncular Scotsman. He had entered the fray as the brother of John's wife, Myra Humphreys, and quickly became known as the Umbro man in English football, appreciated for his guile and wit. 'He was a Humphrey Bogart figure,' said his nephew Charles, John and Myra's son. 'He was a master of the one-liner and could put people in their place in a heartbeat if necessary. He called everyone son, including his own secretary.'

To impose Adidas on English pitches, the contacts built up by Umbro proved decisive. Players still had to buy their own boots and, although leading clubs often agreed to defray such expenses by up to 50 per cent, boots still represented a considerable expense for the players, whose weekly earnings were capped at £20 until the maximum wage arrangement imposed by the Football League was finally abandoned in 1961.

While the cost of a pair of boots is the least of a modern Premiership footballer's concerns, no one at the time would have believed that boot companies would ever fork out millions of pounds for players to wear their brand. 'We were always fishing for boot contracts but I never got one, even though I played on the national team for nearly six years,' sighed Bobby Robson. 'When I was given a pair I thought, gee-whiz, that was a stupendous deal.' In the absence of large cheques, the leading contenders competed on the strength of their boots, as well as small favours and personal relationships.

When Umbro began to sell Adidas boots in 1961, they turned the market on its head. The heavy boots favoured by the English players all but disappeared, to be replaced by the lighter and low-cut boots. Just a few years after Roy Gratrix and Jimmy Gabriel had been derided for their 'carpet slippers', almost the entire League seemed to be wearing them. Backed up by Umbro, Adidas benefited most from this stunningly fast turnabout. When he was on his rounds for Umbro, Jim Terris never failed to bring along a few pairs of Adidas boots. He had built up such tight contacts with retailers that the three stripes suddenly appeared in shop windows all over the country.

The only English manufacturers to survive were those who swam with the tide. Among the smartest contenders was Gola, which was set up at the beginning of the century but began to appear on English pitches in the thirties when it was taken over by Botterill & Sons in Northampton. Just like the Dasslers, the Botterills had a nose for marketing. They were the first English company to try out low-cut boots and from the fifties they introduced their own trademark, the Gola wing, which could be spotted from afar. Then they invested in large-scale advertising, covering the sides of buses with a slogan proclaiming that 'Gola means goals!'.

Another to enjoy some success was Mitre, which made its own balls and boots up in Huddersfield. They grabbed a few headlines with Denis Law, the Scotsman who enthralled the crowds at Old Trafford alongside George Best. But as the Adidas and Umbro managers settled in at the Coburg, they could rest assured that they would quash all of their English rivals at the World Cup.

Terris was almost certain that most of the England players would agree to wear Adidas. He had cultivated a particularly close relationship with Bobby Moore, the commander who had been designated team captain, but by then Terris knew only too well that personal loyalty was unlikely to be sufficient motivation: the England players would almost certainly have heard of the payments handed out in countries such as Italy and Brazil for on-pitch endorsements. Predictably the England players wanted to get their slice of the cake.

As they prepared for the World Cup, the Umbro men had already made sure that their brand would be everywhere. They had begun to outfit international teams in 1958, when the Brazilian squad agreed to wear shirts made in Wilmslow. Eight years later, Umbro achieved exposure that would seem unthinkable in later years. 'My father was gone for six weeks,' recalled Charles Humphreys. 'He went all round the world and when he came back, he had signed all but one of the sixteen teams that would take part in the finals.'

At the same time, the World Cup organizers were grappling with their own equipment problems. The event would involve hundreds of ball boys, stewards and officials, all of whom would need their own kit. In later years suppliers would be battling for the privilege to obtain such deals, but at the time the organizers were fully expected to pay for the equipment. They feared that the bill would be astronomical, and hoped that their usual shirt supplier, Bukta, would agree to a small discount. To handle the deal they approached Ron Goodman, the sports retailer in Southgate. After all, he was the intermediary for nearly all the leading English clubs, and he could surely obtain favourable terms.

Fortunately for Adidas and Umbro, Goodman was entirely devoted to their cause. The good relationship between Goodman and Adidas had been forged one day in the late fifties, when the retailer had been driving through Bavaria with his German wife to visit relatives. He had spotted a sign post for Herzogenaurach and decided to drop by.

Since it was late afternoon, Käthe Dassler immediately sat the Goodmans down at the dining table. 'These people had never heard of us, yet there we were in the middle of the family dinner,' Ron Goodman recalled. 'It would never have occurred to any of the English suppliers to treat us with such informal warmth.' The evening wore on and Käthe insisted they could not continue their drive but must stay for the night.

From then on, Goodman promoted Adidas forcefully and he severed his ties with Bukta to work more closely with Umbro. When the Humphreys drove down to London they never failed to stop over at Goodman's, and they were all regularly invited to Herzogenaurach and Landersheim.

So when the Football Association turned to Goodman for their shirt and boot arrangements, he eagerly introduced the Umbro managers. The retailer personally accompanied John Humphreys and Jim Terris to Lancaster Gate, where they were to meet Alf Ramsey and Denis Follows, the FA secretary.

As the two FA men explained, they needed suppliers for the England team. Then there was the matter of the opening ceremony at Wembley, to be attended by Queen Elizabeth II. They were mooting an elaborate welcome, with the obligatory bands and hundreds of young flag-bearers in full football kit. Bukta had made a little effort, offering a discount of 20 per cent on their standard shirt prices. But if the Humphreys offered a better deal on Umbro shirts and Adidas boots, the contract was theirs.

To Ron Goodman's amazement, John Humphreys didn't hesitate. 'I thought of him as a cautious manager, but this time he immediately realized that the deal would be worthwhile,' he recalled. 'He agreed to provide all the kit and boots for nothing, which was completely unheard of at the time. The people at the FA could not believe their luck.'

The agreement was settled without delay. It marked the beginning of a decades-long relationship between Umbro and the England team, and guaranteed unprecedented exposure for the three stripes.

Puma prepared their ground with equal zeal. In the sixties they teamed up with Alfred Reader, a company in Kent that specialized in cricket equipment. They had the right introductions among English sports retailers, but the problem was that none of the managers at Readers had anything like the quality of contacts the Humphreys had in the football business. To get closer to the British players, Armin Dassler needed his own fixer.

The person that came to mind was Derek Ibbotson, a Yorkshire runner. In Melbourne, 'Ibbo' had gladly picked up his pair of Adidas spikes from Horst Dassler, but a few years later he had switched to Puma, which had offered him more equipment. At the request of Armin Dassler, he had convinced a number of other athletes to switch from Adidas.

Ibbotson had just retired from running at the beginning of 1966, when Armin Dassler came forward with another assignment. If he could take a few weeks' leave from his regular job, Puma would hire him to orchestrate their preparations for the World Cup. Although Ibbotson couldn't really afford to take such a long leave of absence, he nevertheless promised to make a few calls.

He began by approaching Bobby Moore. As Ibbotson knew, the players could make their own choices but they were still likely to be influenced by their leader. He explained that Puma would be prepared to pay a sizeable bonus to the players if they decided to wear Puma – a perfectly legal offer. Ibbotson asked Moore to discuss this with the team at the next England game, away against Scotland in April.

To be on the safe side, Ibbotson placed another call to the Everton and England defender Ray Wilson at his home in Huddersfield, offering £100 for every game that he played wearing Puma, and some Puma-goodies for his family. The player agreed and promised to put the offer to his international team-mates when at Hampden Park. Compared with the average earnings of the English players, the offer was substantial. (After lengthy deliberations, the Football Association had grandly offered the team £22,000 should they *win* the tournament, which they decided to split evenly among every member of the squad – in other words they would get just £1,000 each, and that only if they became world champions.)

Unfortunately for Puma, however, Wilson was injured shortly before the April game against Scotland. In his absence, there was no Puma advocate. Bobby Moore apparently ignored Ibbotson's request and acted as a perfect salesman for Adidas. 'Moore just told the others that Adidas wanted the whole team and he didn't bother to give them the Puma offer,' sighed Ibbotson.

The Germans were among the few teams that still had no choice to make. Under Sepp Herberger, it was taken as read that the *Mannschaft* should wear Adidas. He had since retired, but Helmut Schön, Herberger's former assistant and now his replacement, was just as friendly with Adi Dassler. Not only that, but the squad contained many players whom Dassler had personally befriended. Among them was Uwe Seeler, by then a striker for Hamburg. Since they had got to know each other in the fifties, Seeler regularly turned up in Herzogenaurach. The jovial Hamburger was precisely the kind of individual who appealed to Dassler: tenacious and unpretentious, he would not be distracted by fast cars and discotheques.

Dassler was all the more appalled when he heard that Inter Milan had offered Seeler the exorbitant sum of 1.2 million marks to join the Italian club. The proposed deal caused such a furore in Germany that the dean of Hamburg University felt compelled to write to Seeler: 'If you manage to withstand this temptation,' he wrote, 'that would be a radiant signal, giving people cause to reflect on their ways.'

Shocked by the impudent Italians, Adi Dassler hurried to his phone. 'Think about it,' he told Seeler. 'Everybody loves you here, you're a Hamburger, you've got your feet on the ground.' To make the plea more convincing, he offered Seeler a position as Adidas representative in northern Germany. At a time when Adidas boots virtually sold themselves, this was a more than enticing proposal. The footballer quickly made up his mind in favour of Adidas. 'I knew you would,' Adi Dassler mumbled, audibly delighted at the other end of the line.

In exchange for Seeler's faithfulness, Adi Dassler saved the day for the German football team when the player suffered a tear in his Achilles tendon just before the 1966 World Cup. Although Helmut Schön was not known for emotional outbursts, he declared himself 'mortally shattered' by the likely absence of his star striker. To make sure that he could train in spite of his injury, Adi spent hours working on a special boot, with laces at the back, that enabled Seeler to tighten the heel as his tendon healed.

Another of Adi's close friends was Franz Beckenbauer, a fresh-faced teenager at Bayern Munich. Growing up in the misery of the post-war years, he had practised his tricks in leather ski boots. 'There was a cobbler who lived on the ground floor beneath us,' he explained. 'He just sawed off the soles and hammered some cleats into them.' When the young lad was offered his first pair of Adidas, he was so thrilled that he refused to take them off for the night.

Just like Seeler, Beckenbauer got to know Adi Dassler as a youth player. The two jointly developed boots that were precisely suited to the player's game. As a sweeping midfielder who covered long distances on the pitch, he needed boots with light and flexible soles. Beckenbauer regularly dropped by in Herzogenaurach, where he became friends with the entire Adi Dassler family. Beckenbauer, who would become Germany's most revered football player, was barely nineteen when Helmut Schön picked his squad for the World Cup. Some argued that he wasn't sufficiently experienced for such a tough contest, but the protests would soon die down.

Excited crowds cheered and waved in the packed Empire Stadium at Wembley. The eleven players picked by Alf Ramsey for the opening game of the 1966 World Cup watched anxiously as the ceremonial prelude dragged on. They could barely wait for the kick-off of their game against the incisive Uruguayans.

Seated in the main stand, close to the royal box, Horst Dassler beamed with pride. He had been somewhat sceptical about the arrangements for the opening ceremony, but he could not deny that the impact was stunning: each of the boys on the pitch wore a pair of brand-new black Adidas boots, with white stripes that appeared to have been painted freshly for more effect. The boots were so striking that, in the aftermath of the game, they provoked some heated conversations in the FA's corridors. 'It was a very awkward situation,' recalled Stuart Humphreys. 'There seemed to be stripes everywhere, and some people wondered why on earth the FA had to pick a German brand for this occasion.'

There would be plenty more stripes on the screens over the next days. The watchful Adidas men in England held a precise count: they proudly reported to Horst Dassler that roughly three-quarters of the players competed in three-striped boots.

But Armin Dassler had a few cards of his own to play. Reader's, his English partner, had strangely put him up at the Noke in St Albans, far removed from the action, but until the final at least, Puma still managed to steal the show with the most dazzling player of the competition, Portugal's Eusebio.

Originally from Mozambique, Eusebio liked to say he had never seen proper goalposts until the age of twelve. He had settled in Lisbon, playing for Benfica, the club which had electrified the public with its performance at the quarter finals of the European Cup in March 1966. The Portuguese side was defeated that night by a Manchester United eleven featuring George Best and Denis Law, but Benfica was still widely regarded as the best European club of the time, and Eusebio was its linchpin.

The agile player's performance caught the eye of a Portuguese Puma agent, who offered him a small contract. This was a thorn in Horst Dassler's side, because Eusebio's performance at Benfica earned him countless distinctions and Adidas itself had no choice but to invite him to its own party for the Golden Boot Award. Organized by Adidas France and a French football magazine, this rewarded the European player who had scored the greatest number of goals during the previous season – and as much as it pained Horst Dassler, he could not bend the rules to disqualify Puma players. 'I'm sure they were not very happy about it but they put on a great party anyway,' chuckled Eusebio, who proudly kept his two gold-plated Adidas boots.

While England and West Germany ground their way to the final stages of the tournament, it was Portugal that illuminated the contest. All eyes turned to Eusebio after the team's thrilling quarter final against North Korea. The Portuguese side was three goals down when Eusebio came onto the pitch and scored four times. The fouls committed by the

Portuguese in the earlier group-stage game against Brazil, outrageously crippling Pelé, took nothing away from Eusebio's brilliance. In spite of his team's semi-final defeat against England, which left the striker in tears, he was regarded by many as the man of the tournament.

When the whistle was blown for the end of that game, Horst Dassler rubbed his hands in delight. England's victory had deprived Puma of its most prestigious endorsee in the final. Instead the game would pit the hosts against West Germany, guaranteeing that during the final the pitch would be covered in three stripes.

It was a dream fixture for the Adidas side. The English suddenly stood a chance to make off with the highest prize in the game. The fact that they faced West Germany made the final duel even more compelling. There would not be an empty seat at Wembley, and the pundits estimated that the game would be watched by a TV audience of at least 500 million.

With Portugal gone, there was only one thing for the Puma men to do. It was inconceivable that any German player would walk onto the pitch wearing anything other than Adidas, so Puma's only hope was to convince a few of the English players to switch to the cat.

The Puma men were well versed in such assignments. However, most England players remained true to Jim Terris and steadfastly donned their striped boots, but a few were happy to accept Puma payments at the end of each game after Derek Ibbotson had caught their ear.

His most prestigious target was Gordon Banks, the England goalkeeper. The boot companies were always particularly eager to enrol him, because he featured in the most thrilling episodes of the game. Every time the ball came near the goal, all eyes turned to him. The action would be replayed over and over again, with the goalkeeper and his boots often in shot at close range.

Banks, a remarkable goalkeeper who became known as Banks of England because he was as safe between the sticks as money in the vaults of Threadneedle Street, was also a sharp observer. Since the beginning of the tournament he had been struck by the rise of commercial interests. He was somewhat unsettled to find out that the people who sold T-shirts and other merchandise featuring the World Cup Willie mascot stood to earn more than the players themselves. While the FA had offered him

£1,000 to keep the ball out of the English net, he heard that a T-shirt peddler had made about £1,500 during the competition.

On the morning of the final, the other English players knew precisely where to collect their Adidas money. Alan Ball, a short, red-haired midfielder, was sharing a room with Nobby Stiles, a biting defender from Manchester United. Stiles had woken up early to go to church, and upon his return he decided to take a nap. In the meantime, they agreed, Ball would walk over to Jim Terris and pick up the Adidas payment for both of them.

Each player was to earn £1,000 for wearing the three stripes in the final. It was a considerable reward, amounting to several months of comfortable wages. With that, the players who donned Adidas would be doubling the extra income they had been promised by the Football Association.

Alan Ball was somewhat dazed as he returned to his room, carrying a bag full of banknotes. 'Imagine that. I was just twenty-one, playing for England and carrying £2,000 upstairs for wearing Adidas boots. I would have bought my own but this was different,' he wrote. 'I walked into the room and Nobby was still lying in his bed as I tossed all the notes so that they came down all over the place like confetti. The World Cup final against West Germany was only hours away. We laughed like kids.'

Others were badly irritated by the persistent approaches of the Dassler envoys. They felt that the money talk was disrupting their preparations and this was not the right time to bother them about the boots they would be wearing. Jack Charlton got so annoyed about the dealings that he threatened to embarrass them all by donning one Adidas and one Puma boot.

When the twenty-two players ran onto the pitch and the crowds erupted in rapturous applause, the eyes of the bootmakers scanned the grass. The entrance brought a satisfied smile to the faces of the Puma men. The final would not be entirely three-striped: along with Ray Wilson, Gordon Banks was wearing Puma boots.

It would all seem insignificant over the next hours, as the two teams battled it out in the hard-fought final. Geoff Hurst's hat-trick and the elation of Kenneth Wolstenholme would remain etched in English consciousness, as the team at last reached the pinnacle of its own game.

13. Gordon Banks, one of the few English players who agreed to wear Puma during the 1966 World Cup final.

For Horst Dassler, the triumph was just as complete. While those four Puma boots remained an eyesore, the final was otherwise striped like an Adidas exhibition game. The endless replays constituted as many commercials for the brand. They signified a tremendous accomplishment by Jim Terris, and an invaluable endorsement for Adidas – paving the way for many years of undisputed leadership.

In one memorable game, Adidas had swept nearly all the other contenders from the pitch. Yet the behind-the-scenes dealing of the Dasslers in the football business smacked of good-humoured competition compared with what they had to get up to elsewhere.

9

Dirty Tricks in Mexico

Long before the opening of the Games in Mexico City, it had become clear that the 1968 Olympics would be mired in controversy. They formed another stage for the virulent mood of protest then abroad in a world buffeted by the Vietnam War, the assassination of Martin Luther King and the Soviet invasion of Czechoslovakia that had just put a brutal end to the Prague Spring. The Mexico Olympics also provided the backdrop for the most devious quarrels between the Dasslers – leading to the collapse of the amateur athletics world.

At the centre of the tumult was a group of vocal black American athletes from California. Embodying the refractory spirit of 1968, they were determined to stand up for their political rights, and to shake off the legacy of what they alleged to be the bigots who ruled track and field: a caste of wealthy businessmen and elderly European aristocrats who seemed out of touch with reality. As the protesters saw it, these people stuck to high-minded principles that prevented athletes from making money from their talent while ignoring the blatant injustices that continued to be visited on the underclasses.

Until shortly before the Games opened, on 12 October 1968, it remained uncertain whether any of the protagonists would make it to Mexico at all. Tommie Smith, John Carlos and Lee Evans, the most promising runners on the US team, were also at the forefront of the Olympic Committee for Human Rights, which rallied support for a proposed boycott of the Games.

The movement was set up by the huge Harry Edwards, a 25-year-old black sociology lecturer at San Jose State College. Disgusted by the notoriously racist policies on the campus, which included mealtime segregation, Edwards first threatened to disrupt college games. Then he took his protest one step further by persuading several outspoken black sprinters that they should not run for a racist country. 'It's time for black people to stand up and refuse to be utilized as performance animals for a little extra dog food,' Edwards thundered. The boycott idea was later dropped, but some leading black athletes were still determined to voice their protest.

Among the targets of their scorn were the Olympic rules which forbade payments to athletes. Rudolf Dassler had opened a can of worms during the Rome Olympics in 1960, when he paid Armin Hary to wear Puma spikes for his winning 100-metre dash. From there on, athletes began to make escalating demands in increasingly flagrant violation of amateur rules. The black American athletes were among those who sharply denounced the hypocrisy of it all. If officials nailed all the leading athletes who dealt with shoe companies, they argued, the Mexico Olympics would turn into a second-rate track meet.

The dogged rivalry between the Dassler cousins was a boon for those who were determined to cash in on their performances, like one group of American runners who honoured an invitation by Adidas in Landersheim, a few months ahead of the Mexico Olympics. Although two of them were longtime Puma wearers, they were wined and dined at the plush lodge for an entire week. As they whinged about their lack of money, an Adidas executive offered them a contract to wear Adidas spikes in exchange for $500. Horst Dassler was away at the time, but he was told precisely what happened: 'They got the money, signed the paper and then received a copy of the paper they had signed. I would not have given them the copy,' Horst sighed. 'They took it straight to Puma.'

Since the payments were illegal anyway, there was no way that the Adidas chief could complain about the duplicity of the athletes. His company had just been conned by young people who were in tune with their times – unwilling to adhere to the rules set by their elders. Such audacity was partly inspired by the revolutionary mood that prevailed at the time, as long-haired students proclaimed the end of the Establishment and fought for the right to live by their own rules.

This was alien to Dasslers *pères*, who stayed well away from Mexico. Rudolf had just turned seventy and he entrusted mundane business dealings to his son. Adolf still enjoyed socializing with some of the sporting in-crowd, but the incident with Armin Hary had made it clear to him that the purely sporting days of athletics were over. He had no desire to mix with the new breed of assertive athletes. Just like Rudolf, Adolf figured that his son was better equipped to handle their demands.

For Adidas and Puma, the stakes were enormous. The ruckus around the Mexico Olympics upped the pressure on all the protagonists. The spread of television guaranteed world-wide coverage. More than any other Games over the previous decades, the Mexico Olympics were a matter of prestige for the world's two leading shoe companies – and an opportunity for the Dassler cousins to pit their wits.

Armin's trump card was Art Simburg, a former student at San Jose. While working as a sports writer, Simburg topped up his earnings by peddling Puma shoes. A likeable young fellow, Simburg was the butt of many jokes among other shoe companies. He was regularly left stranded at US track meets, when Adidas people called hotels and car-hire companies to cancel Simburg's reservations. The lonely silhouette of poor Art Simburg lugging his bags from one hotel to the next in the hope of finding a spare room became a familiar sight on the US athletics circuit. Despite such pranks, Simburg had built up an unrivalled network of contacts. It helped that he was engaged to Wyomia Tyus, a black sprinter who won gold in the 100 metres at Tokyo and looked set to repeat the feat in Mexico City. Tommie Smith, John Carlos and Lee Evans were all on Simburg's buddy list.

His opposite number at Adidas was Dick Bank, a real-estate developer from Beverly Hills. But Bank, a staunch believer in the amateur rules, was reluctant to take any part in the payoffs that had begun to proliferate in international athletics. At a meet in San Antonio, a few weeks before the Olympics, Horst Dassler watched in dismay as most of the American athletes strode onto the track in Puma spikes. Bank was quietly sidelined. Horst needed slicker promotion to beat his cousin.

Staged high above Lake Tahoe in September 1968 (to replicate the altitude in Mexico City), the US Olympic trials constituted a full-dress rehearsal for the runners, as well as the officials and the shoe companies. The locker rooms were littered with brown envelopes. As the cynics joked, the true losers at Lake Tahoe weren't the athletes who failed to qualify for the Olympic team, but those who failed to negotiate a sponsorship deal.

Among the most impressive performances was that in the 400 metres by Lee Evans, who smashed the previous world record for the distance in 44.06 seconds. Horst Dassler noted that the black athlete was wearing the latest running shoe from Puma – the 'brush shoe' – which, instead of the customary nail-like metal spikes, was fitted with scores of much smaller steel needles. Horst knew that the rules allowed a maximum of six spikes per shoe, and lodged a protest. Puma argued that the needles could hardly be described as spikes, but Horst Dassler stuck to his guns. To the consternation of the San Jose clan, Lee Evans' record was promptly disallowed.

Meanwhile, thousands of more traditional German-made Puma shoes were sailing to Mexico. The container arrived along with Armin Dassler and some other Puma managers. The Adidas delegation, led by Horst, had already set up shop in Mexico and it had arranged a Dassler-style welcome for the Puma men. Three years earlier, in what seems to be a blatant violation of the most elementary fair-trading rules, Horst had struck a deal giving Adidas exclusive rights to shoe sales in the Olympic village. Most would be manufactured by a Mexican company, but Adidas would be granted a special licence to import another allotment of shoes from Germany for free. Puma, on the other hand, would face a stiff import tariff of about $10 per pair to get its German-made shoes into Mexico.

Exasperated by his conniving cousin, Armin apparently plotted a little trick of his own to avoid the import duty. The shipment of Puma shoes that reached Mexico in the last days of September looked intriguingly like a container of tax-free Adidas shoes. A telegram from Air France identified the incoming shipment as urgent Adidas business, and the boxes were marked 'AD, Mexico', the customary code prefix for Adidas shipments. But Horst was one jump ahead. When the Puma men headed for the customs storage centre to pick up their shoes, the pre-warned customs officials smirked and shook their heads. 'The whole container had been impounded,' recalled Peter Janssen, a former Puma board member. 'Just days ahead of the opening we were all sitting there in Mexico City, unable to get any shoes out of the customs office.'

Armin Dassler was in for another shock when uniformed men burst into his hotel room. 'They came to fetch us in the middle of the night and accused Armin of handing over forged papers to the customs authorities,' Janssen recalled. Interrogated for several hours, Armin argued vehemently. He couldn't help it if Air France had made a mistake and that his initials were AD. But his protests fell on deaf ears. He was firmly advised to leave the country.

The problem was partly fixed through another envelope. 'I placed it in my handbag, then took a cab for a long ride from our hotel to the airport and handed it over to our sports promotion manager, who found the right man to bribe,' said Irene Dassler, by then Armin's new wife.

'It cost us several thousand dollars to get just fifty pairs of shoes out of the customs depot.' However, a group of British athletes agreed to smuggle out some more spikes. 'They walked over to the customs with empty shoe boxes, insisting that they should be let into the depot because the spikes didn't fit and they had to fetch another pair,' she explained. 'If any guard had bothered to open the boxes, we would have been in an awful lot of trouble.'

Several days later Art Simburg was walking around the Olympic village in Mexico, clutching a bag full of Puma shoes, when two undercover policemen grabbed him by the arms. They ignored Simburg's pleas and drove him away without any further explanation. Wyomia Tyus frantically searched for her fiancé. Given the political climate in Mexico City, where scores of students had been shot dead in a demonstration just days before the opening of the Games, there was no telling what might have happened to Simburg. 'She cried her eyes out, thinking that I was dead,' Simburg recalled later. 'I just disappeared from the face of the earth.'

Detained in a Mexican cell, Simburg was given no reason for his arrest and he was not allowed to make any telephone calls. 'The detention was dreadful,' Simburg said. 'One day there was a guy next to me who was suffering from acute stomach cramps. They just pushed him into a corner until he stopped yelling.' When Puma and US officials finally located Simburg, they were told that he had been arrested for doing business while travelling with a tourist visa. It took a vigorous intervention from the State Department to get Simburg released after five days of detention which destroyed his digestive system. From then on, whenever Art Simburg was offered a spicy dish, he thought of Horst Dassler.

This didn't put an end to the distribution of illicit payments, however. American reporters spotted athletes lining up outside both Armin's and Horst's hotel rooms, to collect their money. In a revealing cover story in *Sports Illustrated*, titled 'The $100,000 Payoff', one athlete recounted how he earned $10,000 by running from Adidas to Puma and back. Another switched to Puma just before he won a gold medal and headed straight to Armin Dassler, who rewarded him with $6,000. 'Why should I sit around like a hermit when everybody is making money out of these people?' he asked. There was a commotion when one of the athletes attempted to cash in a hefty traveller's cheque received from Puma at a bank in the Olympic village: fearful of hold-ups, local banks didn't keep that kind of money in their tills.

David Hemery, a British hurdler, was among the most coveted athletes. At a recent meet in the United States he had beaten Geoffrey Vanderstock, the American who held the world record for the 400 metres hurdles. During the heats in Mexico, it had become clear that Hemery was in great shape, making him an obvious target for the shoe men. He was none the less stunned when, the night before the final, a Puma representative approached him in the Olympic village with a £3,000 offer. Hemery had always worn Adidas; in line with regulations at the time, he could accept five free pairs per year. But the local Adidas manager was equally quick off the mark, dropping by to say, 'Whatever you've been offered, we can match it.'

David Hemery didn't waste much time thinking about it. 'My parents had taught me to operate with integrity,' he said. 'I turned it down because I didn't want to get caught cheating, and I could not have lived with it anyway. During the whole run I would have been wondering if everyone was looking at my feet.' He went on to thrill the crowds by winning the hurdles final by an astonishing margin of more than seven metres.

Among the most enduring Olympic memories was that year's 200 metres final. Tommie Smith and John Carlos had both broken world records in previous heats, but Carlos seemed to be favourite after Smith picked up a minor groin strain in the semi-final. Smith, however, ran a near-perfect race, covering the distance in yet another world-record time of 19.8 seconds. John Carlos was third behind an Australian, Peter Norman.

As the three men headed for the podium later that day, 16 October 1968, a gasp rippled round the packed stadium. The two black Americans stood in black socks, with black scarves draped around their necks. As 'The Star Spangled Banner' sounded out they dropped their heads and each raised one arm to the sky, the fist curled and covered in a black glove. Symbolic of the glaring injustice and poverty suffered by many blacks in the United States, the gesture shocked the Establishment and got Smith banned from athletics. Much later his raised fist would be pictured in history schoolbooks as a poignant symbol of black emancipation – a gutsy expression of Black Power. But for all his political commitment, Smith kept his sponsors in mind: as he walked to the medal

DIRTY TRICKS IN MEXICO

14. *Tommie Smith makes a stand for the rights of black Americans in the United States at the Mexico Olympics in 1968.*

ceremony he brought with him a single Puma spike, which he laid down carefully on the podium.

In the excitement of the competition, other deals were struck in the catacombs of the Olympic stadium. The most spectacular about-turn took place on the rainy day when the long jumpers turned up for their final. Bob Beamon, a raw black athlete from New York who spent part of his adolescence in jail, was among the athletes whom Simburg had won over for Puma. The fourth out of seventeen jumpers in the final, he tore down the runway towards the takeoff board, hit it perfectly and sailed through the air at what seemed an improbable height. Beamon went so far and hit the sand so hard that he ended up outside the pit.

It was such an awesome jump that the optical measuring device had not been set up to cover the point of impact. Stupefied judges had to call for an old-fashioned measuring tape. The verdict was 8.90 metres, pulverizing the previous record and setting another that would hold for more than twenty years. When Beamon realized what he had done, he was felled by a cataplectic seizure. Arguably the most extraordinary athletic achievement of all time, Beamon's jump transfixed millions of viewers, over and over again. Much to Armin Dassler's chagrin, however, the three stripes on Bob Beamon's shoes were clearly visible from every angle.

Only a handful of athletes remained immune to the Dasslers' cash appeal. An upcoming American athlete, Dick Fosbury, had his shoes hand-crafted by Adolf Dassler himself. A keen high-jumper, Adi had heard in amazement that a part-time engineer from Idaho had come up with a new technique. While others jumped from their inside leg and curled the other over the bar, Fosbury rolled over it head first with his back to the ground. When Fosbury inaugurated his weird flop he was derided by other athletes and officials, but Adi Dassler immediately picked up his phone.

Several weeks later Fosbury was thrilled to receive a package from Germany, containing handmade shoes that were exactly right for him. For added distinction, the left and right shoes were differently coloured. He wore them in Mexico City, when he stunned onlookers with a jump that propelled him over a bar set at 2.24 metres. The Siberian-born Valery Brumel's world record was slightly higher, but at Mexico City Fosbury's effort was enough to earn him gold. 'It was just amazing that this German cobbler would spend hours on spikes just for me,' said the high jumper. 'I was extremely grateful and certainly wouldn't dream of accepting cash to wear them.' The Fosbury Flop is now the standard technique for high-jumpers.

The bundles of dollars handed out liberally in Mexico deeply upset the supporters of the amateur rules, and they had no doubt who was to blame: 'The entire Dassler family would have to be deported to Siberia', one suggested, for the practice to end. Many pragmatists, however, acknowledged that the outdated rules should be abolished. Sensing weakness, emancipated athletes began to raise the stakes unashamedly.

Meanwhile, Horst Dassler's status had also begun to change. No longer was he the affable young German with the holdall full of spikes but a respected entrepreneur, the international face of Adidas. From his French stronghold, Horst Dassler was planning to seize control of his parents' brand.

10

The Overgrown Son

Back in Herzogenaurach, Adolf and Käthe Dassler watched their impetuous son with growing unease. While they contentedly filled out orders,
Horst pushed ahead with increasingly bold moves. The contrasting
attitudes led to rancorous discussions between Horst and his parents,
but he staunchly refused to be held back by their conservative ways.

Although Horst deeply respected his father, he was often at logger-
heads with his mother and he was altogether exasperated by the pre-
tensions of his four sisters. They were all still living in the compound
and meddling with the business with varying degrees of seriousness.
Yet none of them could match the commitment of their brother, and
many employees felt that the Dassler daughters would never have
attained their position if they had been subjected to a normal job
interview.

Given his drive and achievements, it seemed obvious that Horst was
best equipped to take charge of the business one day, but his family was
not in a hurry to admit it and Horst didn't have the patience to sit about
waiting. He felt that his parents were wasting precious time, while the
sports market was changing at breathtaking speed. Permanently on the
lookout, Horst saw opportunities for the three stripes everywhere and
he could not bear to let them pass by.

To wrest control of the company from his parents Horst needed to
spread his influence beyond the French borders. Adidas was mostly sold
in other countries through distributors, who bought their products from
Herzogenaurach. But Horst knew that, if he could convince the distributors to buy more products from his French operation, his turnover would
take off. 'All that mattered was size,' said one of his aides, 'because that
meant more weight against Herzogenaurach.'

Horst effectively resolved to compete against his parents. To this end
he transformed Landersheim into a parallel organization with its own
development, production, marketing and export units. They would
produce their own lines of Adidas trainers and offer them independent
of the German ranges. The French managers all knew what was expected of them: 'Forget Puma and the other brands,' said Günter

Sachsenmaier, former French export manager. 'For us, the competition was Herzogenaurach.'

When the managers in Landersheim began to offer their own lines, Horst and his parents agreed that they should be displayed at the same time as the German lines, at regular product meetings in Herzogenaurach. The weightiest distributors would be invited to inspect samples from both ranges. Then they would take their pick, ordering a mix of products from Landersheim and Herzogenaurach. The meetings caused some awkward exchanges, as the French and German managers assiduously courted the distributors and unashamedly competed for their orders.

This weird arrangement stemmed from the inextricable interests of the two sides. Horst could hardly build his business without the assent of his parents, but they owned the three stripes, which were still the strongest asset of the Landersheim operation. As for Adi and Käthe, they had to acknowledge that their son's acumen benefited them all. At a time when Herzogenaurach was struggling to keep up with international demand, it seemed absurd to thwart the expansion of Landersheim. By holding joint meetings in Herzogenaurach, the Germans would at least retain some control over the sprawling French business and its aggressive leader.

Predictably, distributors in the French-speaking countries placed most of their orders in Landersheim. Then Horst more or less annexed Spain, where he forged many personal and business ties. He was particularly at ease in the peninsula since he spent a few months as a youngster learning Spanish with a family in Oviedo.

His understanding of Spanish mores helped him to deal with Leon de Cos Borbolla, a shrewd Spaniard who specialized in the registration of existing brand names. This caused awful headaches for Adidas as well as Puma, for which de Cos Borbolla had obtained Spanish rights. No matter what they invested in Spain, Adidas and Puma could be certain that de Cos Borbolla would at least partly benefit from it. Armin Dassler refused to negotiate with the Spaniard, so preventing Puma from truly exploiting the Spanish market for many years, but Horst offered a deal: if de Cos Borbolla surrendered the rights to the three stripes in Spain, he would be given a licence to make Adidas bags. This amicably solved the matter and established Horst's influence in Spanish-speaking countries.

Yet Adidas in France and Germany competed head-on for orders from other countries, which were open to offers from both sides. The highest prize was the United States, where sales of Adidas products were taking off at dizzying speed. The original deal for this huge territory came about in 1955, when Simeon Dietrich dropped by in Herzogenaurach. The owner of a small hardware business in Michigan, Dietrich was running an errand for a friend, a track coach who needed Adidas spikes. He left Herzogenaurach with exclusive rights to distribute three-striped products throughout the entire United States. Just like many other Adidas partnerships at the time, the agreement was sealed with a hand-shake – later confirmed in a written contract that contained just two paragraphs.

Several years later Dietrich admitted that he could not cover the United States by himself. By 1968, the country was carved up between Dietrich's heir and three other distributors: Doc Hughes, a full-blooded Texan, was covering the south-east; Bill Closs, once a basketball player with the Phoenix Pistons and a former Converse salesman, had taken the whole West Coast from the Severn brothers; and Ralph Libonati obtained the East Coast. Gary Dietrich, Simeon's nephew, retained the Midwest.

The four American distributors relished their meetings in Europe – the warmth of Käthe's welcome, the convivial entertainment that was arranged for them. They were once taken on a one-week tour that included overnight stays in magnificent French castles and dinners in some of the country's finest restaurants. Some of them enjoyed the trappings of a considerable fortune, built on the back of Adidas. They were offering such a distinctive product that the shoes almost sold themselves. 'The growth was exponential,' recalled Gary Dietrich. 'For several years I spent most of my evenings at the office, just filling orders.'

The understanding between Horst and his parents was that the French would be allowed to sell their own lines on the condition that they would not make up more than half the export orders. But Horst was far too hungry to abide by this rule. To grab more orders from his parents, he shrewdly exploited their weaknesses.

The biggest problem was that the Adidas pipeline was choked. Through-out the fifties, Käthe Dassler had sealed scores of distribution agreements with people who just dropped in at the right time. Following Adidas triumphs at international level, the requests kept streaming in. It had always been a struggle to adjust production in Herzogenaurach, and once demand for Adidas began to rocket, the company could no longer keep up. It got caught in a chaotic spiral, with scores of distributors clamouring for stock.

The shortages drove the Americans and other distributors to despair. 'We were ordering one year in advance and the products would still come in late,' said Gary Dietrich. 'It was constant. It was hell.' They were bombarded with phone calls from irate retailers who were having to turn customers away.

'I once requested an entire container and sat waiting for months,' recalled Bill Closs. 'Our contact person at the export department eventually admitted that it had gone missing. They simply could not locate it. I suspect that they just decided to divert it to someone else.'

The Americans became increasingly frustrated. They complained incessantly but felt that the Germans were ignoring them. Horst Dassler rightly saw that, if he could make up for some of the German shortages with more timely and adequate French products, the distributors would turn to him with open arms.

To begin with, Horst Dassler sought production deals that would enable him to make three-striped shoes at unbeatable prices. The point was that the distributors made a living on the margin between the price of the products bought from Adidas and the price they obtained from the retailers. The smallest reduction that Adidas France could offer on the purchasing prices would go straight into the pockets of the distributors.

Since he had been shunted off to Dettwiller, Horst Dassler had acquired several other plants in the Alsace and in the Landes, close to the Spanish border. The French production costs were slightly below the German levels, and to push his advantage Horst came up with an audacious plan. He sent his production manager, Charles Hesse, to explore manufacturing deals in east European countries.

At a time when the Iron Curtain was still tightly sealed, this was no small undertaking. On behalf of the French organization, Hesse sat through endless discussions with communist bureaucrats. At considerable cost to his liver, he struck production agreements with suppliers in Romania, Hungary and Czechoslovakia.

These complicated arrangements paved the way for privileged relationships with communist sports authorities while at the same time enabling the French organization to cut its costs of production to an estimated 40 per cent below the German levels. 'The internal competition stimulated us to constantly seek cheaper production,' said Hesse. 'The whole purpose of the set-up was to beat the Germans, by any means at our disposal.'

The Germans desperately attempted to compete by stepping up their own production. They enlarged their plant in Herzogenaurach and acquired several others around Germany. The expansion was supervised by Alf Bente, husband of Inge, the eldest of the four Dassler sisters. To speed up production, in the early seventies he sealed a large-scale contract with a shoe manufacturer in Yugoslavia that concentrated on cheap football boots. The ploy initially provoked a barrage of complaints from distributors as the Yugoslav-made Adidas products quickly fell apart.

Bente explored further partnerships in Taiwan, where he met the Riu brothers. They would become close partners over the next decades, with up to twenty plants churning out three-striped products – most of them shipped to Europe and the United States. The precise arrangements with the Rius remained hazy, but the Riu brothers certainly made a fortune on the back of Adidas, enabling them to build up a conglomerate with such assets as the luxury Sherwood Hotel in Taipei.

The distributors often felt uneasy at their meetings in Herzogenaurach, when German and French managers openly competed for orders, but many of them gladly exploited the situation by pitting the two sides against each other. After their regular get-together in Herzogenaurach, they would sneak off to Landersheim to take a closer look at the entire French range, and to negotiate purchasing prices. 'Once we had finished in Herzogenaurach, we would drive them to the Nuremberg airport for their return flight,' said a former export manager in Herzogenaurach. 'But as soon as we turned our backs they'd walk out of the airport again and head straight for Landersheim.'

The Germans fiercely defended their patch, but the more ingenious French managers still snatched large chunks of international business from under the nose of head office. One of their decisive advantages was that, in his drive to out-sell his parents, Horst was permanently on the lookout for the next big thing. His parents seemed unbeatable in track and football, so he grabbed his orders elsewhere.

*

When Gerhard Prochaska drove from Landersheim to Herzogenaurach for the regular meetings with international distributors, his German colleagues eyed the French marketing manager's large holdall with suspicion. The chances were that it would contain yet another nasty surprise for the Germans.

Prochaska had rehearsed his act many times over. 'Horst thoroughly prepared for the meetings. From his talks with the distributors, he knew precisely what they wanted,' he recalled. 'When we started reviewing products the Germans would display a few models, which were never quite right. Then I'd fumble in my bag, hesitantly pull out a sample and say, "Oh look, we just happen to be working on the kind of shoe you're describing. Would that be all right for you?"'

The most startling invention to come out of the French bags was the Superstar. Until then, basketball had been more or less owned by Converse, the American shoe company of All Star fame. Like all the other basketball shoes on the market at the time, Converse high-tops were all canvas. With the launch of the leather Superstar, in 1969, Converse was almost squeezed out of the American basketball business.

The move was inspired by Chris Severn, one of the six brothers who had laboriously peddled three-striped spikes in the American West in the fifties. The Severns lost their Adidas contract in the late sixties, when Horst felt that they were not growing fast enough, and the rights for the region were now in the hands of Bill Closs. But Horst Dassler had forged personal ties with Chris Severn and eagerly listened to his insightful suggestions.

As Severn observed, basketball shoes had barely changed over the previous decades. Their abrupt moves on the court and the poor grip of their canvas shoes regularly combined to give players ankle and knee injuries. With an upper made entirely of leather, the Adidas shoes would provide a much firmer base. To protect the front of the foot, Severn devised a weird-looking shell toe. Another distinctive feature was the outsole: lined with thin grooves, this herringbone pattern would become a reference in the shoe business.

When Chris Severn proudly turned up in the locker rooms with his Superstars, the players weren't too sure if they should take him seriously. 'They had played in Converse canvas shoes all their lives. The Superstar looked completely alien to them,' explained Severn. 'They weren't even getting paid by the manufacturer, it was just a habit.' While Converse was working with an entire army of salesmen, often former players, Severn was hawking his shoes all by himself, with just a few introductions and no budget at all.

Horst's special envoy was getting discouraged when he met up with Jack McMann, then manager of the San Diego Rockets. He was more than receptive to Severn's pitch, because three of his players were suffering from slip injuries. He convinced nearly all of the players to give the leather Superstars a try. At the opening of the season, Chris Severn was sitting in the bleachers with his fingers crossed. He had heard that a Converse man had made the trip to San Diego and that the players had been offered some money to stick with the canvas shoes. 'When they ran into the arena, lo and behold, they were all wearing three-striped shoes,' said Severn. 'It was a real thrill and it caused quite a stir among the public.'

The Converse men still weren't shaking in their canvas shoes. After all, the San Diego Rockets were the lowliest team in the league. What they failed to grasp was that, whatever position they occupied, the Rockets still had to play every other team in the league. By the end of the season, every professional NBA player had been confronted with the startling sight of the leather shoes on the feet of the Rockets. Chris Severn's phone began to ring.

The second year after its introduction, word had spread to such an extent that the Superstar was worn by most members of the Boston Celtics. Their victory in the American championship that same year opened the floodgates, and the flood was phenomenal: less than four years after the launch of the leather shoes, about 85 per cent of all professional basketball players in the United States had switched to Adidas.

Converse retaliated with player contracts, giving rise to a multi-million-dollar endorsement industry. Some of the players grabbed the cash and reverted to their canvas shoes, but Chris Severn convinced Horst Dassler to sign up some emblematic players on the Adidas side. Towering over them was Kareem Abdul-Jabbar (formerly known as Lewis Alcindor), a seven-foot-two giant who rose quite literally to fame at the Los Angeles Lakers. 'The nice thing about Kareem was that he had always turned down offers to wear Converse,' said Severn. 'He just figured that he played better with Adidas, and his performance mattered more than any Converse deal.'

15. Kareem Abdul-Jabbar signs a deal to endorse the Adidas Superstar in February 1976 – an unprecedented contract. He is flanked by Horst Dassler and Chris Severn, the man behind the best-selling basketball shoe.

The Dasslers reluctantly agreed to cough up $25,000 per year for Abdul-Jabbar, the first basketball player to be contracted by Adidas. With his patented hook, he went on to set multiple records in an unparalleled twenty-year career, most of them in Adidas. The only problem he caused the company was when he showed up in Landersheim: the managers of the Auberge had to saw off the footboards from his bed so that the player could fit in.

Just as Horst intended, the Superstar massively inflated the orders posted by the American distributors in Landersheim. By the early seventies basketball made up more than 10 per cent of Adidas sales – and was 100 per cent under the control of Adidas France.

Horst dealt an even more devastating blow to the German operation in the early seventies, when he decided to hijack the tennis market. As the French managers observed, tennis was undergoing a radical change. No longer monopolized by upper crust men in pressed trousers and women in starched dresses, tennis courts had been taken over by a more diverse cast of players.

Until the sixties, the sport was reserved to well-heeled amateurs who safely locked the gates of their country clubs to players of less distinguished descent. They organized the major tournaments, which could be entered only by fellow amateurs – players who were wealthy enough to train hard without any prospect of a financial reward.

Once they retired, some of the amateur players still sought to cash in by affixing their name to tennis clothing ranges. René Lacoste, a former French tennis champion, built a sprawling international business on tennis shirts adorned with nothing but a small crocodile – the nickname given to the Frenchman due to his tenacious style. Launched in 1933, Lacoste was the first line of branded tennis garments to feature a logo of any kind. Fred Perry, the last British man to have won a singles title at Wimbledon (in 1936), had another upmarket line of shirts named after him, with a laurel stitched on the breast.

But the segregation between amateurs and professionals became largely artificial in the sixties, as the major tournaments were infiltrated by supposedly amateur players who found ways to earn a living from their performance: if they could not earn prize money, they could at least pay the rent by lending their names to a shoe, a shirt or a racket.

Until then, the shoes worn by tennis players were basically plimsolls, low-cut shoes with flat rubber soles and canvas uppers that became popular in England in the nineteenth century along with seaside holidays. They are the ancestors of such brands as Dunlop and Uniroyal, whose parent companies turned out tennis shoes as a sideline to their rubber business. Yet rising enthusiasm for tennis prompted other companies to invest in the sport, unofficially paying players to promote their products. A new word entered the sporting lexicon: 'shamateurism'.

Adidas France hit the ground running with Robert Haillet, one of just two French tennis professionals in the late fifties. Just as he was contemplating retirement, Haillet was approached in 1964 by Horst Dassler to design a tennis shoe. Like most other French players at the time, Haillet had been wearing Spring Court, a French brand which had been around since the thirties, made of canvas with rubber soles. But Horst Dassler had something else in mind: the Robert Haillet would be the first-ever leather tennis shoe.

'It was damned complicated at the time,' Haillet recalled. 'It took us at least one year to get them done, and then the soles still kept coming unglued.' The technical headaches eventually paid off. When the Robert

Haillet made its debut in 1965, the small cadre of tennis professionals who emerged at the time widely agreed that it was by far the best shoe on the market. Along the same lines as the Superstar in basketball, the leather provided more support, which prevented twisted ankles and other slip injuries.

In the interim, tennis continued to draw swelling crowds. The changes became most apparent in 1968, when Wimbledon gave up its exclusively amateur status. It ushered in the open era, allowing self-declared professionals to dominate the game. This meant that tennis could openly seek sponsorship deals. The all-white decorum was partly abandoned (except at Wimbledon) and tennis became more egalitarian. Suspecting that the market was about to explode, Horst decided to turn tennis into a cornerstone of his business.

By now Robert Haillet had retired from the game, to become a sales representative for Adidas in the south of France, and his profile was no longer in line with Horst Dassler's searing ambitions. The hungry heir therefore decided to launch roughly the same shoe under the name of a more prominent player, who could generate publicity throughout the tennis world.

Donald Dell, a former player himself and the most influential agent in the tennis business, offered him Stan Smith. Due to his huge, Viking-style frame, the American champion was sometimes dubbed Godzilla. He rarely smiled on court and refused to provide any other entertainment than his game. Yet Smith topped the international tennis charts for most of the early seventies, repeatedly leading the American team to Davis Cup victories.

Smith had previously worn canvas shoes by Converse and by Uniroyal, an unpretentious American brand which contracted him as part of an entire team. With Adidas it was another story: they promised Smith a separate contract and promised to back it up with large-scale marketing investments. They were eyeing a large slice of the appetizing American tennis market. Smith was delighted to obtain royalties on a shoe bearing his own name.

While the Robert Haillet had been hobbling along, the Stan Smith raced to another dimension. Sales began to mushroom shortly after the switch, in 1971. The player himself was somewhat baffled to see many of his opponents wearing his shoes. 'I got really annoyed the first time that I lost a match against a guy who was wearing them,' he said.

With his next volley, Horst Dassler swept his German rivals off the court. An impetuous young Romanian called Ilie Nastase was enthralling the crowds with his stunning touch and his on-court antics. When he emerged as an international player in the early sixties, Nastase turned up at Roland-Garros for the French Open with entirely flat-soled canvas shoes made by Chinese comrades, causing many slides and falls. He beamed with pride when René Lacoste offered him matching shirts and shorts.

Once he had become a notorious haggler in the early seventies, the Romanian was approached by Nike, an American upstart. In 1972 they offered him a $5,000 contract and gave him shoes with 'Nasty' embossed on the heel. His doubles partner, the American player Jimmy Connors, obtained his own pair with 'Jimbo' on the heel. The market was still so fresh that Connors gladly wore his personalized Nikes for free.

Many at Adidas felt that Nastase was ill-suited to endorse the German brand. Prone to arguments with umpires and other tactics that bordered on foul play, he was likely to damage the brand's reputation. 'My friend Horst just turned around and told them that was precisely why he picked me,' recalled Nastase. 'That shut them up.' The player switched to Adidas in 1973, when the company offered him a four-year contract for about $50,000, a substantial sum at the time, to use the full Adidas tennis range. From the shirt down to the socks, Nastase wandered onto the courts in three stripes.

Though Horst Dassler courted many athletes, his relationship with Nastase turned into a personal friendship. Unfailingly, the Romanian player received full cartons of Adidas equipment for his family and personal gifts from Horst at Christmas. When Nastase went through his first divorce, Dassler called to comfort him. With the apparent naïveté that endeared him to his managers, he proudly exhibited a precious watch offered by Nastase: 'To my friend Horst,' read the message engraved on the back.

The all-encompassing Nastase deal was signed at a time when the player had reached his peak, but Adidas France still drew huge benefits from the tie-up. The white and blue Nastase shoe was worn by an entire generation of tennis amateurs. Although the Germans felt compelled to come up with their own tennis shoe, the upscale Wimbledon, they could not compete with the unbeatable duo of Smith and Nastase.

The two really took off in the seventies, when students began to match their jeans with tennis shoes. With its plain, all-white design, the 'Stan Smith' was particularly well-suited for this trend. Unlike other Adidas shoes, it featured the stripes only in the shape of small ventilation holes, neatly aligned in three rows. It could be worn with almost any colour of trousers, just like the Nastase. While the two players faded into retirement their shoes attained cult status, with sales of close to 40 million pairs for the Stan Smith and 20 million for the Nastase over the next decades.

With the tennis explosion, the French export business assumed such proportions that Horst Dassler pleaded with his managers to truncate their figures. Between the basketball and tennis sales, combined with cheaper football boots, Landersheim reached a turnover of about 10 million pairs per year. 'Horst asked us to disguise the fact that our exports were growing much faster than the business in Herzogenaurach,' said Günter Sachsenmaier, former export manager in Landersheim. 'He was always afraid that his parents would freak out.'

As the French operation continued to spread, Käthe Dassler went to humiliating lengths to keep the situation under control. She tolerated some of the rivalry between the French and German organizations, because it evidently stimulated the company. However, Käthe firmly intended to rule over international operations at Adidas, which provoked increasingly frequent and public clashes.

Since Horst had begun to build his own organization, his mother had kept him under close surveillance. French managers who travelled to Herzogenaurach were often subjected to sharp questions by 'La Mutti'. Others did their best to avoid her at trade fairs. No matter what they had been up to, there was a fair chance that Käthe would nab them for suspected breaches of German–French arrangements.

The situation was particularly thorny for French executives who, following orders, constantly overstepped the German rules. Günter Sachsenmaier in Landersheim drew many complaints from Herzogenaurach. Horst instructed him to ignore the reprimands, which left him constantly on edge. 'Horst told us to race ahead regardless,' said Sachsenmaier. 'He would protect us and deal with his family behind closed doors. But we still suffered a lot from the twisted relationship with Herzogenaurach, which was very stressful.'

Günter Sachsenmaier was just as embarrassed by the envious remarks of his German colleagues. 'When they came to Landersheim they marvelled at our set-up,' Sachsenmaier recalled. 'And when we were over there they kept moaning about the German Dasslers. They were jealous of the independence we enjoyed with Horst. In Herzogenaurach, they told us, they couldn't do anything without consulting the entire hierarchy.' It could not have been more unlike the situation in Landersheim, where Horst sent his aides on the warpath with clear instructions, but then trusted them to reach their objectives more or less as they saw fit.

Many other French managers suffered from the company's schizophrenic situation, and at least one of them could not be rescued from German wrath. Günther Morbitzer, former head of the export department, strongly overplayed his hand. While other managers strove to protect Horst from any unnecessary aggravation in Herzogenaurach, Morbitzer was fed up with all the contortions. The French subsidiary had gained such clout in the international market that he could no longer be bothered to grovel at meetings with the Germans, pretending to care for their opinion. When Morbitzer made this all too blatantly clear, Käthe Dassler demanded his removal.

The tensions between Käthe and Horst also began to taint relationships with distributors. When she gave welcoming speeches to distributors visiting Herzogenaurach, Käthe rarely failed to point out, with thinly veiled bitterness, that Germany was to be regarded as the point of reference for the company's international business. The distributors, who had often planned extensive stays in the Auberge du Kochersberg afterwards, shuffled uncomfortably in their chairs.

Some of them felt so awkward that they resolved to move on. For Peter Lewin, the Adidas distributor in Spain, the decision came after a very lively dinner with Käthe in Barcelona. 'The next day I received a phone call from Horst, asking me to describe what was said in the most precise details,' Lewin recalled. 'I no longer wanted to be caught in the middle of their crazy relationship.'

Back in Herzogenaurach, Adi Dassler watched the business with increasing detachment. In his early seventies, he was tired of the relentless complaints from his managers, his wife and his daughters. One of his assistants recalled that, to avoid responding, he sometimes drove his car from the entrance of the factory to his home, a distance of less than a hundred metres, to spare himself from unwanted encounters. Yet, there were some affronts which even Adi Dassler was not prepared to tolerate.

11

From Head to Toe

The Dassler family could hardly have dreamed of a more momentous occasion than the Munich Olympics which opened in August 1972. The two behemoths from Herzogenaurach could not fail to shine: the Games were being held in their own backyard and they knew all the people who counted in the organization. All being well, the contest would turn into a crowning moment for the Dasslers.

The Adidas managers prepared meticulously. They cajoled the likely medallists to make sure they would wear the right shoes. They set up talks with coaches and dignitaries who were certain to drop by in Munich. But perhaps most importantly, they struck a deal with the organizers of the Games: this time Adidas would not only grace the feet of the athletes, it would also feature on their chests.

With this foray into clothing, Adidas turned the sports business into a whole new ballgame. From then on, the Dasslers could chase deals that would enable them to gain exposure through shirts as well as shoes. The bulk of their business would shift from sports to leisure, and they would suddenly become part of urban fashion, drawing celebrities that had never set foot in a sports club.

The move may have seemed obvious, but Adidas was long held back by Adi Dassler's reluctance to deal with clothing. When he began to order three-striped tracksuits in the early sixties, it was mostly as a favour to football coaches. At one of the national team's training sessions he bumped into Willy Seltenreich, the manager of Schwahn, a small-time German supplier. Once they got talking, Dassler asked Seltenreich to make about a thousand tracksuits for Adidas, 'with three stripes running down the pipes just like that'.

Once the warm-up suits had been adopted by Bayern Munich in 1962, the few boxes of tracksuits quickly turned into huge deliveries. Other football clubs and retailers eagerly ordered their own. Since they already got their boots from Adidas, it was just as easy to buy shirts from them as well. After a few years Adidas had elbowed out most of Schwahn's other customers, and the Dassler family resolved to buy the company.

By the early seventies, Käthe Dassler had convinced her husband to introduce a more plentiful range of Adidas shorts and shirts. Intended for football, other sports and general leisure, the garments were to be adorned with a fresh emblem. The assignment was entrusted to Hans Fick, owner of a small design studio which already handled some catalogues for the German side of the company. The Dasslers' choice fell on three leaves that were striped horizontally at the bottom. Inspired by the crown on the jackets of Swedish athletes, it became known as the trefoil.

The investments in clothing were to be rewarded with massive exposure at the Munich Olympics. After drawn-out discussions with the organizing committee, Adidas had obtained a compromise agreement: it was deemed unacceptable that athletes should appear on the track covered in three stripes, but for the first time they would be allowed to wear clothes that were clearly branded. This was where the trefoil came in: the International Olympic Committee would not object to a small version of the emblem on the vests of the athletes.

Until then, Olympic athletes had worn nondescript and often shabby singlets: at best they featured the colours of their country's flag or its emblem. No other companies had begun to explore clothing in earnest, but Adidas signed endorsement deals with several national athletics federations and supplied them with thousands of shirts that were branded with the trefoil.

The company's clothing was even more visible outside the track, where athletes freely walked around in three-striped tracksuits supplied by Adidas – green for the women and lavender-blue for the men. In a frenetic effort to curb the presence of large companies at the event, Avery Brundage, still head of the IOC, sent his men around the Olympic village to seize airport bags featuring the Lufthansa logo. However, he overlooked the ubiquitous three stripes.

Adi and Käthe Dassler invested most generously in the Munich Olympics. They realized that they would not be able to deal with the influx of athletes who turned up on their doorstep in Herzogenaurach, and therefore ordered the construction of an entire hotel for their guests. The Sportshotel was built on the hills above the Adidas factory. It was initially laid out as a dormitory, an annexe to the Olympic village, but later upgraded to welcome worthy guests from all round the world.

To deepen their contacts with international athletes, the Dasslers further asked Ray Schiele, head of their Canadian subsidiary, to return to Germany. While Horst Dassler worked with multilingual managers, none of his family members in Germany could effortlessly chat with English speakers. Schiele would help to make them feel at ease. The relationship between the Dasslers and the Schieles had grown so close that he was allowed to buy some land next to the factory in Herzogenaurach and to build a house that became part of the Dassler compound, ready for the Schieles to move into a few months before the Olympics.

Horst Dassler still managed to upstage his parents at the Olympic village, where he arranged to set up an Adidas store. Under the Olympic rules, it was officially forbidden to sell or hand out any three-striped shoes within the village, but the enforcement of these regulations was becoming increasingly farcical. 'Every athlete in Munich knew that there was a special room at the back of our tent where we just handed out spikes,' said one of the Dassler aides.

But this time, the Adidas stand no longer welcomed athletes alone. The company's managers made time for other prominent people who thought it cool to be spotted in three-striped clothing. Princess Grace of Monaco was among the luminaries who turned up at the VIP lounge. In tune with the sporty fashion that began to emerge at the time, the three stripes were stepping off the pitches and straight onto the covers of celebrity magazines.

The Puma Dasslers looked on enviously. They barely had any clothing to offer and were still concentrating entirely on wooing athletes to wear their shoes. The company made some German front pages with Klaus Wolfermann, a German javelin thrower who took gold in Munich and went on to work in Puma's sports promotion department. Derek Ibbotson, the former runner who worked for Puma in England, secured some more triumphs: the most memorable of them was Mary Peters, the Ulsterwoman who won the gold medal for the pentathlon. There is no evidence that Wolfermann or Peters took money to wear Puma shoes.

Armin Dassler had rented out an entire villa on the Starnberger lake, south of Munich, to entertain Puma athletes. But Armin no longer had to deal with his cousin alone: along with Adidas he was suddenly confronted with a far less familiar foe.

There was a new kid on the block, an American newcomer marketed by a tiny company called Blue Ribbon Sports. The operation was run by Philip Knight, a lanky middle-distance runner and graduate of the

Stanford Business School. Then known as 'Buck', Knight had always worn Adidas, but he thought it outrageous that American students should be more or less condemned to buy expensive German shoes. In his Stanford paper he outlined a business plan to set up a competing brand. 'Can Japanese sports shoes do to German sports shoes what Japanese cameras did to German cameras?' he asked.

The question was still at the back of Knight's mind when he left Stanford and began to work as a chartered accountant. On a visit to Japan in 1962 he obtained an interview with Kihachiro Onitsuka, owner of the Tiger brand, which still specialized in running shoes. Although he didn't have any business to his name, Knight cheekily introduced himself as an American distributor, instantly making up the Blue Ribbon Sports name. He bluffed so convincingly that Onitsuka gave him an exclusive deal to sell Tiger in the United States.

The partnership demonstrated that there was huge US demand for cheaper and more flexible running shoes. Knight quickly figured that, if he sealed production agreements with the same manufacturers as Onitsuka, he could introduce a brand of his own. In 1972 he began to sell copies of Tiger shoes under another name. Knight intended to call it Dimension Six but a former running mate and employee came up with Nike, the goddess of victory. A design student earned $35 to draw a brand sign that looked like an inverted comma, later dubbed the Swoosh.

The other person behind Nike was Bill Bowerman, former coach of the track and field team at the University of Oregon, a training ground for many of the country's most remarkable runners and jumpers. Tinkering in his garage, like Adolf Dassler in his mother's laundry, Bowerman came up with astonishing novelties. One of them was known as the Vagina ('looking scary but feeling wonderful inside'). Another startling invention was the Waffle trainer, so called after the kitchen appliance which Bowerman had used to mould its soles.

Knight and Bowerman repeatedly stated that they had entered the business for one single purpose: to beat Adidas. As he travelled to the Munich Olympics, his arch-enemy's home turf, Bowerman was in combative mood. He had been appointed as coach of the American track and field team, and this was his chance to show the Germans a few tricks. Bowerman bitterly complained about the marathon route laid out by the organization, which included an uncomfortable section of gravel. Asked why he should have a say in this, he reportedly held up two fingers and replied: 'World War One and World War Two'. Still, Nike failed to impress and the American team's performance proved disappointing.

To make matters worse, one of Bowerman's protégés declined to wear Nike. Knight and Bowerman both regarded Steve Prefontaine, an American long-distance runner, as an emblematic athlete for their brand. With his dashing good looks and outspoken ways, 'Pre' was a crowd favourite who set multiple records as a student. But Prefontaine had been assiduously courted by Mike Larrabee, the man in charge of Adidas promotion among American athletes.

A former mathematics teacher, Larrabee himself had run a stunning 400 metres at the 1964 Olympics in Tokyo. He had burst from fifth position at the final bend to gold medal at the finish. When he retired four years later, Horst Dassler immediately hired him to hand out Adidas spikes. Larrabee stored them in his garage in Santa Monica, and his home became a meeting point for athletes from all around the region. By the late sixties Adidas had become such a coveted brand that retailers on the West Coast drew up huge waiting lists, and even celebrities had to wait several months for their deliveries. Margaret Larrabee, Mike's wife, once opened the door to Michael Jackson and his family, who had driven all the way to Santa Monica just to pick up a few pairs.

Larrabee went about his job with such dedication that he personally befriended many American athletes. He steadfastly refused to give them cash to wear Adidas, but he often offered personal services and paid for rounds of drinks from his own pocket. Steve Prefontaine was enjoying just such an outing, shortly before the Munich Olympics, when Larrabee brought up the subject of Adidas.

'Pre' was caught between two loyalties: he hated to disappoint his friend Larrabee but he didn't fancy upsetting his coach either. It was therefore agreed that the issue would be resolved through a guzzling contest. If Prefontaine downed his glass of bubbly Portuguese wine faster than Larrabee, he would wear Nike. Otherwise, it would be Adidas. Two rounds were deemed invalid because Prefontaine and Larrabee slammed their glasses so hard on the counter that they broke. The third round sealed an Adidas victory.

As things turned out, Prefontaine finished fourth in the 5,000 metres, behind three runners who all wore three-striped shoes. When the medals were counted, the company boasted that about 80 per cent of the athletes at the Munich Olympics had been competing in Adidas. Between the shoes and the clothing, Adidas crushed all of its competitors.

Adi Dassler could not deny that the move into clothing had hugely benefited Adidas. He didn't have a problem with that, as long as the garments remained strictly functional. But all hell broke loose when Horst Dassler decided to ignore such restrictions.

While Munich's Olympic stadium witnessed some thrilling events, the most stunning feat took place in the swimming pool: the man of the Games was Mark Spitz, a handsome American swimmer who left with a record haul of seven gold medals.

Remarkably self-confident, Spitz himself had predicted that he would return from Germany with a sackful of medals. He was greatly disliked by some of his team mates, who resented his incessant bragging. He had fallen flat on his nose in Mexico, when he felt certain to thrash his opponents in at least six races and failed to win a single gold medal in an individual event. But in Munich, Spitz was in unbeatable shape. That became apparent from the start, when he won the 200 metres butterfly by a comfortable margin, setting a new world record in the process.

The American swimmer looked set to make waves, and Horst Dassler was eager to exploit the phenomenon. After a chat in the Olympic village, he convinced Spitz to turn up at medal ceremonies wearing Adidas shoes. The problem was that swimmers often wore sweat pants with very wide bottoms, to be removed more easily. Dassler therefore suggested that Spitz could carry the shoes in his hands.

That was precisely what Spitz did after his second world-record victory, in the 200 metres freestyle. He arrived for the medal ceremony barefoot, with a pair of Adidas Gazelle in his hand. As 'The Star Spangled Banner' echoed around the pool, he dropped the shoes on the podium. But once the anthem ended he picked them up again and enthusiastically waved at the crowds with the three-striped shoes on display. Enraged by the publicity, the watchdogs of the IOC threatened to investigate the matter. The swimmer's manager was in tears. It took all of Horst Dassler's appeasement skills to settle the matter, and the IOC eventually cleared Spitz of any wrongdoing.

Because he was Jewish, Spitz was flown out of West Germany under tight security escort before the end of the Games. His entourage feared more attacks from the Palestinian terrorists who had sneaked into the Olympic village in the early hours of 5 September, killing two members of the Israeli delegation and taking another nine hostage. Spitz, who had won the last of his seven medals just hours before, had been asleep near by.

The swimmer immediately announced that he would retire, which enabled him to sign personal contracts. Endorsements of individual swimmers were strictly prohibited at the time, but there was nothing that prevented retired champions from promoting any brands they chose. While the drama unfolded in Munich, ending in the deaths of all nine Israeli hostages during a botched rescue attempt, Spitz flew to London with his agent to hold talks with a host of sponsors.

Among them were managers from Adidas France, sent on a personal mission by Horst Dassler. As he saw it, the excitement generated by Spitz created a stupendous opportunity for Adidas to enter the swimwear market. Horst had been plotting this for several months, meeting up with designers and looking for suitable fabrics, but when he heard the suggestion, Adi Dassler was not exactly thrilled: 'Horst, you won't spare me anything!' he burst out indignantly. 'Sure enough, you have done well for us. But bathing suits, never! You have gone completely mad. Never under the Adidas brand!' Adidas was about shoes and swimmers didn't wear any, therefore swimwear was out of the question.

When they floated the thought at an internal meeting in Herzo-genaurach, before the Munich Games, the French managers were treated to another dose of sarcasm by their German colleagues. 'You must be out of your mind,' they told Günter Sachsenmaier, the export manager. 'Next thing you'll be flogging Adidas bras and pyjamas!' At the receiving end of these furious tirades, Horst Dassler retained his cool. It didn't matter, he replied calmly: if his parents refused to launch swimwear under the Adidas brand, he would launch it under a brand called Arena.

Horst had been using this name for several years in Spain. The production of leather footballs by Spanish prisoners had been set up under a company called Arena España – to escape the scrutiny of the Dasslers in Herzogenaurach, who might have opposed the arrangement. The Arena brand name was later used by Horst Dassler to move cheap sneakers in the French market. To protect the reputation of Adidas, which was known in France as a producer of upscale leatherware, Horst preferred to market the cheaper canvas shoes under another label. He negotiated to buy the Arena brand from a French trader, who had registered it for a small business in Nîmes, close to the city's Roman arena.

The French team then designed Arena's three-diamonds logo, to be printed on the canvas shoes along with two stripes. Arena had become a small and unglamorous part of the French company. For Horst, however, it was a back door that would enable him to develop his business without his family's consent. The swimwear range was the first large-scale opportunity for Horst Dassler to set up a business of his own.

The task was entrusted to Alain Ronc, a dedicated manager in the export department. He was called into Horst Dassler's office and furiously scribbled notes as Dassler went through his plans for Arena swimwear. 'He had it all in his head, down to the most practical details, production, marketing, partnerships and everything,' Ronc recalled. 'He sat there talking for two hours. He had given me work for the next three years.'

With Arena, Horst envisaged a raid on the swimwear business. Mark Spitz, who had been wearing Speedo in Munich as contracted between that brand and the American Swimming Federation, was to be persuaded to switch allegiance to a French label that didn't officially exist. Almost single-handedly, Alain Ronc was to set up distribution deals in as many countries as possible. And most importantly, he should keep his Arena files well away from any nosy German visitors.

When Mark Spitz said that he would retire, Horst Dassler was ready to strike. Right after the Munich Olympics, the swimmer agreed to pose in samples of Arena trunks. Horst Dassler spread the pictures so widely among friendly reporters that they were often used in conjunction with articles about his medal haul in Munich. 'This gave the impression that Mark Spitz had won his medals in Arena,' observed Georges Kiehl, the man in charge of international promotion for Arena.

With Arena, Horst Dassler demonstrated just how hard-hitting his French team had become. Barely one year after the confrontation with his father, Arena swimwear duly made its debut at the European championships in Berlin in August 1973. Two years later, at the world championships in Cali, Colombia, roughly two-thirds of the swimmers wore Arena. Horst Dassler invested $100,000 in the championships, a substantial sum at the time. It was spent on team sponsorship deals and an agreement with the organizers: the entire pool seemed covered with

16. Horst Dassler (second from left) establishes Arena, endorsed by Mark Spitz (centre), the swimmer who won seven gold medals at the 1972 Olympics.

Arena diamonds. Speedo, the Australian brand which previously held a virtual monopoly in the swimwear market, appeared completely dumbstruck by the advances of its French rival.

Due to the virulent objections of Horst Dassler's parents, the development of Arena required strenuous contortions. Some of the costs were indirectly borne by Adidas: after all, Alain Ronc was on the payroll of Adidas France. But the managers behind Arena didn't have separate budgets for the brand at their disposal and therefore had to improvise. The snapshots for the first catalogues were taken in the office of Alain Ronc, where a group of Adidas executives gladly stripped off to pose in Arena trunks.

Dassler still couldn't push it too far and he regularly had to scrape for money. The situation once became so tight that he requested a personal loan of at least $1 million from Bill Closs, the Adidas distributor for the American West Coast. The call was deeply humiliating for Dassler and just as embarrassing for Closs. Horst made it clear that he needed the money for his own purposes, and that the loan should not be disclosed to his parents. 'They were putting the squeeze on Horst, and he had been a personal friend for a long time. I went to our bank and sent the money to him,' Bill Closs recalled. 'But I didn't think this through clearly, because it couldn't please Germany at all.'

The personal relationship which Horst built up with Bill Closs proved decisive. While Adi never set foot in the United States and Käthe spent most of her time in Herzogenaurach, their son was constantly on the move. He regularly visited Los Angeles and assured Closs that he could call in at any time. When the former basketball player took Horst at his word, he was not disappointed. Horst personally answered the call and rushed to solve the problem. Besides, like some other distributors whose loyalties were torn, Closs kept in mind that the future lay with the hungry young man.

Many others faced an awkward dilemma when Horst approached them to sell Arena. Borsumij Wehry, which had been selling Adidas shoes in the Netherlands since the sixties, pretended to ignore the family tensions. They readily agreed to sell Arena, only to be sternly rebuked by Käthe Dassler at a trade fair in Cologne. The Dutch were presented with a clear choice: either they stopped selling Arena or they would lose the distribution deal for Adidas. They didn't hesitate to drop Arena.

Horst was in such a hurry to build up his brand that he sealed deals with almost anyone who came along. One of the chosen partners was a small-time Canadian coach who claimed to have a sizeable distribution company. Over dinner, Horst Dassler entrusted him with the exclusive distribution rights for Arena in all of Canada and the United States. Alain Ronc, who sat in on the dinner, was somewhat worried about this rash decision. His concerns appeared more than justified when it turned out that the operation of the Canadian coach consisted of a few boxes of goggles in his California garage. 'In our frenetic drive to expand Arena, we regularly fell flat on our noses,' said Ronc. 'But the whole sports market was still so fresh that we still progressed at incredible speed.'

Irked by Arena's rapid expansion, the German side of the company resolved to retaliate by setting up Adidas swimwear. 'The situation was crazy enough for us to launch a swimwear line when we didn't have the slightest competence in this business,' conceded Peter Rduch, then export manager in Herzogenaurach. 'The Germans felt they had to have this, just because Horst had it.'

Back in Wilmslow, the Humphreys brothers watched the three-striped foray into textiles with suspicion. Until then, the British partnership between Umbro and Adidas hinged on their complementary offering, with Umbro covering clothing and Adidas restricted to shoes. Now, all of a sudden, the partners were head-on competitors.

Robbie Brightwell, a lanky British runner, was right in the middle of this thorny situation. He got to know Horst Dassler at the Tokyo Olympics in 1964, where he narrowly missed a medal in the 400 metres. His fiancée, Ann Packer, made up for this disappointment by taking silver in the 400 metres and gold in the 800.

Dassler was struck by Brightwell's savvy and asked him to promote Adidas among his fellow athletes. While the runner was still employed as a university lecturer, he spent many of his weekends trackside persuading other runners to wear three-striped spikes. But towards the end of the sixties, Horst Dassler pleaded with Brightwell to take on a more substantial role.

When the Umbro contract came up for renewal in 1971, one of the conditions imposed by Dassler was that the Adidas business should be run from a small, separate operation. Established in Poynton, this would be headed by Brightwell. The unit was called Umbro Footwear International and the runner was paid by the Humphreys Brothers, but he was unequivocal about his loyalties. 'My brief was to pump up Adidas sales without antagonizing Umbro,' he explained.

Brightwell admirably fulfilled the first part of the mission. When he joined the company, Adidas sales in the United Kingdom stood at roughly £600,000. Before the end of the decade they reached more than £15 million. Previously concentrating on spikes and football boots, it entered many other sports, from rugby to boxing, and sold three-striped clothes by the millions.

However, Brightwell was unable to ease the tensions with Umbro. The concerns of the Humphreys brothers turned into outright consternation once Adidas made it clear that it was serious about the clothing business. 'They became completely paranoid,' he recalled. 'It was major hassle, like going down a minefield.'

The equation was further complicated by the fact that Umbro could barely afford its Adidas deal. With the clothing business the three-striped range widened enormously. The Humphreys brothers profited from the expansion of Adidas, which earned them more than their own brand, but at the same time the explosion of the Adidas business placed Umbro in a parlous financial position. Their finances became so stretched that Adidas offered them extended payment terms and helped them to set up new banking arrangements.

Umbro still had to admit that it could not handle all of the sprawling

Adidas range. It therefore agreed to give up its exclusive tag, handing over some rights to Peter Blacks in Yorkshire. A manufacturer of underwear and luggage, Blacks began by supplying Adidas bags. The deal was later extended to include large chunks of sales through mail order and department stores. The agreement triggered another sales hike for Adidas, but it caused yet more frictions with Umbro.

The Humphreys brothers fully realized that they had a tiger by the tail. By sticking to Umbro as a distributor, Adidas drained the resources of a leading contender. Yet the brothers were still eager to retain some control over the German brand.

Regardless of such conflicts of interest, the investments in apparel proved more than worthwhile for Adidas. For all Adi Dassler's disdain, it quickly made up nearly half of Adidas sales in Germany. There was such huge demand for sports clothing that Adidas hardly bothered to take orders. 'The retailers would have taken almost anything,' said Joe Kirchner, former head of the German textile unit, 'so we could fill out the orders ourselves.'

The explosion came at a time when the lines between leisure and sports clothing became increasingly blurred. It was no longer unseemly to mow the lawn in Beckenbauer shorts, or to walk around town in a tracksuit. Fashion prompted phenomenal sales of Adidas jackets and plain classics like the Swinger, a three-striped tracksuit turned out by the million in a factory in Kassel, in the centre of Germany.

The Adi Dasslers had the German sports clothing market nearly all to themselves. They complemented their own production with the acquisition of Erima in Reutlingen, an established specialist in team sports clothing. Neither Puma nor Nike bothered to come up with a full-fledged apparel range until the late seventies. Yet again, the fiercest competitor to Adidas Germany was just across the Rhine.

Unencumbered by his father's misgivings, Horst eagerly delved into the clothing market. Just like their neighbours in Germany, the French managers sold millions of three-striped shorts and tracksuits. But this was merely the skeleton of a bustling apparel business that out-created the German equivalent many times over.

The French business was orchestrated by Jean Wendling. A former football player at the Stade de Rheims, he had been recruited as a textile manager by one of his erstwhile team-mates, the legendary Raymond

Kopa, who had set up his own sports business. By the time Horst Dassler poached him in the early seventies, Wendling had both unrivalled contacts and expertise in sports clothing. Shortly after his recruitment, Adidas France was turning out hundreds of distinctive lines from regular football shirts to elaborate leisure ranges. Some of them were adorned with the three stripes but Adidas France just as easily used the trefoil.

The French operation largely owed its edge to Ventex in Troyes, a former supplier which Adidas France gobbled up. Previously owned by a chemicals company, the Ventex research and development laboratory was the envy of the industry. 'When German managers asked to be shown around at Ventex,' said Jean Wendling, 'I made sure that the lab remained tightly sealed.' As textile sales boomed around the world, the more creative and colourful French offering turned into another strength for Landersheim in its war of attrition with Herzogenaurach.

To Adi Dassler, the whole clothing business remained a sore point. He didn't mind selling a few three-striped tracksuits, but he certainly didn't care much for the French leisure ranges. 'The boss sometimes told us that he wondered what his son was up to,' said Uwe Seeler. 'This fancy clothing business was foreign to him. He was and remained a shoemaker'. By then in his seventies, Adi Dassler was still at the forefront of his trade. But he was increasingly unsettled by the unashamed demands that began to proliferate in the sports business.

12

The Pelé Pact

As the stakes rose in the football business, Horst and Armin Dassler strove to avoid a repeat of the Mexico episode. Alf Bente, Adi's son-in-law, was repeatedly dispatched to the other side of the Aurach to discuss informal arrangements with Armin Dassler regarding German football. Horst Dassler came to further understandings with his cousin Gerd, established just down the road from Landersheim as head of Puma France.

Football players remained an enticing target for monetary offers, because they guaranteed unparalleled exposure. No other sport drew such large audiences every week, both in the stadium and on television.

Off the pitch, some players were emerging as celebrities in their own right, appearing on chat shows and in magazines. And just as importantly, the football market was huge: the shoes made by all the Dasslers at the time were still intended chiefly to be worn for sports, and football was by far the most popular sport of all.

Undercover payments looked set to cause unrest again in Mexico, at the 1970 World Cup. But this time, before the competition, Horst and Armin Dassler had sealed an astonishing deal. There was one player, the enemy cousins jointly decided, who would remain entirely off limits to both companies: a bidding war for Pelé, the unique Brazilian, was certain to trigger a monetary explosion that neither of them could survive. They called it 'the Pelé pact'.

Pelé had burst to prominence in 1958, when he made his international debut as a 17-year-old at the World Cup in Sweden. He stunned other players with his deftness and agility, helping Brazil to win its first World Cup. Wealthy European clubs offered huge sums to buy the young genius, but to prevent his export, the Brazilian government declared Pelé a national treasure. He stayed true to his club in the Brazilian seaport of Santos, which cashed in on Pelé's fame by organizing regular exhibition tours and handing over a large share of the revenues to the player.

Pelé exited the next two World Cups early, injured by particularly brutal tackles. That didn't take anything away from the adulation he enjoyed in Brazil and elsewhere: as leading football players began to be treated as celebrities, 'King Pelé' was a living legend. Watching him in action, a broadcaster once suggested a new spelling for the word God: 'P-e-l-e'. The player himself joked that there was just a small difference between him and Jesus Christ: 'Jesus Christ may be lesser known in some parts of the world'. As the world's greatest players prepared to congregate in Mexico, all eyes were on the Brazilian again.

To prepare for the 1970 World Cup, Puma had hired a plucky German journalist to infiltrate the Brazilian team. Hans Henningsen had long covered Brazilian football for an array of international newspapers. He regularly shared a beer with the players and he could easily deliver most of them for Puma. But to his amazement, Henningsen was firmly instructed to ignore Pelé.

The situation was deeply embarrassing for Henningsen, who knew the player well. Pelé kept nagging the journalist, clamouring for an offer from Puma. He had obtained a small contract with Stylo, an English company, but he was puzzled that he couldn't get a juicier offer from the Germans, while all the other Brazilian players had long-since signed their deals. Just days before the start of the competition, its most spectacular contender was still without a contract. Henningsen felt that 'the situation was just too ridiculous'. He resolved to ignore 'El Pacto', offering Pelé $25,000 for Mexico and another $100,000 for the next four years, with royalties of 10 per cent on Puma boots to be sold under the Pelé name.

For Armin Dassler, the opportunity was irresistible. He knew that his cousin's wrath would be devastating, but the prospect wasn't scary enough to make him turn down the deal concocted by Henningsen.

The tie-up had an awesome impact for Puma. Before one of the knockout games in Mexico, Henningsen and Pelé came up with a ruse to gain some extra exposure. It was agreed that, just before kick-off, the player would have a chat with the referee and ask him to hold on for a moment. Pelé would then kneel down and slowly tie up his laces. For several seconds, Pelé's boot filled millions of television screens around the world.

The exposure was unique, as Pelé helped Brazil to another World Cup triumph in Mexico. Tarcisio Burgnich, the Italian defender who marked Pelé during the finals, didn't understand what was going on. 'I told myself before the game, "he's made of skin and bones just like everyone". But I was wrong,' the Italian told reporters after his team's 4–1 defeat. Puma would exploit the relationship to the full: although the deal lasted only four years, the ranges it produced, such as the King and the Black Pearl, secured steady orders for many more years.

Predictably, Horst Dassler was not amused. Before he left Mexico, Hans Henningsen got caught up in a most unpleasant meeting between an embarrassed Armin and an irate Horst, flanked by three square-shouldered aides who clearly hadn't tagged along for a friendly chat. From then on, the gloves were off.

The tie-up with Pelé confirmed Armin Dassler's thinking. In its relentless battle with Puma, Adidas was willing to outfit almost any football player skilful enough to tie up his laces and run. Armin figured that Puma should take another tack: concentrate on just a handful of international and charismatic players, the ones who grabbed all the headlines.

The strategy was partly dictated by the fact that Puma didn't have the

17. As part of a unique peace agreement, Horst and Armin Dassler agreed to stay away from Pelé. But Armin couldn't resist and in the end the Brazilian superstar gave his name to several Puma boots.

resources to compete for any and every German player, and Armin Dassler rightly saw that, in the era of football superstars, the media zoomed in on just a few inspiring personalities. Contracts with such heroes were costly, but they could still achieve much better returns than a spate of smaller deals with average players who never made it to the front pages.

Puma's most promising catch was a scrawny Dutch player called Johan Cruyff. He had been hawked by Jaap and Cor du Buy, the Dutch brothers who held the distribution rights for Puma in the Netherlands. Under the deal, signed by Cruyff's mother in January 1967, the 20-year-old player was to earn 1,500 guilders to wear Puma boots at each game and training session. As part of the agreement, he allowed Puma to sell boots called 'Puma Cruyffie', his nickname at the time.

Unfortunately the relationship quickly turned sour, as Johan Cruyff suddenly insisted that the Puma boots hurt his feet. He began to turn up at games in Adidas and demanded that his deal with Cor du Buy should be rescinded. Du Buy derided the claim as 'complete codswallop'. Johan Cruyff's feet were very special indeed, but surely Puma could still find suitable boots for him. After all, their range contained at least forty models and they would be delighted to produce others to measure for the Dutch star. Jaap van Praag, the Ajax chairman, confirmed that the club had never issued any instructions to Cruyff regarding his boots. However, the young player stood firm.

After several failed attempts at mediation, Cor du Buy filed a complaint for breach of contract. Cruyff was ordered to pay hefty damages of 24,500 guilders to Puma: 250 for each of the games and training sessions which he had attended in Adidas. When Cruyff refused to pay up, du Buy obtained the seizure of his earnings from Ajax football club.

The case went to appeal in Amsterdam. Unimpressed by the player's allegations, the court confirmed du Buy's rights. 'The truth of the matter is that [Cruyff] wants more money,' the presiding judge summed up at the hearing on 3 September 1968. Cruyff may have lost the case but, by the end of the year he had obtained a vastly upgraded deal with Cor du Buy. The contract guaranteed him at least 25,000 guilders annually for the next three years.

Intriguingly, Johan Cruyff still seemed to prefer Adidas boots. Just weeks after he signed the fresh deal, one of du Buy's aides peered at a picture in *De Telegraaf*, a Dutch newspaper. With an expert eye, he noticed that Cruyff's left boot was an Adidas, identifiable by the special white cushioning on the heel. 'We would be grateful if you agreed to disguise this element, for example by painting it over in black,' wrote the Puma distributor. 'Of course it would be even better,' he added sheepishly, 'if you wore a Puma boot on your left foot.'

The squabbles between Cruyff and Puma were perfectly in line with the overall perception harboured by many that the player was both a quick-witted footballing genius and a conceited, self-centred nit-picker. In contrast to players before him, Cruyff openly argued that football was his job, and he should be properly rewarded for it.

He was ardently backed up by Cor Coster, a gregarious Amsterdam businessman who had become Cruyff's agent – yet another phenomenon that came with the rise of the football business. In this case, Cor Coster had entered the fray via his daughter, Danny. When Danny Coster became Mrs Cruyff, Coster decided to look after his new son-in-law's business interests. A feisty wheeler-dealer, he soon came to represent several other players, battling for rights that would benefit them all. His hardball tactics terrified even the most hard-headed football club managers.

As Puma's upgraded contract with Cruyff came to an end, Cor Coster kept all his options open. He gladly accepted an invitation to Landersheim, where he was wined and dined extensively. Shortly afterwards, in April 1972, Horst wrote a personal letter to Coster, with an unbeatable offer of 1.2 million guilders for a tie-up with Cruyff over the next five years. A shrewd businessman, Cor Coster knew exactly what to do with the proposal: four days later, a copy of the Adidas offer landed on the desk of Gerd Dassler, then in charge of international affairs at Puma.

Gerd rushed to his typewriter. 'Lieber Horst,' he wrote. 'We understand that you approached Herr Coster, to obtain a contract with Cruyff'. As the Puma man explained, however, his own company already had the Dutchman cornered. The small print of his contract with Cor du Buy gave the Dutch agents exclusive and unlimited rights on the use of his name. Cor du Buy had duly registered Cruyff and a flurry of derivatives as its own trademarks. 'We are therefore convinced that you have attempted consciously, or at least negligently, to influence the player Johan Cruyff, encouraging him to breach his contract,' Gerd angrily wrote to his cousin.

'Lieber Gerd,' began the reply, as Horst Dassler confirmed that he was 'a personal friend' of Cruyff. He argued that du Buy's registration of the Cruyff name would not prevent the player from wearing Adidas boots, 'especially since he has always preferred our boots, due to technical reasons and out of our friendship'. Since Puma had breached the Pelé pact in Mexico, Horst wrote, he could not be expected to abide by any informal rules.

Just as Horst intended, the exchange forced Puma to improve its contract with Cruyff again. He had just used a well-worn business tactic: he knew that he could not get a deal with Cruyff, but he could at least weaken his competitor by driving the price up and thus forcing him to punch a large hole in his budget. In a combined deal with Le Coq Sportif, French producers of football clothing, Puma offered him at least 150,000 guilders a year. From then on, the hard-headed Dutchman showed unswerving loyalty to his partners at Puma.

This caused splitting headaches over the next years, as the Dutch prepared for the 1974 World Cup, to be held in Germany. By the early seventies Holland had a stunning line-up that included some of the most coveted players in the world. It would lean most strongly on the Ajax squad that was then dazzling the football world with its fast and unpredictable style known as 'total football'. The headaches came because the Dutch football federation, the KNVB, endorsed Adidas. Under the agreement, Cruyff and all the other players were meant to walk onto the pitch in three-striped tracksuits and shirts, but Cor Coster insisted that Johan Cruyff could hardly be expected to wear a three-striped shirt in breach of his contract with Puma, which expressly forbade him to promote any other sports brand. The debate came to a head at a tense meeting between Coster and KNVB executives at the Hilton Hotel in Amsterdam. They knew all too well that Cruyff was stubborn enough to leave the team unless they caved in.

Much to the relief of the Dutch federation, Adidas agreed to strike a deal. They could easily picture the furore if it turned out that they had caused the absence of Johan Cruyff, the linchpin of an extraordinary Dutch team. The compromise was an orange shirt emblazoned with the Dutch lion and just two stripes running down the sleeves.

Adidas exacted a minor revenge when the Dutch team was called up for its official team snapshot. Henny Warmenhoven, the man in charge of football promotion for Adidas in the Netherlands, was so well-connected with the Dutch officials that he was always welcome on the team bench. When the team was set up, while chatting with one of the players, he discreetly placed an Adidas bag right in front of Cruyff's Puma boots.

The Dutch clash was typical of the upheavals that were taking place elsewhere, as football pitches were taken over by a cast of assertive (and usually long-haired) players. Even the otherwise obedient German side was not immune to such changes. Players were no longer prepared to take small handouts from the national league while their peers elsewhere in Europe were pampered and generously rewarded. They wanted sizeable win bonuses and lucrative endorsement deals.

The German squad that warmed up for the 1974 World Cup contained some remarkable players. They received rare acclaim in 1972 following a victory in the European championships in Switzerland, during which Günter Netzer enraptured the crowds with his wild mane and Franz Beckenbauer's supreme control inspired his nickname 'der Kaiser'. The side was uncharacteristically praised by the European press for playing with 'elegance', 'inventiveness' and 'genius'. The players, however, were interested in more than compliments.

18. The Dutch football federation endorsed Adidas, but Johan Cruyff had a
lucrative deal with Puma. Cruyff refused to wear three stripes, so Adidas
agreed to remove one from his shirt.

Intriguingly, the personalities of the team's two most prominent members could hardly have been more different. Günter Netzer was regarded as a renegade, a wild-haired attacker who revelled in the controversy of his racy lifestyle. Long before football players became a tabloid staple, Netzer enjoyed gallivanting with a string of leggy blondes behind the wheel of flashy sports cars. Like George Best he was among the first players to have his own night club. He called it Lovers Lane. The dashing rebel from Mönchengladbach regularly snubbed the German football federation and blatantly ignored the plea by Helmut Schön, the national team trainer, that all international players should stay in the domestic game. Just before the 1974 tournament the Puma star had gone and signed a deal with Real Madrid.

By contrast, the Adidas man on the national side seemed almost bland. Since his international debut in England, Franz Beckenbauer had become the most-admired star in German football. He would not turn down a beer, but he still polished his reputation as a smart player who was destined to shine long after his career was over. He built up business interests and bought a season ticket for the opera.

Established several decades earlier, the relationship between Adidas and Beckenbauer had deepened over the years, and in the early seventies was set in stone with a ground-breaking contract. Beckenbauer was to earn a sizeable commission on Adidas boots, shirts and shorts that bore his name. The shiny Beckenbauer shorts, a favourite around European campgrounds, sold in their millions. The payments reached such heights that Käthe Dassler began to protest. She was even more appalled when Robert Schwan, Beckenbauer's longtime manager, came up with more demands. Under pressure from Schwan, Adidas had to arrange at least two large payments to avoid losing their crown jewel. Horst Widmann, Adi Dassler's personal assistant, made sure that such dealings would remain hidden from his boss. 'He didn't want to know anything about such things,' said Widmann.

When, inevitably, the scales fell from his eyes, Adi Dassler was shocked to discover that players were bluntly demanding payment to wear Adidas. Since the 1954 Berne triumph, Dassler had attended nearly all of the national side's training sessions in Germany. It seemed natural that he should be invited to Malente, a resort close to the Baltic Sea where the German squad congregated ahead of the 1974 World Cup. But for the first time, Adi Dassler felt out of place. The players no longer cared about his boots. Everything seemed to revolve around money.

The unprecedented demands of the German players led to a full-scale revolt. It was only a few years earlier that their league had begun to accept professionals, several decades later than their European counterparts. The time had come to catch up. Through Franz Beckenbauer, they demanded a payment of at least DM100,000 per player from the federation. After an entire night of haggling, they ended up settling on DM75,000. The incident left Helmut Schön on the verge of a nervous breakdown. The coach was so appalled by the attitude of his players that he packed his bags. It took all of Beckenbauer's powers of persuasion to convince the trainer to stay.

Adi Dassler was equally dismayed. Two years earlier, Adidas had sealed a deal with the German football federation which made it obligatory for all the national side to wear the three stripes in international matches. Puma predictably sued, arguing that Adidas had abused its leading market position and that players should be entitled to choose their own boots. The anti-cartel judges in Berlin got so tired of the bickering that they seriously proposed that the team turn out in all-black boots.

To avoid such ridicule the Adidas deal with the federation was cancelled. The players no longer had any obligation to wear the three stripes, and they made sure to impress that on Dassler. Just days before the competition started, some of the players were still threatening to black out the stripes on their boots unless they obtained a suitably sizeable bonus. Just like Helmut Schön, Adi Dassler was so disgusted that he packed his bags – and he could not be held back. While he brooded over the incident in Herzogenaurach, Alf Bente and Horst Widmann were dispatched to take care of the German players. The Adidas men managed to patch things up with the national team, with 'some extra money'.

The championships provided the Germans with their second World Cup triumph, twenty years after the Miracle of Berne. The superior Dutch had become complacent and the Germans had beaten them to the trophy with a decisive goal by Gerd Müller. But for Adi Dassler, the tournament marked the end of a personal relationship that had propelled Adidas to the overwhelming leadership of the football business. Back in Herzogenaurach, his ageing brother was equally disillusioned.

While Germany basked in the euphoria of Gerd Müller's cannonball winner, Rudolf Dassler had become an angry old man. Prone to increasingly erratic behaviour, he continuously berated his eldest son and repeatedly made amendments to his will. As Rudolf's family learned later that year, he was in the early stages of lung cancer.

Rudolf Dassler had long faded from Puma's management, but was still updated regularly on his company's dealings. One of the problems that tormented him in his last months was Puma's French subsidiary. It had always been a struggle for Gerd Dassler, Rudolf's youngest son, to establish the brand in the French market. Wherever he turned up, Gerd Dassler discovered that Horst had been there before him with Adidas. And whatever Gerd offered, it could never match the reputation of the Auberge du Kochersberg. 'It was phenomenal, and people talked about it all the time,' he sighed.

With a mix of frustration and curiosity, Gerd Dassler once accepted an invitation to check out Landersheim by himself. He felt even worse when he left: glad to plant a little intrigue, Horst whispered in Gerd's ear that his brother Armin was hatching a plot to undermine him. As

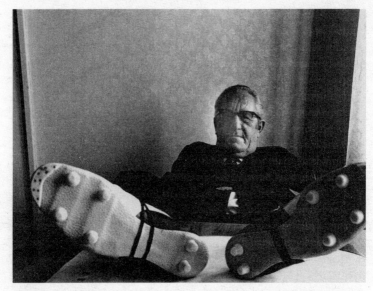

19. Rudolf Dassler, relaxed and happy in the early 1970s. Soon after this photograph was taken, he caused another rift in the family by amending his will.

things turned out, Gerd Dassler soon ran into deep troubles. The French subsidiary sank into the red, with weak sales and disproportionate expenses, allegedly funding the lavish lifestyle of the Dasslers. Rudolf agreed to cover the debts of the French subsidiary but the French banks demanded that his son should be removed from the company's management. 'It was a thorny matter,' said Armin's wife, Irene. 'The rescue of the French business placed the whole company under financial strain, and my husband basically had to fire his own brother.'

The incident occurred just as Rudolf Dassler was beginning to feel unwell. In September 1974, it became clear that the illness was serious. Rudolf hurriedly returned from a break to change his will yet again. Under the statutes of the company, a limited partnership (or 'KG' in Germany), it had long been established that, upon his father's death, Armin would inherit 60 per cent of Puma's shares, against 40 per cent of the shares and all the remaining assets of the family for Gerd. But in the grip of his illness, Rudolf suddenly felt that this split was wrong.

In the last hours of Rudolf's life, a zealous chaplain attempted to put his agitated mind at rest by forcing a reconciliation with his brother.

The pair had continued to pester each other long after their split. In the aftermath of the Mexico Olympics, Rudolf received a restraining order which had apparently been filed by Adolf precisely on his seventieth birthday. Since then, however, unknown to most other family members and employees, Adolf and Rudolf had apparently met up several times. Horst Widmann, Adi Dassler's assistant, said that he arranged four lengthy discussions between the two men in the early 1970s, at the Grand Hotel in Nuremberg and at Frankfurt airport.

The night of Rudolf's death, the chaplain placed the call to the Villa himself. Adolf declined to cross the river and embrace his brother one last time, but he conveyed his forgiveness. Rudolf Dassler passed away shortly afterwards, on 27 October 1974. In line with its haughty attitude towards its smaller rival, Adidas issued a lofty statement: 'Out of piety, the family of Adolf Dassler will not comment on the death of Rudolf Dassler.' Käthe and Adi's eldest daughter, Inge Bente, was sent to attend the funeral service on her parents' behalf.

Several days later, Armin and Gerd sat down at the notary's office for the opening of their father's will. The clerk sighed heavily as he struggled to decipher all the scribbles and amendments, but long before he had finished, Rudolf's intentions had become perfectly clear: the ownership of Puma had been entrusted to Gerd, and Armin had been entirely left out of the will. 'My husband was devastated,' Irene Dassler recalled.

Since Gerd Dassler refused to settle, Armin and his wife consulted several lawyers, enquiring under what conditions the last-minute amendments could be declared void. They were told bluntly that they would have to respect Rudolf's wishes. But in January 1975 they obtained an appointment with a Düsseldorf-based lawyer, Jürgen Waldowski, who had recently hit the headlines in a high-profile case involving a pharmaceuticals company.

With a reassuring grin, the lawyer pulled out a copy of a Supreme Court verdict. 'You don't need to worry at all,' he told Armin and Irene Dassler, going on to explain that the ruling dictated that the statutes of a limited partnership prevailed over a will. 'That was the end of the story,' Irene Dassler said. In line with the unamended statutes, Armin was appointed as *Komplementär* (a partner with unlimited liability) with 60 per cent of Puma's shares, while Gerd was a *Kommanditist* (a partner with limited liability), owning the remaining 40 per cent along with the remainder of Rudolf's estate.

This bitter dispute over, Armin could run the company as he pleased. It was the beginning of a remarkable run for Puma, with sales multiplying fivefold in a decade, yet Armin still couldn't keep up with his cousin Horst, who was worming his way into the most influential spheres of the sports business.

PART II

Champions of the World

1974–1990

13

Politics

As he built up his business, Horst Dassler acquired some startling habits. John Boulter, in charge of international promotion in Landersheim, began to notice them in the mid-seventies when he travelled to London with Horst for Wimbledon. A former Olympic runner, Boulter was trotting out for a jog in Hyde Park when he spotted his boss sitting alone in the lobby of their hotel. Upon Boulter's return, Horst was still in exactly the same position, opposite the lift doors. 'I'm fine, John,' Dassler explained. 'I'm just sitting here in case someone important walks by.'

Wherever he was, Horst Dassler seized every opportunity to reinforce his friendships among sports officials, or to seal new ones. While others regarded schmoozing as a tiresome obligation, Horst went about it with almost fanatical zeal. This was perfectly in line with one of Horst Dassler's adages, that 'everything is a matter of relationships'. He had the right skills to make friends all over the world: he was fluent in five languages, displayed an affable manner, never asked any awkward questions, and he was amazingly considerate.

To begin with, the rationale behind this tireless lobbying was to obtain favourable treatment for Adidas. The rewards could be greatest with national sports federations: among many other things, they picked the shirts and other equipment to be worn by their national team. Unfortunately for Horst Dassler, footwear was exempt from most such agreements because it was regarded as technical equipment, of which athletes should be allowed to make their own choice. Yet by dealing with federations, Adidas saved all the hassle of cajoling individuals and satisfying their escalating demands.

If Horst Dassler obtained a contract with the French handball federation, for example, the entire team would be outfitted with three-striped shirts and shorts, not to mention warm-up suits. That could be much more interesting for Adidas in terms of exposure than a deal with a single player, which perhaps required several weeks of negotiations and might still be worthless if the athlete was injured or underperformed. The advantages were even more obvious in athletics, where amateur status still forced athletes and shoe companies to strike technically illegal deals, at great risk to the individual. By signing an official contract with a national athletics federation, Dassler could be assured that the three stripes would feature on the sleeves of all the team's athletes without breaking any rules.

The next step up were international federations, which had sprung up from the beginning of the century to represent the interests of their sport and manage it at international level. They were often headed by an unpaid chairman, with a handful of paid staff and representatives from national federations. Among the weightiest were Fifa, the international football federation, and the IAAF, the chief guardians of the amateur principle in international athletics. But Horst Dassler got to know countless officials from much smaller federations, covering anything from judo to rowing and weightlifting.

As he knew all too well, decisions taken by the international federations could have huge repercussions for Adidas. Such bodies set the rules for the sport that they covered and organized the international competitions that mattered most. They determined to what extent commerce could become involved in their sport and they could agree contracts that enabled Adidas to outfit hundreds of officials during international competitions, making sure the three stripes would be everywhere.

The Olympic galaxy was another target of Horst Dassler's courtesy. It revolved around the International Olympic Committee (IOC), which supervised the organization of the Games and enforced its strict amateur principles. By the seventies, the movement comprised more than 150 national Olympic committees which dealt with their country's team and had a voice at international gatherings. They were chiefly led by people who had earned their stripes among the country's elite, sometimes in sports but just as easily in business or politics.

Then there were situations where it was simply good to have the right friends in the right places. Horst had repeatedly experienced how useful it could be to have the ear of sports chieftains, the ones who could put in a favourable word for him and bend the rules his way – such as the apparently ludicrous decision to ban the Puma brush shoes in Lake Tahoe.

To some extent, Horst Dassler began to establish his stranglehold on the sports establishment from the moment he disembarked in Australia for the Melbourne Olympics in 1956. Some of the young athletes with whom he chatted as a young man had retired from competition to rise through the ranks of the most influential sports organizations. The twenty years of groundwork done by Horst made him unbeatable. But, as his aides noticed, Dassler also thrived on the politicking.

At a time when sports federations were still run with the same ethos as local snooker clubs, his dedication made a huge impression. 'There were these general secretaries, who were often retired and toiled away for nothing,' recalled Gerhard Prochaska, a former Adidas marketing manager. 'All of a sudden they were propelled to the front of the stage, pampered and respected. Horst grasped such things much earlier than others.'

Auberge du Kochersberg turned into the nerve centre of this operation. Gault Millau rated the cuisine with two toques, while the Michelin Guide expressed its appreciation with one star. Bill Siebenschuh, the sommelier, had one of the most enviable jobs in the region. With up to 30,000 bottles, his cellar was regularly rated as the richest private cellar in the Alsace. After a while he had to rent out a second cellar near by, which held up to 60,000 more bottles.

The French managers in Landersheim precisely budgeted the stays of their guests. A team of rugby players would get the standard treatment: a couple of nights at the lodge, hearty food and abundant supplies of local beer. The worthiest guests, however, would be ushered into the magnificent suites on the upper floor of the Auberge. For meals they would be seated in a separate room, and they would dine off gold-decorated plates. 'The gold service put quite a strain on our budget,' recalled Prochaska. Such stays sometimes came with a full weekend reception, complete with hunting excursions.

Horst Dassler's most intimate guests would be taken down to the cellar, where they could savour anything from Château d'Yquem and Petrus to the finest Armagnac. On particularly intense nights, Horst enjoyed sharing the bench in the cellar to smoke a cigar, accompanied by a glass of wine or cognac. While the racks contained the most prestigious wines, his personal treat was the relatively obscure Château de la Chaise from southern Burgundy. One of his neatest touches was to offer guests a bottle of wine from the year of their birth. To take care of all the arrangements, Adidas France had established a fully operational travel agency on the ground floor of its offices in Landersheim. They had an entire fleet of limousines at their disposal to pick up the guests at the local airport, and to chauffeur them around the Alsatian hills.

A stay at the Auberge became an inevitable rite of passage for anybody with ambitions in the sports business. 'Those who had never been invited to Landersheim were nobodies,' said one of Dassler's former guests. Along with the predictable sports people, they included aspiring members of international sports federations, Olympic committees and politicians of all colours who gravitated around sports.

The plush conference rooms in the Auberge were sometimes used to host internal meetings of underfunded organizations, such as the International Weightlifting Federation. 'Once they had finished their meetings during the day, we spent entire evenings smoking cigars with them in the cellar of the Auberge,' explained John Bragg, one of Dassler's American sports diplomats. 'By the end of the week, they had helped us to develop an Adidas shoe for weightlifting and they had adopted regulations that excluded any other shoes. This was not a lucrative market, but you never knew. From that point on these people were beholden to Horst Dassler.'

Another option for international guests was a stay at the Adidas premises in Paris. The company's French managers held offices on the rue du Louvre, above a small restaurant. Its menu could not compete with the delicacies at some of the adjoining eateries, but if there had been a guest book at the bar, its late-night entries would have read like a directory of the world's leading sports executives. For those who stayed overnight there was the Terrasse Hotel, where Adidas had a running account. At the foot of Montmartre, the rooms were relatively modest but the rooftop restaurant offered a stunning view of the capital. Most importantly, Horst Dassler took on the services of a dedicated barman, Jacky Guellerin. While the hotel bar officially closed at midnight, Guellerin kept a back room with a bar open for the Adidas crew and their guests. He would turn away other potential customers while continuing to serve drinks until Horst Dassler had finished his meetings – often in the early hours of the morning.

Conveniently, the Terrasse Hotel was located at a stone's throw from several temples of adult entertainment in Paris, particularly Le Moulin Rouge. Jacky was equally discreet when it came to requests of private entertainment: they were quietly passed on to the concierge, and Jacky only reported to Horst when things got out of hand. 'There was one of the Adidas people who tended to overdo it,' said Jacky. 'He would embarrass us all by rolling down the stairs, completely plastered, yelling that he wanted more whores.'

Like many other Adidas friends, Jacky was content to be rewarded with boxes full of sports clothing. Back in Landersheim, the French managers had an entire warehouse full of freebies for their guests. They would be invited to play a game of tennis, for which they had to be outfitted, and of course would pack the clothes in their suitcases. Before their departure, they would be taken to the warehouse to pick a pair of trainers and a few shirts. Given the relatively small value of the gifts, the Adidas managers just thought of this as a nice gesture, yet when entire delegations raided the warehouse the presents could amount to a considerable expense. Some visitors exhibited remarkable greed, such as the Olympic official who claimed to have seven wives and drove off with an equal number of bags.

With guests from all cultures, the trickiest part was to find the right balance for each individual – which happened to be Horst's forte. 'He had the amazing ability of always knowing what would influence an individual,' observed Patrick Nally, one of Dassler's partners. 'He was an absolutely charming person who would be up until the early hours of the morning, drinking, talking, to get to know and understand people. It was a matter of getting to know what was right and what was wrong and never to cause offence. If it was right for the person to give him a bit of cash, or a lot of cash, then it was right for that person.'

Just in case his phenomenal memory failed him, Horst Dassler created detailed files for each of his contacts. Meticulously updated, they contained the names of the person's closest family members, their ages, clothes measurements, special likes and dislikes, the subjects that were discussed during the latest meeting, the presents they had received. Horst Dassler's aides were taught to keep track of their contacts in the same way. 'At the end of an evening when you'd think we'd keel over comatose, we would still keep a pretty good diary of notes,' said Nally. 'All these people were trained to take notes, they were very disciplined in giving Horst complete information.'

Among the most efficient reporters of the dealings in sports organization was Karl-Heinz Huba, the editor of *Sport Intern*. Many readers were unsettled by the details contained in the green newsletter. Huba was told about decisions at international sports organizations before the members themselves – if he didn't help to engineer them in the first place by mounting blatant campaigns against people who stood in Horst Dassler's way. It was later alleged that Huba had been on the Adidas payroll, but the allegation was never substantiated.

Horst himself revelled in his reputation as the supreme businessman who knew everything. 'On the rare occasions that he didn't know before everybody else, he still pretended that he knew,' said John Bragg. 'That gave him an aura of omniscience.' To begin with, the purpose of this intelligence remained innocent. The strategy was to make as many friends as possible, across the entire spectrum of sports and on all continents. But as time went by, these investments acquired a manipulative purpose.

Yearning for yet more influence, Horst Dassler resolved to build up an unofficial team that was entirely dedicated to international sports relations. While all his disciples were taught to make friends, the sports politics squad, patched together in the seventies, went much further. Their activities were entirely geared towards the infiltration of leading sporting organizations.

The whole venture was based on the premise that, in the most influential organizations, each country had one vote, regardless of its weight or size. Decisions that mattered to Adidas could hinge on the votes of a handful of delegates from insignificant far-flung countries. Horst Dassler's sports diplomats therefore strove to cover the entire world – offering plane tickets and other resources to make sure that their friends in the remotest countries could take part in crucial deliberations.

The most accomplished lobbyist hired by Dassler was Christian Jannette, who joined Adidas immediately after the Munich Olympics in 1972. As chief of protocol for the Munich Games, dealing with all the arrangements for officials, Jannette had been courted by countless Olympic friends. Since he was in charge of allotting tickets, some of them had grovelled shamelessly to obtain tickets for their extended family and friends. He was owed more favours than the Auberge could ever dispense. His leading assignment was to strengthen Horst Dassler's ties with his Soviet friends.

Owing to his sharp observations and affable manners, Horst Dassler had exceptional entrées in the otherwise impenetrable Soviet Union. Adidas executives boasted that a white bearskin rug in one of the suites in Landersheim had been offered to Horst Dassler by Leonid Brezhnev, then comrade-in-chief of the Soviet Union. Horst had hired a Russian-speaking assistant, Huguette Clergironnet, who accompanied him on many of his trips. He cherished a private collection of Russian icons, and he genuinely enjoyed the company of his Russian friends. But the most interesting aspect of the Soviets was that they provided reliable votes, dictating policies for delegates from the entire communist bloc.

The only problem that haunted Horst Dassler in Russia was that his family in Herzogenaurach had earmarked it as its own territory. While his two eldest sisters concentrated on sports promotion and advertising, Brigitte Baenkler, the third of Adolf and Käthe's daughters, pleaded with her parents to let her learn Russian. She was fascinated by eastern Europe, with a particular affinity for Hungary and Russia.

While Horst Dassler made personal friends in the Kremlin, Brigitte established herself as the official envoy of the Dassler family in the Soviet Union. She regularly travelled to Moscow on behalf of Adidas – never failing to bring along trolleys full of Western goods. In the early eighties, Brigitte's efforts would help Adidas to set up one of the first factories in the Soviet Union that was at least partly controlled by a Western company.

This shared interest forged a bond between Horst and Brigitte which came much closer to respect than his relationship with any of his three other sisters. Still, the involvement of the German Dasslers in eastern Europe sometimes caused huge frustration in Landersheim. Horst went ballistic when Brigitte was caught at a Soviet airport attempting to smuggle out some icons. He had warned her many times to refrain from such foolishness. To avoid a diplomatic incident and get his sister safely out of the country, Horst Dassler used up many favours.

His relationship with Soviet officials was generally costly. As the company's sports diplomats acknowledged, Soviet sports dignitaries were among the greediest in the world. Christian Jannette distinctly remembered walking around the Place Vendôme in Paris, holding a bulging wallet while a Soviet delegation raided the square's most refined jewellery stores.

Through their production and equipment contracts, the Dasslers cultivated close contacts with many other east European dignitaries. Erich Honecker, head of the East German state, personally signed a totalitarian deal with Adidas. The three stripes became a distinctive sign for the country's international athletes – set against the two stripes of Zeha, the regime's own sports-shoe brand. The deal related in the main to equipment supplies but it was still very precious for the East Germans, who invested massively in the prestige of their sports stars. Sport was regarded as an integral part of East German education and the regime pumped unparalleled resources into sports-related studies and medical science. As the East German rulers saw it, buying Adidas was just another way to make sure that their athletes would be best-equipped to perform. Adidas was of such undeniably superior quality that the East Germans were prepared to turn a blind eye to its capitalist origins.

One of the advantages of this all-encompassing deal was that Adidas executives could rest assured that the East Germans themselves would ensure it was respected. Georg Wieczisk, former head of the East German athletics federation, explained that the country's athletes and sports officials weren't inclined to risk the loss of their privileges. 'Others had to wait at least four years for a Trabant,' he said, referring to the boxy cars produced by the East German state. 'For us the wait was a little shorter.'

Adidas could not expect to make any sales in East Germany on the back of the endorsement deal, since imports of most Western consumer goods were prohibited and East Germans could not have afforded them anyway. On the other hand, East Germany produced a stunning proportion of medal winners, taking the three stripes along with them to the podium. The results were partly obtained through the kind of financial support and full-time training that should have qualified them as professionals (they were thinly disguised as 'students' and 'military personnel'). It didn't seem to matter at the time that many record-breaking performances were obviously substance-assisted.

Over the years there were just a handful of brand defectors, like Walter Cierpinski, the East German marathon champion. Just before one of his races he agreed to wear another brand, which also happened to be the sponsor of the marathon in question. Adidas and the East Germans kicked up such a fuss about it that the organizers suggested a weird compromise: just before the start of the race, they placed little stickers on the shirts of the runners, covering up the logo of the offending company.

The ties between Adidas and the East German regime did not prevent the Stasi from closely watching Horst Dassler. One of their most prolific sources was IM Möwe. As things turned out much later, the man behind this code name, meaning 'informant Seagull', was Karl-Heinz Wehr, a relatively obscure East German sports official. Wehr regularly updated the Stasi on the dealings of Horst Dassler's aides for more than two decades. 'My opinion is that this sports political department, led by Dassler personally, is also the most important unit of sports espionage in the capitalist foreign world,' he wrote.

As Wehr recalled, Horst Dassler began to cultivate closer contacts with the East Germans in the seventies, when communist representatives conquered some leading positions in international organizations. Sport had become another stage of world politics, in which the two superpowers of the Cold War kept each other in check. The communist countries were keen to make their voice heard, and international federations were careful to preserve a representative balance of power in their boards.

Horst regularly held talks with Manfred Ewald and Günther Heinze, the two most influential dignitaries in East German sport. In an apparent effort to please the two men, Horst Dassler obtained Karl-Heinz Wehr's appointment as a general secretary of AIBA, the international boxing federation. From this position, IM Möwe closely observed Dassler's crew. He thoroughly described their *modus operandi*, from the delegates of international organizations who were 'softened' by Adidas to the 'drink orgies' organized by the company. 'We are faced with the fact that, in the current sports world, nothing happens without this company – and that, in my eyes, many things happen under the influence of this group,' he wrote.

The Puma Dasslers watched in frustration. As reported by Wehr, the East Germans were once approached by the company's public relations manager. This man stated that Puma would be 'immediately prepared' to match or improve the contract with Adidas, which apparently earned the East Germans about DM700,000 each year. However, the Puma

Dasslers could never get a foot in Honecker's door. 'There was nothing we could do,' sighed Gerd Dassler. 'Horst Dassler had it all sewn up.'

Among Horst's most intimate communist friends were the Hungarians. In line with his insidious approach, the interests of Adidas and the sporting supremos in Budapest were intertwined. Through its production assignments to Hungarian shoe factories, Adidas provided the government with badly needed currency. In return, the Hungarian regime gladly signed with Adidas and saw to it that its leading athletes sported the three stripes. The Adidas chief commanded such influence in Budapest that he obtained the release of an executive who was arrested for drink driving. His recklessness had killed at least one person. Any other West German citizen arrested in such circumstances might have expected to spend the rest of his life eating goulash, but after a few phone calls by Horst Dassler, the culprit was soon back in Germany.

As his aides observed, the Dassler heir felt particularly at ease in east European countries where power could be exercised firmly. He didn't seem to care much for the political opponents who risked their lives to liberate their fellow citizens from the yoke of communism. 'I was somewhat shocked,' said one of his former executives, 'when Lech Walesa unleashed his Solidarity movement in Poland. Horst spoke of Walesa as the worst of thugs.' Otherwise, Horst Dassler made a point of refraining from any political judgements at all, under the untenable assertion that politics should stay out of sport.

Among the other most likely targets of the Adidas diplomats' largesse were African sports delegates. In many of the continent's emerging and economically fragile nations there was no way that the average citizen could afford a pair of Adidas shoes. Although only a handful of African countries could be regarded as markets, Horst Dassler invested heavily to spread the three stripes and exert more influence on the dark continent. Dassler's interest in Africa stemmed partly from the fact that it had produced some stupendous athletes. Several African countries had sent large contingents since the Rome Olympics in 1960, when an Ethiopian, Abebe Bikila, had stunned the crowds by winning the marathon (unfortunately for the Dasslers, barefoot). From then on, runners from Ethiopia, Kenya and Morocco were regularly among the front runners in long-distance races.

To some extent, the Adidas diplomats assisted in the development of sports in the emerging nations of Africa. They convinced politicians to invest in facilities, arguing that sporting victories unleashed more popular fervour than any political project. To affirm their political standing they needed high-performance athletes. Adidas was there to help them: although there weren't many African sports federations that could pay for an endorsement deal, Horst Dassler had them showered with three-striped equipment.

Some of Dassler's aides were convinced that, in many cases, he acted out of sheer philanthropy. Yet in the long term, the grateful contacts he built up were certain to pay off, as Africans began to take seats in international organizations. 'When a sports official has received unfailing support from Adidas for many years and Horst Dassler advises them to back this or that person, is there any way they could refuse?' asked Gerhard Prochaska, former marketing manager.

Blago Vidinic, the coach of the Moroccan football team, was among the beneficiaries. Tall and square-shouldered, Vidinic started his career as a remarkable goalkeeper for Yugoslavia, occasionally quoted in the same breath as Lev Yashin of the Soviet Union. He then moved on to coaching. His first assignment brought him to Morocco, which had wrested its independence from France in 1956. Vidinic was asked to form a decent squad ahead of the 1970 World Cup in Mexico, for which the national team had qualified for the first time in its history. During that year, Vidinic was startled to receive scores of Adidas boxes filled with shirts and boots. Although the federation couldn't afford such swish equipment, the boxes kept coming right up until Mexico, where yet more boots were waiting for the Moroccans.

After the squad's predictable elimination in the first round, Vidinic and his team hung around Mexico City for a few more days to watch other games. While Vidinic was sitting in his team bus in front of the Maria Isabel hotel, waiting to leave for the hour-long drive to Azteca Stadium, a young man asked if he could hop on. Vidinic agreed and the two started chatting. It had been tough for Morocco to patch together a proper team in time for the championships, Vidinic conceded. 'Fortunately we received unbelievable support from Adidas,' he added. 'Throughout the tournament they gave us boots and tracksuits. I don't know what we would have done without them.' The man next to Vidinic held out his hand. 'That's an extraordinary compliment,' he said. 'I'm Horst Dassler. From now on, your family and mine shall be friends.'

The handshake provided Horst with a devoted African-based informant.

Admittedly, it was hard to tell how much of the equipment donated by Adidas reached the athletes themselves. This came to mind when Thomas Sankara, former president of Burkina Faso, in west Africa, asked for a container of footballs to be delivered to his palace. Although the request seemed odd, even by Adidas standards, the company duly sent the balls to the embassy in Paris. They couldn't help chuckling in Landersheim a few years later when newspapers reported the circumstances of Sankara's murder. The presidential palace had been ransacked and, to their delight, the rebels had found 3,000 Adidas balls in the cellar.

The company's high-ranking African friends were unashamedly flattered in a publication called *Champion d'Afrique*. When it was launched by English-speaking journalists in 1974, it covered African sports with incisive reporting. In the late seventies, however, the banner was taken over by the Tunisian Colonel Hamouda. He had met Horst Dassler at the Melbourne Olympics and later become involved as an official in one of the competing bodies that ruled over the tumultuous boxing scene. With *Champion d'Afrique*, he became an integral part of Dassler's diplomatic team and was on Adidas's official payroll.

The magazine was promptly transformed into an Adidas pamphlet to the glory of Horst Dassler and African sports officials, using the sort of eulogizing prose that would make an independent publisher cringe. Most of the space was taken up by photographs of African dignitaries shaking hands with Dassler and other sports supremos. It barely contained any stories on actual sports, but all the more editorials congratulating African friends for their supposed vision.

The editorial that opened the first issue of the new *Champion d'Afrique* was written by Jean-Claude Ganga, Congolese member of the IOC. 'One of the main weapons that we have at our disposal to lead the fight against under-development is sports,' he wrote grandly. 'The main point is to foster strong and healthy men.' Much later, Ganga was expelled from the IOC after it turned out that he had pocketed $250,000 in reimbursements of fabricated travel expenses, medical costs and other gifts.

Among the African leaders most frequently pictured in *Champion d'Afrique* was Mohamed Mzali, who once held nearly all the positions that mattered in Tunisian sports. He started off in the sixties as a sports

director in the Tunisian government and twenty years later he made it to prime minister. Along the way, he picked up assignments as head of the Tunisian football federation, leader of the Tunisian Olympic Committee and member of the IOC. Subscribers to *Champion d'Afrique* could be forgiven for thinking that Mzali was the greatest political leader of all time.

These African contacts would prove most useful for Dassler when he sought to influence the decisions of international sports organizations. Much like the rest of the world at the time, they were often split between the communist bloc and the capitalist forces of the West. In many cases, the African vote could tip the balance.

Another style was required in the United States, where Horst Dassler relied on the resourcefulness of Mike Larrabee and John Bragg. The former had been recruited by Horst Dassler to promote Adidas among American athletes. To back himself up, Larrabee introduced John Bragg, a longstanding friend who was becoming bored with the small family business which he had dutifully taken over.

From the late sixties, the two continually dodged the rules of the American athletics federation and found ways to cajole athletes without offering them cash. To make sure that they would not get in trouble, they made friends in the right places. It certainly didn't hurt that Mike Larrabee had won his second gold medal at the Tokyo Olympics in the 400 metres relay on the same team as Ollan Cassell, who went on to become the executive director of the American athletics federation and vice-president of the IAAF. 'Horst always helped Ollan to advance at the international federation,' Bragg recalled. 'That made it easier to work things out somehow.'

While Larrabee dealt mostly with athletics, Bragg often handled other tricky issues. He caught Horst Dassler's eye when a crisis emerged with Muhammad Ali in December 1970, on the eve of a fight with the Argentine boxer Oscar Bonavena in New York's Madison Square Garden. For several years he had been wearing boots made by Adi Dassler himself. But all of a sudden Ali had been persuaded to wear all-black boots, in line with his spiritual credo.

When Adi Dassler dispatched one of his German envoys to New York to resolve the problem, Ali sent him packing. Sent to the rescue, John Bragg tried another tack. 'Adi Dassler would like to design the greatest boxing boot in the world,' he told Ali at his New York hotel. 'We need the advice of the greatest boxer in the world.'

After a pause, Muhammad Ali talked of the female dancers he had watched the previous night in a New York club. They had been wearing short skirts with tassels, which moved elegantly as they shuffled. For his fight against Bonavena, he wanted Adidas boots with tassels. Over the next hours, Bragg frantically scoured the backstreets of New York to find the tassels and a sewing machine. Ali was overjoyed when he unpacked the boots at his hotel that night, but he firmly instructed Bragg to keep them under wraps. At the weigh-in, 'The Greatest' refused to answer the questions of the assembled reporters about the upcoming fight. All he would talk about was the 'secret weapon' which Adidas had prepared for him. He pointed to Bragg, screaming that this man had come all the way from Germany to deliver the weapon that would make him unbeatable. 'It was as if we had written a script for him,' said Bragg. The tasselled boots, called the Ali Shuffle, made miles of copy.

From then on, Bragg performed many diplomatic assignments for Horst Dassler in the United States. Among the contacts cultivated by Bragg was Colonel Hull, head of the International Boxing Federation. When the world boxing championships were held in Cuba, a country almost inaccessible to Americans, Horst Dassler confidently picked up his phone. Sure enough, Colonel Hull arranged for John Bragg to travel along as a member of his technical staff.

There was not much that Armin Dassler could do to counteract his cousin's friendships. The Puma chairman didn't have the stamina, the personality or the platform to build up such contacts. Although Armin was sly and crafty, he could not compete with the refinement of his cousin. 'Horst had an incredible intellect and he could adapt to any kind of situation. He was completely unflappable,' said John Bragg. 'He could be quite a charmer, focusing entirely on what he was trying to do. He would have been a great ambassador.'

In some of Dassler's dealings, it was hard to draw the line between courtesy and bribery. Without openly encouraging them to act unfairly, Horst Dassler made it clear to his executives that he was not against bending the rules. In the early days, some former Adidas executives felt uneasy about the manipulative aspects of their supposed friendships. 'Don't worry, we're controlling them,' they often heard Dassler say. He

20. *Muhammad Ali in his own three-striped boots with red tassels, made for the fight against Oscar Bonavena in New York.*

rarely discussed manipulation, yet those who worked closely with him could not fail to observe that some doors unlocked with unnatural ease. 'We never saw it and he never talked about it, but we knew it was going on. They couldn't all be bosom buddies,' as one of them put it. Abundant press investigations later uncovered sickening abuses by high-ranking members of the Olympic movement, as well as odd bank transfers.

Jean-Marie Weber was probably the only person who could keep track of all of Horst Dassler's dealings. Hired as an accountant at Adidas France, this unostentatious and refined man soon turned into one of his closest aides. Weber was sometimes described as Dassler's 'right-hand man' but often more prosaically as his 'bagman'. Adidas executives joked that his shoulders were bound to dislocate one day, because he was always hauling at least one large sports bag full of personal documents. It was rumoured that, when the load became too heavy, he rented a barn in the small village of Landersheim, to make sure the papers would not fall into the clutches of any potential raiders.

By the mid-seventies, Horst Dassler's diplomats relied on a wide network of friends and informants in the international sports world. They had placed their pawns in scores of relatively modest sports organizations. But all the efforts that they deployed in the process would become worthwhile only if they managed to infiltrate the organizations that truly ruled over international sports. The time had come to cash in.

14

The Bountiful Game

Horst Dassler was in a celebratory mood in June 1974. As he walked over to the bar of his Frankfurt hotel he felt assured that he could continue to bank on his privileged contacts in international football. It appeared certain that, the next day, his English friend Stanley Rous would be elected for another four-year term at the head of Fifa, the sport's international federation.

In about three weeks the greatest football players of the moment would battle it out on West German pitches, but the game's officials were bracing themselves for another hard-fought contest. The fight for the Fifa chairmanship was regarded as a potential watershed for world football, pitting former colonial rulers, supposedly hearty and just, against a slick, brazen new world.

The incumbent, Sir Stanley Rous, an impeccable Briton, prided himself on his gentlemanly behaviour. A former teacher, he had distinguished himself as an outstanding referee who helpfully updated the rule book. Horst Dassler became friendly with Rous back in the early sixties, when he was secretary of the English Football Association and the Adidas chief was working his way into the country's football business.

At the head of Fifa since 1961, Rous had adeptly dealt with the rising enthusiasm generated by football, the spread of television coverage, the swelling crowds that streamed to games, the organization of World Cups that turned into planetary events. He coped honourably with the pressure of politicians who sought to profit from the game, and the money that began to swirl around it. The 61-year-old seemed out of touch, however, with the upcoming football nations of the post-colonial world. He certainly didn't have the flair or the right connections to deal with the aggressive campaign of his charismatic opponent, João Havelange.

While Rous serenely relied on the support of longtime friends, Havelange thoroughly prepared the ground for the election. The tall Brazilian had observed the working of sports organizations since 1936, when he took part in the Berlin Olympics as a water-polo player. While he remained part of the Brazilian team for two decades and acceded to the International Olympic Committee in 1963, Havelange ran a sprawling business in his homeland. Consisting mainly of investments in industrial and transport companies, this generated enough returns to fund Havelange's exhausting Fifa campaign. As the official South American candidate for the chairmanship, he visited eighty-six countries – often flanked by Pelé, the greatest crowd-puller the continent had to offer.

Havelange's manifesto unashamedly pandered to the wishes of emerging football nations. Among his eight election promises, he vowed to increase the number of participants in the World Cup from sixteen to twenty-four, enlarging the quota for non-European countries. He would organize a junior championship, to be held outside Europe. He would fund the construction of football grounds in developing economies, as well as training and medical centres. Unlike Rous, Havelange further pledged that, under his chairmanship, South Africa would be firmly banned from Fifa until the end of apartheid rule.

In contrast with the buttoned-up Rous, Havelange excelled at sports diplomacy. Part Belgian (he was baptised Jean-Marie Faustin Godefroid Havelange), he had grown up as a cosmopolitan young man, a polyglot who gladly and easily mingled with officials from all continents. With far more political nous than his opponent, Havelange used all the means at his disposal to swing the vote in his favour. As one observer wrote, 'the struggle was between a decent man who has served football loyally and been rewarded by just being there, and a slippery one who has no illusions about the true nature of the world and coveted glory for himself.'

To be on the safe side, Horst gave contrasting instructions to his aides. Christian Jannette was told to take good care of João Havelange and the African delegates who appeared certain to support him. Then again, John Boulter was told that Adidas should bet on Stanley Rous: he had a reassuring track record, and Europe's grip on football was still too tight to allow the election of a South American upstart. As he headed towards the hotel bar on the evening before the vote Horst Dassler was convinced that Europe would prevail. His friends would remain in place and they would surely remember the support offered by Adidas. Just to be certain, he called up his friend Blago Vidinic for a few drinks downstairs.

Since their encounter in Mexico, Vidinic had moved on to coach in Zaïre. With the personal support of President Mobutu he scoured the remotest corners of the country to assemble a team of healthy and lean youngsters. Mobutu was just as pleased as Vidinic and the players when they received their free kit from Adidas, with a leopard's head emblazoned on their shirts. Entirely three-striped, the Leopards went on to win the 1974 African Nations Cup, held in Egypt, that had qualified them for the upcoming World Cup in Germany.

The Leopards returned to an ecstatic welcome by the people of Zaïre: they would be the first black African team to take part in a World Cup. 'I left the celebrations early, saying that I was tired, because there were all these delirious people chanting my name, which is a little awkward when you're standing next to Mobutu,' said Vidinic. The qualification still earned him 'a sack stuffed with banknotes', delivered by one of Mobutu's goons.

The night before the Fifa presidential vote, Vidinic gladly joined Horst Dassler at the bar of the Frankfurt hotel where most of the officials were staying. Horst was confident that Stanley Rous would win, but Vidinic was adamant that he was wrong. In Egypt, on the sidelines of the African Nations Cup, he had witnessed a meeting of the African football federations. 'They all promised to back Havelange,' Vidinic told Dassler. The Brazilian had obtained the support of the African federations through his position on South Africa. Deeply unsettled, Horst pondered his next move. Although it was getting late, Blago Vidinic urged him to change his tack right away. 'Here's Havelange's room number,' Vidinic said. 'Tell him you had been backing Stanley Rous but you have been defeated, and from this moment you will be at Havelange's disposal.'

This turned out to be an inspired suggestion. As João Havelange had found out over the previous weeks, Horst Dassler could be a mighty opponent. By backing Stanley Rous, the German had nearly undermined Havelange's conquest of Fifa. It seemed much more comfortable to have Horst Dassler on his side, and his resources would be invaluable to fund Havelange's plans. When Dassler returned from his chat with Havelange, he was beaming. 'He reckoned that I deserved champagne,' said Vidinic.

The next day, after some tumultuous debates and two rounds of voting, João Havelange was elected as chairman of Fifa by a thin margin of 68 to 52 votes, applauded by Horst Dassler. In the wake of the congress the two struck a deal that would reshape the football business: Havelange would hold the door wide open for Dassler in international football, provided that the German helped him to garner the funds that he needed to make good his costly election promises.

There was just one little hitch: Horst Dassler was already stretching his budget to such an extent that he certainly didn't have any loose millions for Fifa in his pockets. To keep his side of the deal he would have to find a way to raise some funds.

As it happened, Dassler observed that several agents had begun to take a close interest in sports. They had come to realize that the large crowds drawn by international sporting contests formed an interesting audience for large companies, even if they were selling completely unrelated products. Until then, the only companies that could be described as sponsors were the ones that had their names placed on shabby billboards around the pitches and tennis courts. But other forms of sponsorship began to emerge in the early seventies as an alternative to advertising: the investments would forge the sponsors' reputation as good corporate citizens, linking them with the supposedly clean and prestigious values of sport.

Dassler soon realized that, in this business, there could not be any more interesting product to sell than football. It remained by far the most popular sport of all, drawing vast audiences and creating excitement that reverberated around the globe. If he could only build a bridge between football and international companies, he would raise Havelange's money in no time. He therefore turned to John Boulter. The former English runner, in charge of sports promotion at Landersheim, had exhibited all the flair necessary to deal with leading executives of multinational corporations, but after a few meetings it became clear that Boulter could not handle this new business all by himself: everything had to be invented!

While he began to study the business, however, John Boulter discovered an interesting little outfit which had made a name for itself in London by shrewdly exploiting the nascent concept of sports marketing. West Nally was built on a partnership between Peter West, a former BBC commentator, and Patrick Nally, a former advertising manager: while West provided the contacts in sports and the media, Nally established a reputation as a relentless salesman.

What West Nally proposed was to act as an intermediary between events organizers and companies that were eager to be associated with sports. To begin with, they would help organizers to package their event in a way that made it more enticing to broadcasters and sponsors. Then they would convince international companies to cough up the sponsorship money – and reap a hefty commission on the sums they were able to raise.

This was a textbook example of the right concept at the right time. Since the borders of consumer-goods markets were becoming increasingly blurred, international companies eagerly explored new ways of building up a global brand reputation. Sports sponsorship could have a more positive impact than advertising, because it could be regarded as a less obviously commercial investment. The opening offered by West Nally was particularly interesting for tobacco companies, which were no longer allowed to use traditional advertising in many countries.

The execution was just as remarkable. A few years into the partnership, West Nally had convinced large companies such as Gillette and Benson & Hedges to invest in cricket and snooker. By the early seventies, the agency employed about forty people and it was beginning to open overseas offices, but West Nally's plucky young advertising manager believed that, with the right connections, he could move on to a much larger stage.

While Peter West brought in many of the contacts with event organizers, it was Patrick Nally who put the deals together. A dashing man in his early twenties, exuding youthful charm and enthusiasm, Nally wooed hard-nosed international executives to unlock stacks of commercial dollars. As they liked to say at the agency on Berkeley Square, Patrick Nally could sell fridges to Eskimos. So when John Boulter called, Nally eagerly agreed to meet Horst Dassler in Landersheim. The two men were to be introduced by Boulter shortly after Havelange grasped the leadership of Fifa. And once they had shaken hands, they barely stopped talking for two days.

Patrick Nally was deeply impressed by Horst Dassler's operation and his drive. Seated behind his desk in Landersheim, he seemed constantly busy. 'He fired instructions to his four secretaries and picked up the phone to speak to executives and dignitaries around the world, often in their own language,' Nally marvelled. 'He was an unbelievably intense and charismatic man.'

Horst Dassler was equally charmed by Nally's boldness and quick wit. He soon came to realize that, between the two of them, they could stamp a huge and exciting business out of the ground. On the back of his talks with Havelange, Horst Dassler could easily obtain rights for the sale of marketing deals in international football. A tireless and highly creative salesman, Patrick Nally could rake in millions.

Once Dassler obtained Havelange's go-ahead, Patrick Nally set to work. For several months he jetted around the globe, convincing some of the world's largest companies to invest in football. His most rewarding catch was Coca-Cola: after several rounds of intense negotiations in 1975, they became by far the most generous Fifa partner.

The company's money was poured into the organization of the youth championships pledged by Havelange, in exchange for huge billboards around the pitches. In line with Havelange's promises, more Coke dollars were invested in football academies that were set up in developing countries to grow them as footballing nations, supported by European trainers and physicians.

The real prize, though, was the next World Cup, to be held in Argentina in 1978. To begin with, Horst Dassler coaxed the Argentine organizers into a promising partnership. They awarded him the rights attached to 'Gauchito', the Argentine mascot for the World Cup, but six months later the nascent tie-up was stymied by the murderous generals who seized Argentina's leadership. Protesters vehemently argued that the World Cup could not decently be organized by a regime which sanctioned torture and eliminated political opponents by the truckload. Fifa rejected the pleas, but the rustling rifles and click-clacking army boots made poor sales arguments for Patrick Nally.

As they toured executive boardrooms to sell their marketing plans, Dassler and Nally constantly struggled to fund their informal partnership. For several years they would have to invest substantial sums in a venture that would not begin to turn a good profit until after the World Cup. Since Horst Dassler had kept the business well away from his family, he could hardly fund it blatantly with Adidas cash. The demands of the Argentine generals made the venture all the more awkward. Still, the two young men weren't about to give up. They knew that they were onto something.

Along the way, the dashing sports marketer forged an uncharacteristic complicity with Horst Dassler. He relished Nally's bubbly company and his mischievous streak. Nally quickly grasped the workings of Horst Dassler's business and he could contribute to discussions on almost any sport- or business-related subject. Horst was genuinely pleased to have Nally at his side. 'He didn't have anyone around him whom others would describe as friends, but Patrick Nally came closest,' observed Didier Forterre, who managed the finances of Dassler's business with Nally.

To get around their funding issues, the young partners established a partnership in Monte Carlo, called SMPI. The joint venture was run by Patrick Nally and West Nally, his company, held 45 per cent of its shares, but the partnership was still controlled at 55 per cent by Horst Dassler. The exact provenance of the joint venture's income and funds was aptly disguised through a financial carousel that made the money spin from Switzerland to Monaco, the Netherlands and the Dutch Antilles.

Shortly after it was established, in February 1977, SMPI obtained extensive rights from the organizers of the Argentine World Cup. In exchange for a guarantee of 12 million Swiss francs, blithely provided by Coca-Cola, Dassler and Nally could sell advertising boards around the Argentine pitches. The understanding between Nally and the Coca-Cola executives proved decisive. Once the Atlanta-based behemoth had committed, several other international companies followed in its wake. Nally ended up raising about 22 million Swiss francs.

Between the two of them, they had cracked the football marketing business. If they played their cards right, they might soon pull the strings of an entirely new, multi-million-dollar industry.

15

The Clandestine Empire

While Horst scented unprecedented prospects in sports marketing, he suffered from the permanent strain of growing his business far from his parents' eyes. It was almost by chance that he found the solution. As part of a raggedy package to take over Le Coq Sportif, Horst Dassler found just the right partner to build up his clandestine empire.

Horst Dassler had worked closely with Le Coq Sportif since the sixties, before Adidas began to turn out its own clothes. Belonging to the Camuset family, the company was established as a French maker of sports shirts and shorts bearing its rooster emblem. Under the deal with the Camusets, Adidas France and Le Coq Sportif teamed up to offer a complete kit: while Adidas provided the boots, Le Coq Sportif manufactured three-striped shirts and shorts at its expanding plant in Romilly sur Seine, a small town in the Champagne region.

Le Coq Sportif had grown from an ordinary knitwear factory run by Emile Camuset. He often spent his evenings at the Bar Romillon, a meeting place for locals who enjoyed chatting about sport. Over a round of drinks, they suggested that Emile should try to design some sports shirts. Le Coq Sportif was registered as a brand in 1948 and shot to prominence three years later, when it was asked to make shirts for the Tour de France.

Over the next few years, Le Coq Sportif spread rapidly on French tracks and football pitches. Fittingly, the French rooster graced the shirts and tracksuits of French athletes at the Olympics, and the chests of the country's football players. The feather in its cap was the contract it obtained in 1972 with Johan Cruyff, in conjunction with Puma's boot deal.

The tie-up between Adidas and Le Coq Sportif was sanctioned by Käthe Dassler, who repeatedly met up with the Camusets. It worked out so well that they considered drawing Umbro into the agreement. Several meetings were held in Romilly and Wilmslow between the Camusets, the Dasslers and the Humphreys brothers – the weightiest families in the European sporting goods business.

Yet the relationship suddenly soured when Adidas began to build up its own textile range. One of the problems was that Le Coq Sportif, which was making three-striped goods under the Adidas label, had been selling clothes with the same design under its own name. Horst Dassler pleaded with Le Coq Sportif to desist from the practice, but the Camusets staunchly refused, insisting that they held the rights to the three stripes in France. In June 1973, Horst Dassler sued.

The move was fully backed up by the Dasslers in Germany. They couldn't tolerate the fact that Le Coq Sportif caused confusion and unduly benefited from the Adidas image. But the case took a nightmarish turn in February 1974, when a court in Strasbourg ruled in favour of the

French company. The decision unequivocally identified Le Coq Sportif as the owners of the three stripes, thereby undermining Adidas France's entire textile business.

The verdict confirmed a problem which affected Adidas in several other countries. It was unable to register the three stripes as an exclusive trademark in the United States, among other places, because the courts judged that the design was not sufficiently distinctive. Adidas Germany had registered the design with a trademark office in Geneva in January 1970, almost three months before Le Coq Sportif registered it at a commercial tribunal in Romilly. Yet in February 1974, the judges in Strasbourg were adamant that Le Coq should have the rights in France, because it had been using them there before Adidas.

From then on, Horst Dassler fought Le Coq Sportif relentlessly. Adidas France's efficient textile facilities in Troyes worked at full capacity to swamp the market with Adidas shirts. Sales people were deployed on an all-out offensive to squeeze Le Coq Sportif out of the market. Owing to the dispute, Le Coq Sportif was also deprived of its most precious endorsement by the French football federation: the contract had been obtained as part of a deal with Adidas, which supplied boots and left the shirts to Le Coq Sportif. However, the agreement hinged on the personal relationship between Horst Dassler and Jacques George, head of the federation. It only took a few whispers in George's ear to get Le Coq Sportif booted out. A complaint filed by the Camusets in June 1974 was duly rejected by Paris judges, who felt the federation had merely picked its supplier of choice.

Ironically, the move that proved most devastating for Le Coq Sportif was orchestrated by the Camusets themselves. Weakened by heightened competition from the early seventies, they still decided to invest massively to expand their production. They acquired one plant and started constructing another one in Romilly. But under attack from Adidas, Le Coq Sportif continued to lose ground in the market. They were up to their necks in debt and stock – thousands of products turned out by the new factories remained unsold. By March 1974, Le Coq Sportif was besieged by anxious creditors. One month later the Camusets were expelled from the company, and a court-appointed manager led the search for takeover candidates.

Leaving their squabbles aside, Horst Dassler and his parents agreed that it would be disastrous if the rights to the three stripes, owned by

Le Coq Sportif, fell into the wrong hands. Käthe Dassler therefore backed her son's bid to acquire Le Coq Sportif on behalf of Adidas. A competing offer by Groupe Kopa, the sports business run by the eponymous former French footballer, was rejected by the judges, who deemed it shaky. The court favoured the Adidas bid, but it was met with unexpectedly virulent resistance at Le Coq Sportif.

Mireille Gousserey-Camuset, the founder's daughter, controlled just over half of the company's shares. Active in the Resistance during the Second World War, she balked at the thought that Le Coq Sportif would fall into German hands. Her brother, Roland Camuset, was happy to commit his 49 per cent package to the Adidas bid, but Mireille stubbornly refused to surrender.

As Le Coq Sportif edged closer to liquidation, the French government became involved. Romilly was chiefly known for its railway depot, which turned the small town into a citadel of trade union activism. The workers, who had elected a communist mayor, were becoming restless. To prevent riotous scenes, the government came forward with its own buyer for Le Coq Sportif. All breathed a sigh of relief when Mireille Gousserey gave her blessing to André Guelfi, a swashbuckling investor. His father was Corsican, his mother Spanish, and he resided in Switzerland, but at least he was introduced by the French government. In March 1976, Mireille Gousserey surrendered her 51 per cent of Le Coq Sportif to André Guelfi. Adidas France held on to the 49 per cent bought from Roland Camuset nearly two years earlier – ending a two-year stalemate that had reduced Le Coq Sportif to a state of near collapse.

When the request to buy Le Coq Sportif landed on his desk, André Guelfi chiefly regarded it as a political favour. He smelled a very interesting opportunity, though, when a manager at Le Coq Sportif helpfully pointed out the court ruling on the three stripes. Armed with the court papers, André Guelfi consulted Marceau Crespin, a mandarin at the French sports ministry. Through Crespin, whom he had befriended in the army, Guelfi arranged a meeting with Horst Dassler. 'I went over in a bellicose mood, to tell them that they couldn't just walk away with the three stripes,' Guelfi recalled, 'but then we hit it off and decided to become partners.'

The seduction worked both ways. André Guelfi rightly figured that Le Coq Sportif would do much better if Horst Dassler took it under his wing. As demonstrated by the incident with the French football federation, fighting Horst Dassler was a lost cause. As for Dassler, he was instantly charmed by the gregarious Guelfi, and Guelfi had amassed enough money to discreetly back up Horst Dassler's solo ventures.

The two came to a secret agreement. In the eyes of the Dassler family, Adidas France owned just 49 per cent of Le Coq Sportif, but Guelfi gave 2 per cent of his holding to Horst Dassler along with an option to acquire the remaining 49 per cent at any time. The deal was made with Horst personally, as opposed to Adidas. In other words, quite unknown to his family, Horst had overall control of Le Coq Sportif. The agreement marked the beginning of an intense partnership between the two men.

André Guelfi was a dazzling man. In his mid-fifties at the time of the agreement, he had twice lost his fortune and rebuilt it with gusto. Some of the dealings behind his millions remained murky, but he swaggered through his troubles with exuberance and panache.

Growing up in Mazagan, on the Atlantic coast of Morocco, he made his debut as a gofer at a local bank. While he was cleaning up the archive room, Guelfi discovered a stack of files marked 'unrecoverable loans'. He struck a deal with the bank manager, whereby he would get a hefty commission on any of the loans he could recover. After less than a year, the runner was earning more than the bank manager. He amassed enough money to invest in several fishing vessels, which earned him the unglamorous nickname of 'Dédé la Sardine'.

Guelfi's nose for a deal was sharpened during his military service in Indochina during the mid-fifties, when France was unsuccessfully trying to reassert control over what would soon be Vietnam. A reluctant fighter, he spent most of his time scouring the jungle for artefacts. Finding few, he began to deal in cars, a fascination for him since childhood. In downtown Saigon, the Frenchman established a workshop called Le Garage Toulousain. Sadly, he had to leave the region in a hurry when one of the twenty-seven women to whom he became engaged took the promise seriously and sent her family round to speed up the proceedings.

On his return to Morocco, Guelfi made a fortune from fishing and lost most of it when an earthquake devastated Agadir in 1960. Dédé bounced back in Mauritania. There he amassed another fortune, operating the first fishing vessel with on-board processing facilities ('they were frozen alive!' he marvelled) and several more plants ashore. He resolved to give up this business, however, when his flagship caught fire in dubious circumstances.

This time Guelfi fled to France, in trouble with both the Mauritanian government and the Moroccan royal family. The Mauritanians were after him for alleged bribery, although it probably didn't help that, when the Mauritanian prime minister turned up to visit his processing plant, Guelfi had thought it funny to lock him in a freezer for a couple of minutes. As for King Hassan II, he wanted a few words with Guelfi after an attempted coup by General Oufkir, Morocco's brutal interior minister and a close acquaintance of the entrepreneur. Oufkir was killed and his wife, Fatima, and their children imprisoned under abominable conditions. It was widely suspected that, during their detention, Guelfi helped himself to some of the money which the Oufkirs were rumoured to have stashed away in a Swiss bank.

When he resurfaced in France, André Guelfi went on a spending spree. However he obtained it, he had enough money to acquire some of the most renowned luxury hotels in Paris: the Prince de Galles, the Grand Hôtel and Hôtel Meurice. When he applied for a Swiss residence permit in 1975, he reported assets of about 50 million Swiss francs. His mansion in Lausanne was next door to the headquarters of the International Olympic Committee.

His personal life was equally colourful. Guelfi took part in six motor races as part of the team Gordini. By the time he tied up with Horst Dassler he owned a Lear jet, which he flew himself. His yacht was described as 'the fastest in the Mediterranean'. Once they had shaken hands on Le Coq Sportif, André Guelfi regularly popped up at Dassler's side, perpetually suntanned. The jet was almost always at Dassler's disposal, with Guelfi in the pilot's seat.

Some in the Alsatian team frowned upon the new partner, who appeared to have come out of nowhere. His flamboyant style was out of sync with the hard-working ethos in Landersheim. Guelfi's extraordinary glibness was most helpful for lobbying purposes, but he admitted that his knowledge in terms of management was restricted to the notion of 'right pocket, left pocket'. Since he had been brought up by his Spanish grandmother he easily mingled with Latin Americans. Then again, the only English he knew was derived from flight instructions.

The French managers laughed at the wild tales circulated about André Guelfi – often by the man himself. With waving arms, he would recount

21. *To finance his undercover sports business, Horst Dassler teamed up with André Guelfi, a dazzling Corsican. As Guelfi saw it, the two became the 'masters of the world'.*

the sinking of his yacht and how he had managed to save a couple of masterpieces from the wreckage, swimming ashore with a Renoir tucked under his arm. (His insurance company apparently believed him!) Other stories were more worrying, involving secret services and illegal funds transfers. A French judge later described André Guelfi as 'a business parasite', 'an old bandit' and 'a manufacturer of false bills by the kilometre'.

But Horst Dassler ignored all the warnings. He increasingly relied on André Guelfi as a jovial sidekick and a deep-pocketed financier. 'Between the two of us,' said André Guelfi, 'we became the masters of the world.'

Since André Guelfi had thrown Le Coq Sportif into his lap, Horst Dassler pushed the brand with the same drive as when he had contrived to sink it a few years earlier. If the tensions with his family took a dramatic turn, he could always exercise his buy-up option. Le Coq Sportif wasn't just an investment: it was an alternative brand which Horst could use as leverage in the stalemate with his family.

Together with André Guelfi, Horst Dassler plotted far-reaching investments to overhaul Le Coq Sportif. An established player in the French market for sports textiles, it was to become a serious contender in the international sports business, with a full range of products endorsed by some of the most coveted athletes and football teams around the world.

In Landersheim, Horst Dassler briefed his most trusted aides. As far as his parents were concerned, Adidas France owned 49 per cent of Le Coq Sportif. André Guelfi had to invite the Dasslers to official shareholders' meetings and politely consult them about expansion projects, but Herzogenaurach was not to find out about all the efforts that the French team was deploying to push Le Coq Sportif around the world. 'When someone came from Herzogenaurach, the Coq Sportif files were safely locked up in the cupboards,' one of the Landersheim managers recalled.

The instructions to disguise the French managers' direct involvement in Le Coq Sportif led to some odd arrangements. A French executive recalled that, when he was recruited by Horst Dassler, there was an odd side-clause in his contract. He was officially hired by Adidas France, but an appendix in the contract indicated that he was to perform the same tasks for Le Coq Sportif. Adidas France were so anxious to keep the arrangement secret that they asked the executive to sign a confidentiality agreement.

Johan van den Bossche, head of legal affairs at Adidas France, came to realize the bizarre aspect of the situation a few weeks after his recruitment. He received a phone call in an Asian hotel from a Mr Gary Heller. The lawyer thought hard but he didn't remember anybody of that name. He was even more startled when Mr Heller addressed him by his first name and began to issue precise instructions regarding a licensing deal. 'I'm sorry, sir. I can't take instructions from somebody I don't know,' van den Bossche calmly replied. It turned out that Mr Heller was Klaus Hempel, special assistant to Horst Dassler. When travelling in Asia on Le Coq Sportif business, Hempel routinely booked hotel rooms under the name of his brother-in-law.

Horst Dassler and André Guelfi went through elaborate rituals to inform the Dassler family in Herzogenaurach about the progress of Le Coq Sportif in France. 'Horst sometimes pretended to side with his mother, rejecting investments which I advocated,' Guelfi recalled. At the same time, however, the two established a holding company called Sarragan in Freiburg, Switzerland, to regroup all of Horst Dassler's covert activities – including most of the international business for Le Coq Sportif.

The treachery was made possible by the acting talents of all the French executives involved, as well as the opacity of their accounts. Horst heavily relied on Jean-Marie Weber to blur the picture for Herzogenaurach. When he dutifully submitted his reports to his parents, he could rest assured that they would not reveal anything. Dassler's unauthorized dealings were aptly disguised in a maze of Swiss holdings and complex legal documents. 'In such a jumble, even a cat would not be able to trace its kittens,' Weber is reported to have said.

Shortly after the tie-up with Guelfi, Horst Dassler acquired Hungaria, an old-time rival boot and ball company near Orléans. The now-ailing brand name was ditched and the plant began to turn out Le Coq Sportif boots. Production was complemented by two other units acquired by André Guelfi in the Corrèze region, the stronghold of Jacques Chirac. The man who would be president was spotted in Landersheim at least twice discussing the arrangements.

Descente, the Japanese licensee of Adidas, was drawn into the plot. The managers in charge of the Adidas business at Descente seemingly remained loyal to Herzogenaurach, but they agreed to play along with Horst Dassler by also distributing Le Coq Sportif behind Käthe Dassler's back. The Adidas business was handled by Murakawa-san, but the same man had another set of business cards for Le Coq Sportif, where he was known as Nakamura-san.

In the United States, the setting up of Le Coq Sportif was entrusted to Donald Dell, a tennis agent, and his partner Frank Craighill. They built up a brand that was completely at odds with the positioning of Le Coq Sportif in other countries: while it was mostly known in Europe as an affordable football brand, in the United States it became an upscale tennis and fashion label. Aided by Dell's impressive list of contacts in American tennis, Le Coq Sportif obtained high-profile endorsements: in spite of its modest sales, Le Coq Sportif was worn by such prominent American tennis players as Roscoe Tanner and Arthur Ashe.

Another full-fledged Le Coq Sportif operation was hurriedly opened in the United Kingdom by Robbie Brightwell. The British runner had long enjoyed a special relationship with Horst Dassler, who had placed him in charge of the Adidas unit in Britain back in 1971. But in 1978, he was persuaded to switch sides. 'Horst Dassler told me that he was going to devote most of his time to Le Coq Sportif,' Brightwell recalled. 'That was all I needed to hear.'

Privy to the twisted relationships in the Dassler family, Brightwell understood perfectly that the new operation had to be kept away from Herzogenaurach. Le Coq Sportif UK was therefore established in the Cheshire town of Congleton, a few doors away from the Brightwells' home, and funded from their personal accounts. This caused a bit of a panic at the Congleton branch of the National Westminster bank, which normally dealt with small local transfers. 'Mr Brightwell, a very large sum has been transferred from Switzerland to your account,' a nervous bank manager whispered down the line.

Sent by Sarragan, the Swiss holding company set up by Dassler and Guelfi, the money enabled Brightwell to build up a fast-growing operation. A production plant was established for Le Coq Sportif in Macclesfield, a few miles away from Congleton, using the most advanced fabrics and designs from Adidas. Starting from scratch, Le Coq Sportif UK recorded sales of about £12 million after five years. It was endorsed by seven First Division clubs, including Tottenham Hotspur and Everton.

All the contacts Horst Dassler cultivated for Adidas were exploited to boost the international standing of Le Coq Sportif. The brand which had been over the moon a few years earlier to obtain a domestic deal with the French football federation was suddenly adorning some of the world's most revered athletes. Several South American football teams sported French roosters on their chests, including the Argentine world champions.

Still, Horst Dassler acknowledged that Le Coq Sportif alone could never attain the same scope as Adidas. He therefore acquired a string of companies and entered joint ventures that were all placed under the Sarragan holding. The structure was enlarged with an offshoot in Strasbourg and offices on the Champs-Elysées, run by some of André Guelfi's associates.

To organize the entire operation Horst Dassler hired Larry Hampton, a high-calibre American executive. For several months he stayed in a little guest house next to Horst Dassler's home in Eckartswiller. Later, Hampton's office was officially located at Sarragan on the Champs-Elysées, but he spent most of his time jetting around with Horst Dassler. His undertaking was both far-sighted and amazingly devious: they would build up a multi-brand sports conglomerate – behind the Dassler family's back.

*

Among the boldest partnerships under Sarragan was a joint venture with Daniel Hechter. An acclaimed French designer, he cocked a snook at the elite of Paris haute couture by making designer clothes that could be worn every day by increasingly emancipated women. One of his trademarks was a range of blazers for women that could be worn with skirts as well as trousers. But what brought him together with Horst Dassler was the fact that Hechter dabbled in the football business. His investments contributed to the setting up of Paris Saint-Germain, the football club which he established in June 1973 with Francis Borelli, a businessman well known in the advertising world.

To impress Hechter, Horst Dassler set up a meeting in June 1979 at the Beach Plaza in Monaco, at which he arrived aboard André Guelfi's high-speed yacht. Two months later, Hechter returned the compliment by inviting the pair for a second round of talks at his sumptuous villa in Saint-Tropez, and taking them for a cruise on his own boat. Mutually seduced, Hechter and Dassler hatched an agreement to have a line of Daniel Hechter sportswear manufactured and sold by Le Coq Sportif.

The tie-up with Daniel Hechter belonged to Sarragan but it was effectively run by the Adidas managers, backed up by André Guelfi's men. They worked from the Sarragan suite on the fifth floor of a tall building on the Champs-Elysées, which boasted several plush offices as well as a grand showroom. In line with the confusing structure of Horst Dassler's covert business, the plaque on the door said Sarragan, but the managers were formally employed by Le Coq Sportif.

Daniel Hechter Sports had a spectacular start. The line was launched with much fanfare and endorsed by some of André Guelfi's pals – from the actor Jean-Paul Belmondo to Jean-Pierre Rives, the rugby player. The designer introduced sports clothes that were truly original at the time, such as apple green tennis outfits and fuchsia pink ski suits. In its second year Daniel Hechter Sport reached sales of roughly 20 million French francs.

The partnership was strained, however. The problem was mostly attributed to the fraught relationship between the laid-back Adidas managers and the pedantic executives at Daniel Hechter. 'It was the pink-shirted sissies against the roughnecks,' as one protagonist summed it up. 'They just couldn't understand why Daniel made such a fuss about a button that was not exactly in the right place or a fold that was not precisely right.'

Hechter himself professed such admiration for Horst Dassler that he wrote a novel about him. Called *Le Boss*, this featured an impetuous young character named Luca Maltese who single-handedly built up Winner, an international sports brand. The hero's actions deviated for effect from Horst Dassler's in places – when Maltese pursued a steamy liaison with an American actress and ordered the murder of an African journalist, for example – but the storyline featured many other characters clearly based on Dassler's most exuberant partners.

His most secretive tie-up was sealed with Roberto Muller, a flamboyant young man from Uruguay. The dapper executive was the driving force behind Pony, an American sports company established in 1974. A former vice-president of Levi Strauss, he had extensive contacts in the Far Eastern sourcing industry. His plan with Pony was to concentrate on the all-American sports of baseball and American football. Muller quickly grasped the workings of the sports business – and he distinguished himself as a particularly slick operator.

Another swashbuckling character with a Latin temperament, Muller had all the right credentials to seduce Horst Dassler. His father originated from a Slovak brewers' family, his mother came from the Austro-Hungarian aristocracy. On a business trip in Brazil when the Second World War erupted, the Jewish family decided it would be too dangerous to return home and ended up in Uruguay. Roberto was sent to school in Leeds, and on his return joined Uruguay's junior football team. He went on to become one of the country's youngest oil and fashion executives, fluent in eight languages.

There were other aspects to Roberto Muller that weren't mentioned on his CV. One of them was his taste for glitz and glamour: his office was decorated with pictures of himself as a dashing young man, surrounded by stunning women on the steps of a private jet. A fanciful storyteller, he easily captivated his audience. As one former Adidas executive put it, Muller displayed 'flashes of genius and flashes of something else'.

But Horst Dassler was mostly charmed by Roberto's glibness and his sense of intrigue. The two hit it off when the Pony chief agreed to take part in a prank at the US Olympic trials in 1976, by cancelling Armin Dassler's car reservation in Seattle. Shortly afterwards, when Roberto Muller needed financial back-up for Pony, he turned to Horst Dassler.

The deal was set up at Les Pirates, a festive restaurant on a Caravelle that was anchored between Monte Carlo and San Remo. On the boat, Horst Dassler introduced Roberto Muller to André Guelfi. The snapshot that was taken at that dinner would have horrified Horst Dassler's parents: there was their son, flanked by two grinning suntanned men who could have walked straight off the set of *Hawaii Five-O*. Shortly after this encounter, André Guelfi agreed to acquire a large minority stake in Pony. Just as in the case of Le Coq Sportif, however, Guelfi was merely a front man. In an addendum, Dassler and Guelfi agreed that Dassler was entitled to take over Guelfi's shares in Pony at any time.

Backed up by Horst Dassler, Pony became an aggressive contender in the American sports business. Roberto Muller was promptly introduced to the Riu brothers, the Adidas partners in Taiwan. The deal considerably reduced production costs for Pony, encouraging Muller to push the brand in the American mass market. Pony made further progress in American sports, endorsed by sprinter Wilma Rudolph and footballer O. J. Simpson. When his deal with Puma expired and he ended his career at New York Cosmos, Pelé became another Pony endorsee.

But the Pony deal was kept hidden from Herzogenaurach even more diligently than any of Horst Dassler's other outside interests. While Le Coq Sportif and Daniel Hechter belonged to Sarragan, the stake in Pony featured solely in the books of André Guelfi – that is, if he kept any.

There were only a handful of French executives who were fully cognizant of Dassler's dealings with Roberto Muller. Others who encountered the clique unexpectedly were somewhat unsettled by some of the values they discovered. André Gorgemans, former financial manager of Le Coq Sportif USA, was invited for drinks at a New York apartment owned by one of Roberto Muller's business partners. As he entered the flat, Gorgemans was intrigued by an ornamental bowl filled with white powder on the mantlepiece. It wasn't pot-pourri.

Bundled together under the Sarragan holding, Horst Dassler's secondary brands quickly reached combined sales worth millions of francs. Due to the clandestine aspects of the set-up, the operations remained somewhat haphazard, but Jean Wendling, then chairman of Sarragan France, still found himself at the helm of a full-fledged sports conglomerate. As he put it, 'Sarragan became a sort of internal competitor for Adidas.'

As Horst explained to some close managers, the accumulation of side-interests was meant to reach a critical mass that would enable him to survive in the sports business by himself. Remarkably, he managed to hide most of these dealings from his family in Herzogenaurach. But the pressure became unbearable for many managers, who were torn between the frustrated Horst Dassler and his inquisitive family.

Gerhard Prochaska, marketing manager in Landersheim, placed himself in the firing line when he travelled to Herzogenaurach with a tennis racket. This had been identified by Horst Dassler as a promising product, with a special three-pronged design above the grip. Prochaska headed the French delegation that was to obtain approval for the racket at a product meeting in Herzogenaurach. When his turn came he dutifully pulled out the racket and showed it to the assembled German managers. As Horst Dassler had anticipated, the product was inspected with scepticism, and summarily dismissed. In line with his instructions, however, Prochaska spoke up again. 'I understand that you don't wish to sell this racket under the Adidas brand,' he said calmly. 'Under these circumstances, I must inform you that we will sell it under the Coq Sportif brand.' A few minutes later Prochaska was called to the Villa for an amicable but thorough grilling by Käthe Dassler.

The same treatment was used on all visiting French managers who stepped out of line. Käthe Dassler seized every opportunity to learn more about the hidden business of her son. She suspected that it existed, but permanently probed to learn more. Subjected to her questions, the managers went through exhausting contortions to keep their boss out of trouble. 'Sometimes I wondered whether I was in international business or in diplomacy,' said Robbie Brightwell.

The same thought occurred to Dieter Passchen, who headed up the Adidas operation in Hong Kong. He once travelled to Herzogenaurach with a delegation from Descente, the company's Japanese licensees, who had a separate deal with Horst for Le Coq Sportif. The talks between Käthe and the Descente managers were meant to extend their deal with Adidas. Just before the meeting, however, Käthe Dassler discovered Descente's double role with Le Coq Sportif. 'She completely flew off the handle,' Passchen recalled. 'She branded the Japanese as traitors and refused to sign with them again.' It took several days for the dust to settle.

The confrontations were particularly awkward when Käthe Dassler berated her son's managers in public. Alain Ronc, the young man who ran Arena in the early years, was harpooned by Käthe Dassler during an international trade fair, while he was holding talks with officials of the German swimming federation. The Dasslers staunchly opposed the promotion of Arena in Germany, because they felt it caused confusion among retailers. 'But Herr Dassler asked me to enter these talks,' Ronc protested. One of the Dassler daughters shot back: 'Frau Dassler's orders are to be obeyed throughout the world. That counts for Herr Dassler, too.'

The situation became so stressful for Ronc that he resolved to confront Käthe Dassler. He managed to get a seat next to her on a flight from Phoenix to Los Angeles. During the journey he explained what he was doing with Arena, and how this could benefit Adidas. She then opened up and confessed that the tensions with her son were deeply tormenting her. 'I don't understand my son,' she lamented. 'He has all he wants in life, why does he have to spend all of his time annoying his family?' Ronc continued to plead in favour of Arena, but she cut him off. His arguments regarding the financial rewards of Arena didn't mean anything to her. 'Peace of mind is much more important to me than money,' she said.

Later that evening Alain Ronc met up with Horst Dassler, who was staying at the Marriott Hotel in Los Angeles. His mother didn't know that Horst was there, but he had followed her every move in the country. Horst was deeply affected by the conversation which Ronc relayed. 'All these women are paranoid about me,' Dassler sighed. 'I try to explain what I'm doing, but they just don't get it. Their narrow-mindedness is making my life a misery'. He asked Ronc to ignore his mother, but the young man had had enough. Upon his return he announced that he was leaving.

To back herself up in Herzogenaurach, Käthe Dassler attempted to recruit a batch of managers with high international profiles. Among them was Alex Schuster, a German who started up the apparel section of Head, an Austrian ski and tennis equipment brand. Käthe and her daughters invited Schuster for a discreet meeting in Herzogenaurach, without informing Horst. More out of curiosity than genuine interest, Schuster turned up at the Villa. The meeting came to an abrupt halt, however, when Horst stormed into the room. While his mother recovered from the shock, Horst began to grill Schuster, berating his experience and his accomplishments in front of the other family members.

Deciding that being insulted during his job interview was no way to begin a new career, Schuster stood up and left.

Outraged by the sabotage, Käthe Dassler persisted. Her next candidate was Jürgen Lenz, a 33-year-old German with an impressive profile as account manager at McCann Erickson, an advertising agency based in New York. Lenz had been assigned to missions around the world and he had been entrusted with weighty international budgets. He was duly hired from October 1977 as the company's first international marketing manager, based in Herzogenaurach.

Several weeks after his recruitment, Lenz thoroughly prepared his first presentation for assorted members of the management and the Dassler family. He was to outline briefly how he would approach marketing issues in the US. If the family approved, the same speech would be given to the four American distributors who would arrive the next day. Horst Dassler had made the journey for the occasion, accompanied by his new marketing manager, Klaus Hempel.

Hempel himself had joined the French side of the company just six months earlier, and he soon noticed that something was badly amiss in the relationship between the two branches. The suspicion took a very concrete shape during the four-hour drive to Herzogenaurach: Horst Dassler unequivocally instructed Klaus Hempel to demolish Jürgen Lenz. 'Ask him tricky questions,' he told Hempel. 'Counter all of his points. Make him look stupid.' While Lenz held his short presentation, Dassler continuously prodded Hempel to jump into action.

At the end of the speech, Hempel complied. After the second tough question, however, Käthe Dassler stood up in a rage, furiously waving an umbrella. 'Horscht,' she yelled with her thick Franconian twang. 'You are not going to do it again. We will not let you destroy this man!' The meeting ended in another Dassler family slanging match.

Horst Dassler would never resolve the dispute with his father. In his darkest moods he shared his sadness with close colleagues and showed them long, bitter letters in which Adolf Dassler disowned his son. Right until the last months of his life, Adi was permanently harassed by the conflicts between his son and his German managers. One of the last skirmishes erupted before the 1978 World Cup. For the occasion Adi Dassler had discreetly developed a football boot with all the latest enhancements. Horst Widmann, his personal assistant, was sent to present the boot in Argentina. But when he met up with the Adidas France delegation, at the Sheraton Hotel in Buenos Aires, Widmann was stunned to discover that the model the French had brought along was, as far as Widmann could see, a barely disguised copy of the German one. He was fuming, certain that the French had used a mole in the German organization.

Widmann agitatedly called the Dasslers in Herzogenaurach. 'Adi Dassler was livid,' he recalled. 'He gave me the official order to steal a boot from the French delegation to check out how it was made.' Then, the two parties still had to work out which of the boots would be launched by Adidas at the World Cup. 'Adi and Käthe were breathing down my neck, on the phone all the time to make sure I would stand firm,' said Widmann. They ended up reaching a somewhat one-sided compromise, whereby the German team would wear the German boots and Horst Dassler would hand out French ones to all the other players.

Oblivious to the business aspects of Adidas, Adolf continued to walk around with his notepad and to tinker in his workshop. The obsession that perpetually drove him to seek improvements for his footwear never appeared to fade. Over five decades he registered nearly seven hundred patents to his name, ranging from the screw-in studs to minute modifications that would stir only the most fanatical shoe fetishist.

As his hair turned grey Adi still refused to travel but he avidly watched televised sports coverage. Horst Widmann received proof of Adolf's assiduity when he received a phone call from the boss during the 1976 Olympic Games in Montreal. Adolf Dassler had been watching Alberto Juantorena Danger, the Cuban runner. 'Fetch him right away,' Dassler told Widmann. 'I can tell by the way he's running the bends that there's something wrong with his shoe.' When Widmann checked the Cuban's shoes, it turned out that Adi had observed correctly, from several thousand miles away. Juantorena went on to win the gold medals for the 400 metres and 800 metres – once his shoes had been fixed.

In his seventies, Adolf Dassler continued to shy away from the honours that were bestowed upon him. When strangers turned up at the gates in Herzogenaurach, hoping to catch a glimpse of the great man, they were turned away unceremoniously. 'One day he was walking his dog in the compound when someone called him to the fence, asking for Adi Dassler,' recalled Karl-Heinz Lang, another of his close assistants. 'Adi

just shrugged. "Don't know," he told the visitors. "I'm the gardener." '
Clad in his three-striped sweatpants, he tended to look the part.

Adi once confessed to his friend Erich Deuser, medical adviser to the
German team, that he didn't have a clue how many factories Adidas
owned – and frankly he didn't care. Käthe could probably have told
Deuser that, by 1978, the company which her husband founded in his
mother's washroom employed nearly 3,000 people in Germany alone.
About 180,000 pairs of three-striped shoes were produced daily in the
factories which Adidas owned in seventeen countries. They were officially distributed in 144 countries.

By then, Adi had been advised to slow down. He had been gently told
after a medical check-up that he should take things more easily. Since
the warning, Adolf Dassler had dutifully been swallowing coloured pills
by the handful. But to no avail: on the morning of 18 August 1978,
Käthe found him almost motionless in his bed, paralysed by a stroke.
He was rushed to an intensive care unit in Erlangen and lay there for
nearly three weeks, surrounded by all his children. He passed away at
the clinic, aged 78, when his heart finally gave up on 6 September.

The Dassler family strictly followed his instructions to keep pompous
speechmakers and other interlopers at bay. To make sure the funeral
would remain private, Käthe Dassler, her five children and their families
assembled one hour before the time that had been scheduled publicly,
on a rainy morning two days after Adi's death. He was buried under a
plain marble stone in the upper right corner of the Herzogenaurach
cemetery – a spot as far away as possible from the one where his brother
Rudolf had been laid to rest four years earlier.

16

Olympic Friends

By the time the Olympics opened in Montreal in July 1976, Horst
Dassler's sports political group was in full swing. The stage would be
used to reaffirm the supremacy of Adidas, under increasingly virulent
attack from Asian and American newcomers. At the same time, Dassler's
marketing men seized the opportunity to storm the Olympics.

Still supposedly amateur, athletes were increasingly demanding. Their emancipation had risen by another notch after the Munich Olympics in 1972, stimulated by heightened competition. The almost folkloric rivalry between Adidas and Puma continued unabated at the Montreal Games themselves: sure enough, Hans Henningsen, the influential Puma agent from Brazil, was left stranded in a motel about thirty kilometres out of town. Adidas had seen to it that the Puma people were far removed from the action.

The fight for the favours of the best athletes ended up taking a more violent turn. One of the disputes centred around Cuban athletes, who were supposed to wear Adidas but eagerly responded to Henningsen's advances. As the Brazilian recalled, he then received an impromptu visit at his Canadian motel by 'a Cuban delegation, armed with pistols, who threatened to murder me if I continued to deal with Cuban athletes'.

But this time around, the two Bavarian companies faced more aggressive competition from impudent upstarts. Nike had made much headway since the Munich Olympics and had come to regard the Montreal edition as an international launching pad. Their strongest hopes were pinned on Steve Prefontaine, the company's iconic long-distance runner, who had faltered in Munich but looked set to peak in Montreal.

In the meantime, Bill Bowerman had resigned as coach of the American track and field team, disillusioned by the performance of his athletes in Munich, but Nike still managed to get closer to Prefontaine. Since the runner had trouble financing his training he agreed to be placed on the payroll of Blue Ribbon Sports – in another weird instance of technically illegal dealings that were increasingly tolerated by the US federation. There was no way that Prefontaine would wear Adidas this time. Sadly, Nike's hopes were dashed when 'Pre' was killed in a car crash in 1975.

On the other hand, Asics found itself at the centre of a little storm. The brand had just been launched by Kihachiro Onitsuka, the Japanese businessman behind the Tiger brand. His company's international sales had expanded briskly after he signed a distribution deal for the United States with Phil Knight back in the sixties. But the two had fallen out in the early seventies when Knight had begun to make similar shoes under his own Nike brand while he had an exclusive agreement with Tiger. The matter was settled in a court case which Onitsuka lost.

The Japanese came back in Montreal with another brand called Asics (short for 'Anima Sana in Corpore Sano' – a sound mind in a sound body). It immediately hit the headlines when Lasse Viren, a Finnish long-distance runner, waved his Asics shoes under the noses of the cameramen while celebrating his unexpected victory over 10,000 metres. The IOC called him to appear before a technical committee, but its members were greatly reassured when the Finn told them that he had not taken off his shoes for commercial reasons at all – he just removed them because he had a blister. Viren was allowed to compete with his Asics shoes in the 5,000 metres race, after which he took home another gold medal.

To fend off such attacks, Adidas relied on the contacts it had been building with athletes for many years. There was no way that Nike and Asics could match the scope of the Adidas relationships, not to mention the fact that athletes couldn't easily be persuaded to switch overnight from their trusted German spikes to an entirely unknown brand. After all, shoes remained an essential piece of equipment, and many preferred to play it safe.

Regardless of the piecemeal triumphs achieved by their new rivals, Adidas still trounced all their opponents when it came to the absurd exercise of the medal count – the measurement which Adidas routinely used to underline its hegemony at the Games. Among their most remarked-upon endorsees was Nadia Comaneci, a 15-year-old gymnast from Romania who enraptured judges and public alike. She was the first gymnast ever to score a ten in Olympic competition, for her perfect beam routine. The entire Romanian team was clad in sober white tunics with a trefoil on the hip. It was one of the greatest rewards for all the handshakes and hospitality offered to Romanian officials over the previous years.

Meanwhile, Horst Dassler spent most of his time schmoozing with his influential friends. While he could not fail to see that Adidas was under attack in the stadium, he apparently felt that the brand was mighty enough to remain at the fore and he could concentrate on his grander sports political schemes.

Patrick Nally had arranged to rent a private mansion in Montreal, where the two held discussions in a cosy setting. To make the abode all the more welcoming, Nally had hired a British cook. The only guests that were missing were the Africans, who had withdrawn their teams from the Games to protest at the participation of New Zealand, which had sent a team to play in a rugby tournament in South Africa.

Through Christian Jannette, the former chief of protocol at the Munich Olympics who had been hired by Adidas to open doors for

Horst Dassler, the chief executive easily reached the highest-ranking dignitaries. The efficient Adidas diplomat had obtained a room at the Queen Elizabeth hotel, where the IOC members resided, as well as a pass that gave him privileged access to other facilities. In line with his brief, Jannette paid particularly close attention to delegates from Russia. It had been decided two years earlier that the next Olympic Games were to be held in Moscow, and the Adidas men knew that nothing could be left to chance. Just as he had courted Canadian officials ahead of the Montreal Games, Christian Jannette thoroughly prepared the ground for the 1980 Olympics.

One of his trickiest missions in Montreal was to organize an odd journey for Sergei Pavlov, the Russian sports minister at the time. Mikhail Mzareulov, head of protocol for the Russian delegation, let it be known that Pavlov would be thrilled to see the Niagara Falls. It was left to Jannette to make the arrangements. The excursion would have to be secretive since the Russian authorities would have frowned upon their team leader taking a jaunt to a capitalist attraction, albeit a natural one. It was quite a tricky affair, since Pavlov accompanied one of the strongest teams in the Montreal Games and resided in the Olympic village.

Pavlov and Mzareulov were smuggled out of Montreal at four o'clock in the morning, then embarked on a scheduled flight to Toronto, where they transferred to a private jet and finally a car with smoked-glass windows to Niagara Falls. 'Pavlov was like a kid,' recalled Jannette, who accompanied them all the way. The two Russians insisted on having their picture taken behind barrels for a tacky montage – with just their heads sticking out and Niagara Falls in the background.

Sergei Pavlov reciprocated the favour many times over. In the six years before the Moscow Olympics, Christian Jannette made sixty-two trips to the Russian capital. His friends treated him with every consideration, and they made special allowances for him to travel around the country unimpeded. Jannette must have been among the first Westerners in the communist era to travel to the steppes of Yakutia, about 8,000 kilometres from Moscow, an outpost for which Russians themselves required visas.

The preparations for the Moscow Olympics marked a turning point in the relationship between Adidas and the IOC. Over the previous years, Horst Dassler had drawn priceless benefits from his personal rapport with João Havelange, head of Fifa. There was no telling what could be achieved if Adidas obtained the same privileges at the IOC. As it happened, the chairmanship of the IOC would be up for grabs in a vote just ahead of the Moscow Olympics. This time, Horst Dassler made sure that he was on the winning side from the start.

When Christian Jannette arrived in Moscow on one of his numerous trips, he often headed straight to the Spanish embassy. There, he was certain to be treated to a copious meal by Juan Antonio Samaranch, the ambassador. They became such good friends that, when Jannette was taken to a Moscow hospital with a hernia, the ambassador's charming wife, Bibis Samaranch, came to bring him fresh fruit and Spanish dishes every day.

Christian Jannette began to cultivate his contacts with Samaranch shortly after he joined Adidas in 1973. It did not seem to upset anyone that the Catalan had previously shown unrestrained fervour for the Franco regime. Back in the fifties, he caught the eye of Spain's ruling generals by organizing an international contest for roller hockey and a Mediterranean sports festival, at a time when the country was still widely ostracized. The regime deemed him too young and openly ambitious to push him up the political ladder, but changed their minds once he had built up a personal fortune though a textile business and become friends with Carmen Franco, the dictator's daughter. In December 1966 he was appointed minister for sport in Franco's government. He was later elected as a member of the Cortes for Barcelona under the fascist banner – although the ballot had little in common with the basic principles of democracy.

At the same time, Samaranch made his ascent in sports politics, beginning with his election to the IOC in 1966. He gradually reached one of the most coveted positions in the Olympic movement: the chief of protocol. Insiders could not fail to recall that the two previous chairmen of the IOC had held the same position. Jannette was further charmed by Samaranch's smooth manner, his astute business sense and his multiple language skills. 'He distinguished himself from the brigade of smalltime Olympic officials with green blazers,' Jannette said.

Jannette pounced at the wedding of Avery Brundage, former IOC chairman, to Mariann Princess Reuss in June 1973. Between speeches, Jannette asked Samaranch, another wedding guest, if he would be interested in meeting Horst Dassler. Samaranch instantly grasped the potential of the proposed encounter. The date was set for a few weeks later, in September 1973.

Juan Antonio Samaranch arranged an elaborate welcome. Horst Dassler was taken around Camp Nou, the legendary home of Barcelona FC. He had lunch at the private residence of the Samaranch couple. He toured an impressive nautical show in Barcelona. And he was treated to a black-tie dinner with the Samaranchs, in the grandest Catalonian style.

The dinner sealed a lifelong understanding between the two most influential men in the sports world. Both of them were driven by an insatiable thirst for power, and they acknowledged that they could attain it together: if Samaranch reached the chairmanship of the IOC he would open the door to Horst Dassler. In turn, the money raised by Dassler would help Samaranch to reinforce his standing. Together they would rule over the Olympics and turn them into a gigantic money-spinner.

If Horst Dassler knew about Samaranch's close ties with the Franco regime, they probably didn't disturb him. As a young boy his parents had sent him off to live with a Spanish family for several months. He resided in Oviedo, the home town of the Generalissimo, with the Garcías. Horst remained in close touch with the family, which staunchly supported the regime. He even appointed Manuel García, his former Spanish playmate, as head of Arena Brazil.

Samaranch invested heavily to fulfil his part of the unwritten deal. Shortly after Franco's death, in November 1975, at a time when Spain didn't have an ambassador in the Soviet Union, he convinced the government to send him to Moscow. He shrewdly figured that, ahead of the Moscow Games, all the people who counted in the Olympics would spend much of their time in the Russian capital. They would be grateful for the support and hospitality of the Spanish embassy. Given the lavishness of the parties thrown by the Samaranchs, it was widely suspected that they pumped some of their personal funds into the diplomatic efforts.

For its closest friends, the Spanish embassy was prepared to sort out more mundane matters. Adidas had again obtained an exclusive deal to equip all of the officials for the Moscow Games. This turned out to be a monstrous task: while the organizers of the Montreal games required about 10,000 such outfits, the Russians coolly asked for 32,000 pieces. As they joked back in Landersheim, 'For every task there was one chap performing it, another one supervising him, and then the KGB man watching the two others.'

22. *Horst Dassler soaks up the atmosphere at Camp Nou, the legendary Barcelona stadium. He was there with Juan Antonio Samaranch (not pictured), future chairman of the International Olympic Committee.*

Just a few months before the opening of the Games, however, another blazing row erupted between Horst Dassler and his family in Herzogenaurach. All of a sudden, the huge equipment deal for the Moscow Olympics was transferred to Arena. The switch was indicative of Horst's personal clout, but it was also nightmarish for the textile people in Landersheim, who had to come up with an entirely new range almost overnight.

Putting his oar in, American president Jimmy Carter decided to protest against the Red Army's invasion of Afghanistan by ordering a boycott of the Moscow Games. A similar stance was taken by West Germany, Japan and China, among others. All deals with American companies were off, including the contract which Adidas had sealed with Levi's to supply jeans to the Olympic officials. It was Patrick Nally who saved the day with an Italian company that produced denims under the Jesus brand.

Not unlike Havelange a few years earlier, Samaranch campaigned openly for the IOC chairmanship. His unofficial manifesto was partly based on the principle that the amateur ethos of the Olympics should be somewhat relaxed. This position had infuriated his opponents when Samaranch dared to express it at a meeting in Olympia, and it continued to irritate some IOC members, who tended to think of money matters as indecent. However, more down-to-earth members became convinced that the hypocrisy of the existing rules was unsustainable.

Another problem that played in Samaranch's favour was that the Olympic movement was teetering on the brink of collapse. The Montreal Games had punched a massive hole in the city's accounts: its mayor, Jean Drapeau, was quoted as saying that 'the Olympics could no more produce a deficit than a man a baby'. But the Games left Montreal with debts of about $1 billion (rising to $2 billion with interest payments). The reputation of the Olympics was further tarnished by the large-scale boycott of the Moscow Games, which badly disappointed some sponsors and looked certain to deprive broadcasters of millions of viewers.

Controversial as they were, Samaranch's plans concretely addressed this urgent situation. He intended to set up a task force that would concentrate entirely on raising funds. It would help to package the Olympics in a way that made them more attractive for the broadcasters, and it would seek much more comprehensive sponsorship deals. This was where Horst Dassler came in.

On 16 July 1980 the Catalan beat all his opponents – including Willy Daume, the German candidate favoured by executives in Herzogen-aurach. That evening, those who had contributed most to Samaranch's triumph convened to celebrate it in a rented meeting room at the Moskva hotel. Among the fifteen guests around the Samaranch couple were Horst Dassler and Christian Jannette. The caviar was most certainly Russian, but the *foie gras* for this special party had been flown over from Landersheim.

By then, Horst Dassler had become completely fascinated by the mechanisms of power. He had turned into a chief manipulator, influential enough to bend weighty decisions in his favour. He enjoyed rubbing shoulders with high-ranking people, thrived on his role as a puppet-master. He relished the intrigue, building on the life of deceit he had cultivated since the deep disagreements had erupted between him and his parents. But since Horst Dassler had first become involved in international sports politics, both he and it had acquired a razor-sharp edge.

Although Dassler was permanently on his guard, he was particularly suspicious in the Soviet Union. Convinced that he was bugged all the time, the Adidas chief always took behind the Iron Curtain a debugging device, which he used in his hotel room even before he started unpacking his bags. He taught several leading executives to use such devices, and encouraged them to carry disinformative documents in their briefcases.

The suspected surveillance sometimes became so stressful that Horst Dassler relieved the tension with a playful touch. During a dinner meeting he would share a piece of fresh information with his Soviet partners, but then conclude casually: 'Well, you already know this anyway since you've read all the documents.' The hosts remained poker-faced.

With Patrick Nally, Horst Dassler allowed himself more cheeky interludes to shake off the KGB men. Fed up with the constant surveillance, the two jumped into a taxi and ordered it to drive out of town at high speed. The driver sped off without further questions, taking Dassler and Nally to an obscure restaurant that surely didn't feature on the propaganda tour. Back at their four-star hotel the two men burst into fits of giggles – in the bathroom, of course, with the taps turned on full blast.

The obsession was not entirely in jest nor unjustified. After all, Soviet rulers were notoriously inquisitive about capitalist guests, and the stakes of the sports business became so high in those years that the fear of bugs apparently spread to the IOC itself: the Olympic headquarters in Lausanne were rumoured to have one meeting room for sensitive discussions that was guaranteed surveillance-free, constantly swept for bugs by technicians.

Even animals were not deemed above suspicion. Some eyebrows were raised when Thomas Keller, head of the international rowing federation, based in Monte Carlo, received a dog as a present from his Soviet friends. 'We were convinced that they had actually sent Tommy a bugged dog, that was the sort of thing you expected,' quipped Patrick Nally. 'We were very friendly to this dog, just in case.'

Conversely, an American salesman was stunned to discover, while staying at the Sportshotel in Herzogenaurach, that its bar appeared to be wired. By then the hotel had been upgraded and it was regularly used by entire delegations of high-ranking dignitaries, who were most likely to share their impressions of the day over a drink at the bar. The salesman was trying to tune his transistor to the radio station of the US Armed Forces in Germany, but distinctly heard conversations at the downstairs bar instead.

23. *Christian Jannette, a key player in Horst's warm Soviet relations, sits to Horst's left for an evening at the Lido in Paris. With them was Soviet sports minister Sergei Pavlov (front left). The young man at the back is Patrick Nally, who pioneered modern sports marketing.*

The same happened to Jörg Dassler, Armin Dassler's second son, when he was still a teenager in the late seventies. He was sitting in his living room, fiddling with his radio, while Armin was talking on the phone. 'And all of a sudden, I heard my father on the radio,' Jörg Dassler recalled. 'That's how we found out that the phone was bugged. We found the device in the receiver.'

Such methods caused disbelief and outrage, but many felt that they had become an integral part of the sports business. The boycott at the Moscow Olympics aptly demonstrated that sport had come to be regarded as a sharp political instrument. Horst Dassler and his managers operated in the awkward political climate that characterized the period, fraught with suspicion and intrigue. Others were concerned by the extent of the manipulation which Horst orchestrated, sometimes for sheer excitement. When he had some spare time at his hotel, Dassler would sometimes pick up the phone and alarm people with entirely fabricated stories. 'The way they reacted often yielded precious information,' said one of Dassler's confidantes.

As Horst became more deeply involved in the exploding sports business, however, his behaviour acquired an obsessive, paranoid edge. 'He was permanently hiding,' said Klaus Hempel, his personal assistant. 'He would make phone calls from his desk and make people believe that he was at the other end of the world.'

At the zenith of his political might, from the late seventies, Horst Dassler appeared most concerned about the loyalty of those around him. One of Dassler's managers witnessed how the Adidas chief went berserk at a football match when he spotted Franz Beckenbauer at the other end of the stadium, casually chatting to an Adidas competitor. 'The next day Dassler called the German police to find out where he could get hold of long-range microphones, so he could eavesdrop on such conversations,' the aide remembered. 'When I told him he may be overreacting, he rolled his eyes and called me naïve.'

He dismissed several executives on grounds that turned out to be entirely unfair, or grossly exaggerated. Christian Jannette was gruffly rebuked when he asked Brigitte Baenkler, Horst Dassler's sister, for an innocent dance at the annual German sports ball. Frau Baenkler was unaccompanied, and Jannette was just being polite, but Horst didn't see it that way. 'He quizzed me aggressively, asking what we had been talking about, what she told me,' Jannette said. 'It was most unpleasant.'

Jannette, who had served Dassler selflessly for seven years, was unceremoniously dumped soon after Samaranch's election. 'He told me he could not trust me any more but never explained why,' said Jannette. 'Later I discerned a pattern, whereby he would discard people like used tissues whenever he no longer needed them. He was Machiavellian, with an unbelievable thirst for power.'

Those who were ditched by Horst Dassler knew that they would have a hard time finding another position in the sports business – unless they walked over to Puma. 'You could see that he was a very political individual who didn't stop at anything; very manipulative,' said Patrick Nally. 'I would never want to be offside with him.' Unfortunately for Nally, this was precisely what happened.

17

Pitch Invasion

After their Argentine warm-up, Horst Dassler and Patrick Nally were preparing to lock in their sports marketing business. Despite all the hiccups they had had to endure before Argentina, the two felt certain they were onto something.

For Horst Dassler, the sports marketing business had started off as another sideline, when Patrick Nally came along. To begin with he saw it as a means to raise the money that would oil his relationship with João Havelange. It would enable him to earn cash that he could pump into his undercover brands. However, Dassler became convinced that the business of sports rights could grow far beyond his initial expectations.

Patrick Nally had already managed to unlock millions of dollars from international companies in Argentina, under the worst of conditions. And that was mostly for marketing rights: there was no telling what kind of sums Nally and Dassler could raise if they added far-reaching broadcasting rights. If this business was run properly, it could disgorge more cash than Adidas and all of Dassler's other brands put together.

Horst Dassler's interest in sports rights was almost entirely independent from his sporting-goods business. He drove it so personally that, even at Adidas France, only a few managers were privy to the whole picture. Among them was Klaus Hempel, who joined Adidas as a marketing manager but quickly became Horst Dassler's personal assistant in 1978. Another was Jürgen Lenz, the former advertising executive who had been hired by Käthe Dassler as an international marketing manager but changed sides as soon as he got to know her son.

None of Horst Dassler's competitors stood in the way. His mother, his sisters and his cousins at Puma still concentrated on their products and just didn't have the nous to try to exploit more fundamental changes in the sports business. They could not fail to notice the rise of sports marketing, which raised the stakes in the entire industry, but they didn't have the impetus to profit directly from the changes themselves.

This was precisely what distinguished Horst Dassler from his rivals. He never lost sight of the wider picture and he was permanently on the lookout for opportunities on all fronts. He sometimes got his fingers burned, but on other occasions he was inspired by remarkable vision. There is no denying that Dassler saw, much more sharply than others, the prospects of the sports rights business.

With Patrick Nally, he had exactly the right partner to prime it. Straight after the Argentine episode, the two men began to put together an unprecedented package for the next football World Cup, to be held in Spain from June 1982. A football-crazy nation and an enticing destination, it would make an easy sell.

The problem was that another shrewd and persistent entrepreneur had latched on to the concept. Rolf Deyhle dabbled in all sorts of smart business investments, including a London cartoon studio. Watching the developments in international football, the canny German thought that he could combine two of his interests by marketing a football-playing cartoon hero. He therefore asked a Hungarian artist in his London studio to draw up two characters, called Sport Billy and Sport Suzy, which he would attempt to introduce as Fifa mascots. He would then organize the sale of marketing rights to companies that wanted to use the characters.

Armed with rough drawings, Deyhle drove to Villa Derwald, the Fifa headquarters in Zurich. He was warmly greeted by Helmut Käser, Fifa's general secretary. A stoical Swiss with two sleepy dogs under his desk, Käser had become wary of the changes that were taking place at the federation. As he told Deyhle, he resented the influence of the greedy cronies whom Havelange had brought in since his election as Fifa chairman. 'After several meetings Käser told me that he wanted us to take up the fight together,' Deyhle recalled, 'to counter the influence of these people.'

Helmut Käser apparently produced a contract that gave far-reaching marketing rights to Rolf Deyhle. Among others, he could exploit the Fifa emblem and mascots for the next twelve years. In other words, for this entire period he would be entitled to sell products featuring Sport Billy and Sport Suzy. As for the organization's emblem, Rolf Deyhle drew it himself, on the spur of the moment. The drawing consisted of two overlapping globes in the shape of footballs, showing the two sides of the earth. When Dassler and Nally heard about the deal, they could not believe their ears. They thought they had an understanding with

Havelange. After all the investments they had put in to raise money for the Brazilian in Argentina, he had handed over complementary rights to a maverick entrepreneur – and for a paltry sum at that. While Dassler and Nally's rights related mostly to the World Cup itself, Deyhle had been given permanent rights for the emblems. This meant that Dassler and Nally would constantly have to consult Deyhle, to make sure that they did not sign conflicting contracts.

Confronted with Dassler's ire, Havelange protested that Käser had handled the deal all by himself. The two attempted to settle the matter amicably with Deyhle. But when the Stuttgart entrepreneur turned down Dassler's offer, things turned nasty. Out of the blue, it seemed, he received a curt letter from the Fifa chairman. In little more than one paragraph, Havelange informed Deyhle that his marketing rights had been rescinded. He filed for an injunction in a Swiss court and won. From then on, Horst Dassler had no choice but to negotiate with Rolf Deyhle, a notoriously hard-headed businessman. The two men worked together smoothly for a while – both far-sighted executives who shared the excitement of inventing business – yet, given the strong personalities of the two unwilling partners, their relationship was bound to be tumultuous.

Often feeling sidelined, Deyhle repeatedly threatened to walk over to Dassler's mother and to torpedo his undercover business. On other occasions, the somewhat mischievous German could not resist the temptation to stir things up. While Nally had again persuaded Coca-Cola to invest heavily in the 1982 World Cup, Deyhle cheekily approached Pepsi and sold them rights to use the Fifa emblems. All hell broke loose when they found out in Atlanta, and it took all of Nally's persuasive powers to prevent Coca-Cola from storming out.

These headaches convinced Dassler that he needed a more reliable partner at Fifa. As far as he was concerned, he had been cheated by Helmut Käser, the general secretary who mooted the Deyhle deal. He conveniently used the ensuing mayhem to persuade others that Käser was out of his depth in the modern football business.

To remove the hapless general secretary, Horst Dassler turned to his most persuasive henchman. 'Horst asked me if I couldn't work something out to eliminate [Käser],' said André Guelfi. 'I told him that, if he refused, we would make his life a misery, it would be tough.' Helmut Käser initially stood firm, but he soon found out what Guelfi meant.

Käser complained that he was being harassed, even stalked. In the circumstances, the compensation promised by Guelfi seemed an interesting alternative. 'I told him he'd better leave with his head held high and negotiate for his safety,' Guelfi explained.

In the interval, Horst Dassler had identified a replacement for Helmut Käser. As part of his pitch to investing companies, Patrick Nally promised that a competent marketing person would respond to any of their queries at Fifa. While Dassler and Nally were looking around for a suitable marketing man, Tommy Keller, head of the international rowing federation, dropped a name. Keller, then a leading executive of Swiss Timing, a group of Swiss watchmakers who offered joint services at sports events, had spotted an upcoming manager who might be interested in the position.

Sepp Blatter was in charge of public relations at Longines, one of the two leading brands in Swiss Timing at the time. A well-mannered polyglot, the Swiss was far less impressive and charismatic than Havelange, but that suited Dassler down to the ground. He needed a man who would be sharp enough to conduct marketing activities at Fifa, yet sufficiently docile to let Dassler and Havelange rule over the organization – and its income.

For several months Sepp Blatter worked from an office in Landersheim, where Horst groomed him intensely. 'From the beginning, Horst Dassler and myself felt that we were kindred spirits,' said the Swiss. 'He taught me the finer points of sports politics – an excellent education for me.' Since their birthdays were just two days apart in March, they regularly celebrated together at the Auberge. 'That often included smoking a good cigar, another thing that I learned from Horst Dassler,' Blatter recalled.

Others felt that Dassler was blatantly using his new protégé. 'They held discussions in which Horst plainly issued instructions to Blatter,' recalled Christian Jannette. 'Horst openly talked of Blatter as a puppet, he introduced Blatter as one of us,' André Guelfi agreed. 'He was an insignificant character, entirely at Horst's command. When the three of us had lunch together Blatter looked up at Dassler as if he was God, knowing full well that he wouldn't stand a chance to get the Fifa job without Dassler.'

Sepp Blatter was placed into orbit after the ousting of Helmut Käser at a Fifa executive committee meeting, in May 1981. With his opponents

24. Captains of the Fifa team: Sepp Blatter (right) and João Havelange both kitted out by Adidas.

out of the way and his friends firmly at the helm, Horst Dassler could virtually sign his own deals.

Backed up by Dassler, the indefatigable Patrick Nally scoured the globe to find companies that would be prepared to invest in the 'Mundial', as the 1982 competition became known. On one of his flights he elaborated a package – he called it Intersoccer – that outlined precisely what rights could be accorded to the sponsors and how they should be protected. Devised almost entirely by Nally, Intersoccer formed a remarkably clean and creative blueprint for the huge marketing fests orchestrated for World Cups in the following decades.

As part of Intersoccer, international companies could buy rights that would identify them as official sponsors of the World Cup. They could exploit the Fifa name and emblem for their own publicity, supposedly adding to their credentials as vibrant international companies that behaved as good corporate citizens by supporting football.

Emboldened by the millions gained from Argentina, Dassler and Nally agreed to cough up about 25 million Swiss francs for the marketing rights to the Mundial – a sizeable jump compared with the 12 million Swiss francs required four years earlier. But less than one year before the championships, the Spanish organizers came up with another request. They coolly explained that they would need another 35 million Swiss francs, because the enlargement of the championships had sharply pushed up their costs. In line with Havelange's election promises, the number of teams taking part in the 1982 World Cup would be raised from twenty-four to thirty-two. Dassler and Nally eventually had to put down 63 million Swiss francs for the rights to the Mundial, but in exchange for the huge increase they obtained some extra marketing rights from European football's governing body, Uefa, and two football federations, all of which were bundled in Intersoccer.

The set-up behind this whole marketing deal was more opaque than ever. The rights were formally held by a holding called Rofa, based in Sarnen, Switzerland. Only a handful of insiders knew at the time that 'Ro' stood for Robert Schwan, Franz Beckenbauer's manager, and 'Fa' for the player. They both contributed to the acquisition of the rights, together with a bunch of unknown investors. In turn, Rofa assigned SMPI, Dassler and Nally's company in Monte Carlo, to handle and sell the marketing rights.

Less than one year before the opening of the Mundial, however, Dassler stunned Nally with an urgent request. At a meeting in Rome, Horst suggested that Nally could buy up his majority stake in their joint business. He was apparently strapped for cash again, and pleaded with his partner to make an offer as quickly as possible. After several rounds of negotiations, it was agreed in principle that Nally would buy out Dassler at a price of about 36 million Swiss francs. Signed at a Paris airport in January 1982, this letter of intent came to be known as 'the Orly agreement'.

Over the next months, Nally worked doggedly to get the money together, and to make sure that he could continue to expand the Inter-soccer programme over the next years. To begin with, he secured the approval of João Havelange and Sepp Blatter, who agreed to transfer the existing agreements to Nally.

Then, while Horst Dassler had been unable to solve the Deyhle problem, Nally got that out of the way as well by offering a generous settlement: each year until the nineties Deyhle would receive a fat cheque without having to lift a finger. The Briton figured that it was worthwhile because, once he had all the Fifa trademarks, he would be able to offer much more valuable sponsorships to his prospective partners.

Precise budgets were drawn up and submitted to Horst Dassler, detailing projected income for the next four years, with huge contributions promised by the likes of Canon and Anheuser Busch. Nally outlined in detail the price he would have to pay to Fifa and Uefa for their rights, not forgetting to add the usual 'additional' line. He had to admit that, for all the millions they had raised for the Mundial, SMPI would make only a small profit on the whole first Intersoccer package, yet he was adamant that the next instalment would be much more profitable, enabling him to finance the largest chunk of the acquisition.

As Nally put the buy-out together, some of Dassler's managers raised concerns about the messy aspects of the Briton's dealings. 'He used to make calculations on the back of a beer mat, which were extremely sloppy and often turned out to be wrong,' said Didier Forterre, the marketing company's financial manager.

On several occasions, Forterre convinced Dassler that there was something badly amiss with the SMPI accounts. He prepared thick files with documents incriminating Patrick Nally and convinced Horst to summon the Englishman to Landersheim. 'Then during the dinner, Patrick would conquer Horst all over again by telling him about all the people he met,' sighed Forterre. He ignored the warnings and continued the talks for the buy-out: by the end of March, Dassler and Nally had even agreed on the routing of the payment, to go through special holdings in Liechtenstein.

But all of a sudden, Horst called off the deal and accused Nally of attempting to double-cross him. The Briton felt trapped and betrayed, completely puzzled about the motives of his partner. The two men had built up the sports marketing business together, but suddenly Horst refused to talk. Unaccountably furious, Dassler seemed determined to pull the rug from under Nally's feet.

Just weeks before the opening of the Mundial, Horst Dassler placed a short call to Didier Forterre. 'I've had enough of the little twat. I don't want to see him anymore. This is it,' Horst reportedly said. He booked three adjoining suites at the Scribe Hotel in Paris, called a lawyer and locked himself in for several days to unravel his relationship with Patrick Nally. 'He fired off letters and faxes to the whole world, telling them that he didn't want anything to do with Nally again, that Patrick didn't exist any more as far as he was concerned,' Forterre recalled. 'It was a complete mess.'

In those bewildering circumstances, Didier Forterre was asked to pack his bags and take up residence in Spain. In letters to his contacts, Horst Dassler had helpfully indicated that any queries regarding SMPI would be handled by the Frenchman. Forterre suddenly found himself at the helm of an improvised SMPI office, in a Madrid hotel, running a huge programme which had been entirely set up by Patrick Nally.

Having decided to split with Nally, Horst Dassler mooted an alternative scheme to fund his sports marketing business. An unthought-of solution emerged in the shape of Dentsu, a Japanese advertising behemoth. The company's executives observed with irritation that Hakuhodo, the country's second-largest advertising group, was snatching business from Dentsu through its dealings in the sports business. Tetsuro Umegaki, the chairman of Dentsu, therefore came up with an irresistible offer. While the talks between Nally and Dassler had always revolved around a sum of 36 million Swiss francs, the Japanese agency was prepared to let Horst keep half of the business and to invest generously to get back at Hakuhodo. Umegaki was promptly invited for the final of the Mundial, and a firm agreement was sealed shortly thereafter.

While the Japanese deal was taking shape, Horst Dassler formally broke up with Nally. The pioneering partnership came to an end after several uneasy meetings in Frankfurt airport and at London's Brown's hotel. Patrick Nally relinquished his shares in SMPI in exchange for a compensation of just 3.6 million Swiss francs. The money was duly paid, but West Nally never recovered from the split.

Patrick Nally, who almost single-handedly devised the football marketing business, never understood what caused the abrupt *volte face*. He speculated that Horst Dassler was piqued by the relationships which Nally had built up in the sports business, and that he feared for his influence. Another explanation was that Horst turned away from Nally when he was presented with the more generous offer from Dentsu – and from then on Nally had to be removed.

'Horst Dassler had been infatuated with Nally for a while and all of a sudden he was slinging massive lumps of mud at him,' observed Monique Berlioux, former general secretary of the IOC. 'He ranted that Patrick had betrayed him, he saw traitors everywhere, he thought everybody was after him.' As Patrick Nally saw it, Horst Dassler and his cronies did 'everything they could to keep me out of the business'. It was all the more painful for Nally when two of his former assistants, Steve Dixon and Peter Sprogis, defected to the Dassler camp.

They were among the founding executives of International Sport and Leisure (ISL), equally owned by Horst Dassler and Dentsu. Established in Lucerne in the autumn of 1982, it was headed up by Klaus Hempel, Dassler's personal assistant. He was joined by Jürgen Lenz, former international marketing manager at Adidas, but only after an interlude of about three months, in order not to arouse any suspicions in Herzogenaurach.

With a cast of steady managers and Dentsu's backing, ISL went on to capture the football marketing business. Just like West Nally before them, ISL acted as an intermediary between Fifa and international companies, selling rights that would identify the investors as official sponsors of the World Cup. The concept hatched by Patrick Nally was expanded and, just as Horst Dassler had anticipated, the rewards were huge: the rights for the 1986 World Cup in Mexico cost ISL 45 million Swiss francs but they enabled the Swiss sports rights firm to raise 200 million from assorted sponsors.

The money went to Fifa, which spent it on international projects to further the game and enlarged subsidies to national federations. Another chunk of the money was used to fund the expansion of Fifa itself, including the increasingly lavish payments and expenses of the international federation's board members. But before that, ISL was rewarded with a juicy commission, estimated at up to 30 per cent of the sums raised by the agency.

The business became altogether fabulous once ISL was awarded broadcasting rights as well. For several years, huge contracts were issued to it without a second thought, behind closed doors. This hegemony gave rise to widespread suspicions that Horst Dassler shared at least some of the spoils with his executive friends at Fifa and other sports organizations.

Jean-Marie Weber, Horst Dassler's former 'bagman', regularly turned up at ISL in Lucerne to deal with financial issues. He later became known there as the man with the 'blacklist', describing the recipients of unusual bank transfers. Other ISL managers professed innocence in such matters, but they all agreed that the list was long; it is not known to whom payments were made.

Unperturbed by this pervading sleaze, Horst Dassler moved on to his most formidable project. Now that he had conquered football, there was only one fortress left to storm.

The proposition was roughly the same as with football: ISL would sell the Olympic rings to large corporations as an international marketing tool. It should have been easy, since the Olympics were even more universal than football and supposedly occupied higher moral ground. In fact it was anything but, because the rights to the Olympic rings were scattered between scores of national Olympic committees (NOCs).

Under the movement's rules at the time, each NOC could strike deals with its chosen sponsors, allowing them to use the Olympic rings in their country. If large corporations wanted to use the rings more widely, they had to negotiate rights with the NOCs in each of the countries they wanted to cover. This negated the whole purpose of the marketing product ISL was intending to sell: they could persuade international companies to pump money into the Olympic rings only if they could guarantee that the companies in question would be allowed to publicize their affiliation with the Olympics wherever they pleased.

The implications were head-spinning. To be able to offer international packages, ISL would have to convince nearly all of the NOCs to surrender their rights to the Olympic rings. Their leading argument was that the IOC could then draw much larger investments from international companies, which would be partly distributed back to the NOCs. Still, it would take years to meet and convince them all, and the project could still falter if any of the large countries refused to take part.

However, Horst Dassler was not intimidated. The time had come to reap the rewards of the many lonely hours in front of hotel lifts: owing to such relentless lobbying, he knew many of the heads of the national committees personally. The people appointed in his sports politics team had befriended many more.

His most zealous supporter was Juan Antonio Samaranch. Since his election in Moscow, the IOC chairman had avidly pursued his plans to find new sources of revenue for the ailing Olympic movement. The project was steered by the New Sources of Financing Commission, which began to meet in December 1981 and was headed by Louis Guirandou N'Daye from the Ivory Coast.

They identified broadcasting rights as the most promising source of heightened revenues for the IOC. This business had come a long way since the fifties, when broadcasters boycotted the Olympics because they deemed it unacceptable that they, unlike their newspaper colleagues, should have to pay for the privilege of covering the Games. Since then, broadcasters had identified the Olympics as a strong booster for their ratings, and the prices for television rights had gradually climbed to about $102 million for the Moscow Olympics in 1980.

The battle among US broadcasters to obtain Olympic rights reached a temporary climax before the Moscow Games, as some of the contenders unashamedly curried favour with the organizers. ABC and CBS both produced documentaries on Soviet life that could have come straight from the politburo's archives. NBC bought a series of documentaries on the heroics of collective farming and walked away with the rights, at a price of about $85 million.

Samaranch rightly calculated that, if they were properly marketed, the broadcasting rights could still yield much higher revenues. He would make concessions to render the Games more enticing for broadcasters and organize auctions that drove up prices sharply, multiplying revenues to $403 million for the 1988 Games in Seoul. But unlike Fifa, the Olympic Committee judged that it could handle such negotiations itself, to avoid paying large commissions to ISL or any other sports rights agency.

Next in line were marketing rights. Owing to the fragmented control over the rings, the IOC had been unable to draw to the Olympics the million-dollar investments that were spreading in other sports. Samaranch gladly looked to Horst Dassler, his longtime friend, to deal with the practicalities. The Olympian-in-chief vigorously supported Dassler at a session in New Delhi in 1983, where he convinced the IOC to set up an international marketing plan. It barely seemed worth mentioning that the deal would go to ISL.

Once the IOC confirmed ISL's mandate to elaborate an Olympic marketing scheme, Horst Dassler and Jürgen Lenz set out on an Olympic world tour, to strike a deal with each of the national committees. The smaller ones were delighted to be offered a lump sum in exchange for rights which were virtually worthless. Others had running contracts which had to be evaluated and bought out. The stiffest resistance came from the German and American committees, among others, which made it immediately clear that they had no intention of relinquishing their rights.

To assuage the fears of some indecisive committees, Juan Antonio Samaranch sent them all a personal letter to explain the benefits of the sale. It took much politicking and several rounds of drawn-out talks to turn around the wealthiest. Dassler and Lenz called it quits when the United States had given in and all but thirteen of the NOCs had signed. There was no point in entering further talks with the likes of Afghanistan, Albania and North Korea, which held on to their rights for political reasons and were almost meaningless for the sponsors anyway.

This *tour de force* enabled ISL managers to push through an all-encompassing marketing plan for the Olympics. Dubbed the Olympic programme (TOP), it would raise hundreds of millions of Swiss francs for the organization in Lausanne. The selling off of the Olympics would create some appalling scandals over the next decades, as reporters exposed widespread abuses of the funds garnered through TOP. Although some of the revenue funded aid programmes, much also went to fuel the egos and expenses of self-serving IOC members.

But for Horst Dassler, it was the ultimate reward. With the Olympic programme, ISL had established a stranglehold on sports marketing, a business that was expanding at breathtaking speed. In less than ten years, his partnership with Patrick Nally had turned into a multi-million business – the unshakeable leader in a rich and seemingly limitless market.

Horst Dassler protected it fiercely. He had built ISL all by himself, and it would remain his personal patch. He conscientiously preserved it from the nerve-wracking squabbles in his family. They came back to haunt him, however, when his cover was blown.

18

The Return

While Horst Dassler hobnobbed with the masters of world sports, Käthe Dassler continued to share plum cake with her guests on the terrace of the Villa. In the early eighties, many weighty decisions at Adidas were taken during daily sessions of coffee drinking, when Käthe spent long hours chattering with her sister, Marianne, and her daughters.

In line with Adolf Dassler's will, Käthe Dassler inherited control of the company but she insisted on drawing all of her children into the management. Under the family structure, each of the four Dassler daughters supervised her own department. Inge Bente, the eldest, contributed strongly to sports promotion in Germany, but she lost much of her influence after she suffered a stroke that paralysed half of her body. Karin Essing, the second-eldest, meddled with all things marketing. Brigitte Baenkler seconded her brother Horst when it came to relations with east European countries. Sigrid, the youngest daughter, briefly supervised the textile business until she moved to Switzerland with her husband.

Other issues facing Adidas were discussed in informal family meetings, involving the four sisters and their husbands. Alf Bente wielded the strongest influence. He had been integrated into the company for a long time, supervising the expansion of its production. When Adi began to fade out, Bente informally took up some of his duties. Hans-Günter Essing was less involved in the daily running of the business, but he was seen as a reliable person with solid analytical skills. Hans-Wolf Baenkler listened much more than he spoke. Christoph Malms, the last in-law, didn't spend much time in Herzogenaurach. Having honed his skills at Wharton business school in the United States, he took up a job as a consultant. Family decisions were more or less rubber stamped by a formal supervisory board, the *Beirat*. This was composed equally of representatives of Käthe and Adi's children, backed up by a group of friendly advisers, bankers and lawyers.

Some of the family's methods were chiefly designed to keep a tight grip on the management. Among the most outrageous rituals was the opening of the mail. Marianne Hoffmann, Käthe Dassler's sister, spent more than two hours going through every single letter that reached Adidas in Herzogenaurach. It didn't matter if the letters were marked for specific managers – she went through the contents of each package and dispatched them to the recipients of her choice.

Unfortunately, the judgements of the Dassler sisters weren't always in line with the preoccupations of professional managers. One of them was in the middle of an urgent perusal of some intricate files when he was summoned by Frau Essing. 'Come up immediately. Our reputation is at stake!' she said. At the centre of her desk was a single document, an open sports magazine. It featured an ad for a foot-odour remedy, illustrated with a small drawing of a sports shoe. 'And with a magnifying glass, you could just about make out that the shoe in question had a few stripes on its side,' the young manager recalled. He struggled to retain his cool as Frau Essing ordered him to handle the matter instantly – deeming it outrageous that Adidas could be associated with smelly shoes.

On some occasions, the managers had to deal with very private family matters. Hansrüdi Ruegger, head of the company's Swiss subsidiary, thus found several boxes of nappies in a truckload of Adidas shoes. In an accompanying message, Ruegger was asked to deliver the nappies to Sigrid who had then recently moved to Zurich and become a mother.

Most of the managers accepted such obligations. After all, they had joined a family business. This was made clear from the very beginning during the job interviews – routinely conducted in the Villa and interrupted by unruly children who chased each other in cowboy hats. But the family's habits became damaging when they prevented adjustments in the company, which had grown well beyond the scope of a provincial family business.

Jürgen Lenz, the international marketing manager in Herzogenaurach, was among the most frustrated. Having spent several years at McCann Erickson, he knew the power of advertising. But when he joined Adidas in the late seventies, it had never run an advertising campaign that featured anything other than products. The only production that fell under the category of advertising, in the books of Adidas, was a series of sporadic magazine inserts and stacks of catalogues designed by Hans Fick, the small agency in Nuremberg that had been working with Adidas since the fifties. Lenz watched with envy the witty and spectacular advertising campaigns run by Nike almost since their inception.

Shortly after his recruitment he was approached by an established German research company, which proposed to study the sporting goods market. They offered precisely the instrument which Jürgen Lenz had requested since his arrival at Adidas to refine his marketing strategy. He assumed that Käthe Dassler would approve the small investment required for the study. But the reply came in the shape of a short, handwritten note: 'Herr Lenz. Sold out until 1982!' As Käthe saw it, there was no point in market research if the company was struggling to meet demand anyway.

On her own since the death of her husband, in 1978, Käthe Dassler sometimes longed to get away from her complicated family business.

25. Käthe Dassler firmly steered Adidas in Herzogenaurach. Appreciated for her sharpness and warmth, she is pictured here with Helmut Schön, German football coach.

She travelled widely and attempted to make the best of life, even allowing herself some conspicuous flirtations. She raised many eyebrows at Adidas when she 'fell head over heels in love' with the manager of a Brazilian shoe factory. The target of her affections, a married man of Swiss origin, gently rebuffed her advances.

On other occasions, Käthe Dassler simply sought to escape the tense atmosphere in Herzogenaurach. When Hansrüdi Ruegger had new offices built for the company's Swiss subsidiary, she asked him to fix up a small apartment for her. She regularly left Herzogenaurach to spend a few days on her own in the plain flat, in a drab industrial neighbourhood of Zurich.

But La Mutti was most tormented by the troubles that affected her children. On the terrace of the Villa, she poured her heart out to some of the company's long-serving managers, lamenting about the errant ways of her son and the destructive habits of her son-in-law. 'One of them is dealing with gangsters and the other should be in rehab,' Käthe told one embarrassed visitor.

The jibe on detoxification was targeted at Alf Bente, the husband of Käthe's eldest daughter, who notoriously suffered from alcohol abuse.

As some noted, this may well have been caused by excessive loyalty to Adidas. 'When Alf travelled to Hungary and Russia, they started on vodka at ten o'clock in the morning,' as one witness recalled. Alf introduced the habit in Herzogenaurach, where guests were surprised to be offered liquor before lunch. His problem was no doubt exacerbated by the collapse of his marriage to Inge. Apparently, things began to go downhill after the stroke that half-paralysed her. The disagreements between the couple caused some awkward problems at Adidas, where employees sometimes had to follow conflicting instructions.

When it became clear that Alf Bente could no longer function at Adidas, he went missing for several days. Hansrüdi Ruegger, head of the Swiss subsidiary who enjoyed a close relationship with Bente, got a nervous phone call from the owner of the Adidas store at Zurich airport: there was a steaming drunk man in the store, who claimed to be the owner of Adidas and demanded to be picked up. Ruegger rushed to the airport, tucked Bente away at the Dolder hotel and alerted the family. Soon afterwards German tabloids revealed that the Bentes' marriage had come to an end. Alf Bente had moved out of Herzogenaurach and in with a young woman in Nuremberg.

The other part of Käthe's tirade, referring to her son's gangster connections, was targeted at André Guelfi. The Corsican's charm had worked on Käthe Dassler for a while. When he travelled to Herzogenaurach for the shareholders' meetings of Le Coq Sportif back in the late seventies, she welcomed him heartily. He rarely left the Villa without a small present. But Käthe Dassler's trust had waned fast. Her informants soon let her know that Guelfi and her son were jetting around the world together. She began to suspect that Guelfi was playing a substantial role in all the murky deals her son was plotting behind her back. Käthe Dassler was not prepared, however, for all the stories that Guelfi had to tell.

Marcel Schmid anxiously scanned the papers on his desk. A sparkling character, Schmid was the chairman of Sarragan, the Swiss holding that regrouped the non-Adidas interests of Horst Dassler. From his office in Freiburg, he controlled the operations of the sprawling business, covering Le Coq Sportif and stakes in a flurry of other companies. But as he peered at the contracts and invoices handed over by André Guelfi, Schmid became convinced that the figures were wrong.

As Schmid saw it, Guelfi had been cheating Horst Dassler all along. Whenever he signed a deal, the sum reported to Sarragan was much higher than the figure indicated on the contract. Guelfi routinely argued that the differential had been paid under the table, therefore it could not appear in the accounts, but the incidents multiplied at such a rate that Schmid resolved to alert Horst Dassler. Confronted with the facts, Dassler took furious action. André Guelfi disappeared from the scene just as quickly as he entered it. Under his agreement with the Corsican, Horst exercised his offer to take full control of Le Coq Sportif, and he stripped Guelfi of his responsibilities at the company.

Blago Vidinic, the former Yugoslav football trainer, was thus confronted with a puzzling situation at a meeting of Uefa. Vidinic was meant to hold talks with Roger Petit, then chairman of Standard Liège FC and Uefa board member, but then André Guelfi also turned up, to take part in the discussions as chief executive of Le Coq Sportif. 'I'm afraid you have nothing to do at this meeting, since you are no longer in charge of Le Coq Sportif,' Petit coolly told Guelfi.

The dispute ended in the courts, when Marcel Schmid, the Sarragan chairman, angrily described Guelfi as 'an international crook'. Guelfi professed to be outraged. He filed a libel suit in a Swiss court. On the day of the hearing, in line with Swiss guidelines at the time, he was led to a small room at the back of the court (to avoid wasting taxpayers' money, the two parties were brought together in a last-ditch attempt to settle the matter amicably). He was joined there by Schmid, who had prepared a thick file. When the two emerged from the room, the libel case was dropped. After careful consideration, Guelfi apparently felt that the tag of 'international crook' wasn't all that ill fitting.

Still, there was no way that the two parties could be reconciled. They thoroughly disagreed on the sum to be reimbursed to Guelfi for his investments in Sarragan. Guelfi estimated that, since he had struck his confidential deal with Horst Dassler, he had pumped about $30 million into his business. The price for the companies acquired by Guelfi on behalf of Horst Dassler was easy to quantify. But the exercise proved thornier when it came to running expenses. Guelfi argued that he had contributed most of the funds that were required for the development of the brands under Sarragan – and he wanted them back.

Some of the most explosive rows centred on the exorbitant bill presented by André Guelfi for his travel expenses. The Corsican refused to fly in anything other than his Lear jet, and he had meticulously totalled all the hours that he had flown on Dassler business. 'One hour cost about 30,000 [French] francs and I had flown thousands of hours,' Guelfi argued.

When Dassler refused to pay up, his managers were confronted with a series of unsettling events. To begin with, shortly after the rowdy break-up, one of Jean-Marie Weber's bags went missing at Geneva airport. The man who oiled the wheels at international federations on behalf of Horst Dassler permanently carried at least one large holdall full of sensitive documents.

Shortly afterwards, in April 1982, the Adidas building in Landersheim was raided by French customs police. Several managers were peremptorily instructed to leave their offices as uniformed men went through their files. Other officers loudly knocked on the door of Horst Dassler's home in Eckartswiller. A third unit was dispatched to the rue Grimaldi in Monte Carlo to search the offices of SMPI. Patrick Nally was questioned at length by the head of the customs department in Marseilles. Yet another unit fetched Marcel Schmid from his office in Freiburg.

The enquiry centred around illegal transfers of currency. The socialist government that came to power in France after the presidential elections of May 1981 had imposed rules requiring companies and citizens to report any sizeable currency transfers. This badly complicated the operations of all French-based international companies, but given the intricacy and the hidden aspects of Horst Dassler's business, it was simply unthinkable for him to comply.

Some of the managers closest to Horst were convinced that the customs officers had been alerted by André Guelfi. 'The most incriminating documents were found behind the mirror in Guelfi's bathroom,' one of them said, 'planted by him, of course.' Didier Forterre, the financial manager of SMPI, who was detained and interrogated in Marseilles for three days, was allegedly told by the police that the tip emanated from Guelfi.

The case was eventually settled without any disastrous repercussions for the Dasslers. After the tax investigation, Horst moved to Switzerland with his wife and their two teenage children. However, the company was not reprimanded. As several executives pointed out, the man in charge of the French budget at the time was Henri Emmanuelli, a left-wing minister, and one of the plants operated by Adidas France was situated in his Landes constituency. Nevertheless Dédé la Sardine still had one last card to play.

Armed with his documents, André Guelfi made the trip to Herzogenaurach and enthusiastically spilled the beans. To her utter dismay, Käthe Dassler discovered that the charming Frenchman had backed her renegade son for several years, spending millions to build an ancillary business of unexpected scope. Käthe was enraged. She had long suspected her son of cheating the entire family, but the outing of Sarragan was still a devastating blow. It revealed the scope of the investments which Horst had committed to his concealed business, and all the resources that he had diverted from Adidas for his own purposes. It exposed a duplicity of staggering proportions.

The discovery caused such explosive rows that it sometimes became impossible to tackle the ensuing problems through rational discussion. 'There were entire periods when Horst Dassler only agreed to talk to other family members in the presence of lawyers,' said Günter Sachsenmaier, then export manager in Landersheim. 'He was evidently depressed.'

In a fit of pique, Käthe Dassler flew over to the United States to check out the assets which Horst had acquired there without her consent. Don Corn, the man in charge of the textile division at Adidas USA, had not seen her for several years. He was surprised when an aide called and asked him to pick up Frau Dassler at the airport. 'She had fire in her eyes,' Corn recalled. As soon as she disembarked, Käthe launched into a furious tirade and ordered Corn to clean up the New York business.

From then on, it became much harder for Horst to divert investments from Adidas to Le Coq Sportif and other brands. Tensions rose to boiling point before the 1982 World Cup, as Horst Dassler sought endorsements from weighty teams for Le Coq Sportif, which the Dasslers in Herzogenaurach would have liked to draw to the Adidas side. To recruit the football teams for Le Coq Sportif, Horst Dassler again turned to his friend Blago Vidinic. After his stint in Zaïre, Horst Dassler had asked him to move to Colombia. He figured that his privileged relationship with Vidinic as a Colombian team coach would come in useful for the 1986 World Cup, that was scheduled to be held in the country. When the Colombian government admitted that it could not cope with the organization, Horst Dassler rushed to his phone. This time he asked

Vidinic to pack his bags for Landersheim, where he would take care of football promotion for Le Coq Sportif.

For the Mundial, Vidinic's assignment was to arrange sponsorship deals for Le Coq Sportif with at least three national sides. There weren't any objections when Vidinic signed with Cameroon and Algeria, but the Germans began to grumble when they heard that Le Coq Sportif had obtained a deal with the Squadra Azzura. Although it seemed in poor shape, the Italian national team's sponsorship was still one of the most coveted in international football.

Vidinic had a hard time with the Italian football federation, which would not allow any company to display its logo on the Azzuri's shirts. They reached an agreement whereby Le Coq Sportif would be emblazoned on the Italians' tracksuits. 'The Spanish crowds were a little surprised to watch the Italians running out in the blasting heat in their tracksuits,' Vidinic laughed. The arrangement later ignited a furore in Italy, with allegations that the players had received a bonus to wear Le Coq Sportif. It had become the norm for sports companies to hand out such extra payments, but the Italian authorities were concerned that they would not feature on the players' tax bills. Blago Vidinic was called to account by Italian investigators and duly admitted the payments – defending non-disclosure on the grounds that they were too small to arouse interest from the taxman.

The noses of the Adidas managers in Germany were pushed still further out of joint on the day of the 1982 World Cup final, when the Coq-Sportif clad Squadra Azzura thrashed its West German opponents 3–1. Horst Dassler's aides weren't quite sure if they should cheer for Paolo Rossi or Karl-Heinz Rummenigge and the rest of the three-striped team.

In the course of the arguments between Horst Dassler and his sisters, the option of a break-up was repeatedly tabled. Several Adidas managers were told of a bid issued by the Dassler sisters to buy out their brother's share and his operations in Landersheim. Horst rejected the offer, however, and Käthe pleaded with her children to reconcile.

As for Guelfi, after several months of recriminations it was agreed that he would walk away with about 15 million Swiss francs. The brands and shareholdings under Sarragan would fall under the control of the Dassler family. Unwittingly, André Guelfi had smoothed the way for Horst Dassler to return to Herzogenaurach.

*

Bernard Odinet, an executive with a French tyre company, was treated to the obligatory coffee and several helpings of plum pudding on the Dassler terrace in Herzogenaurach. Flanked by Albert Henkel, her trusted legal adviser, Käthe explained that the company needed a manager to take over the chairmanship of Adidas France. Horst Dassler, who still headed the French subsidiary at the time, was about to return to Herzogenaurach. 'We haven't always seen eye to eye,' Käthe Dassler explained with masterly understatement, 'but the time has come for him to take over the reins. No matter what has happened in the past, there is no denying that he is the most suitable person to steer this company.'

After some hesitation, Odinet accepted the position. He went through an introductory period of about six months in Herzogenaurach, then packed his bags for Landersheim. Before his departure, the Adidas lawyer issued some bizarre instructions. 'Don't mess things up,' said Henkel. 'If you make any diplomatic mistake, you're gone.'

Odinet soon found out what this meant. Warned of his arrival, in July 1982, employees in Landersheim had conscientiously pulled down the flags that often flew at the entrance of the Adidas building. 'We wouldn't want this guy to think the flags are out for him,' the office manager quipped. As far as they were concerned, Bernard Odinet was to be sent back as quickly as possible.

'The reception was ice cold,' said Odinet. 'They refused to hand over the files I needed to get my work done and constantly watched me with suspicion.' The defiance sometimes rose to ridiculous proportions: the first time he attended a trade fair with the French managers, Bernard Odinet took time to thoroughly study the shoes that were displayed on the stand. He immediately heard whispers that he was spying on behalf of the Germans.

The alleged spy soon turned. While he endured the petty humiliations inflicted by his French colleagues, Bernard Odinet watched Horst Dassler with increasing fascination. He rapidly came to the conclusion that Käthe Dassler was right, and that Adidas was wasting precious time: under increasing attack from American newcomers, the company needed an undisputed, purposeful leader. There was not the slightest doubt that Horst Dassler was the man.

Several other managers who had been recruited by Herzogenaurach felt the same. Since the apparent reconciliation with his mother and sisters, Horst had become more influential in Herzogenaurach, but they longed for Horst to rid the company of its staid, old-fashioned ways. The unrest escalated when three influential German managers issued an ultimatum. Klaus-Werner Becker, international controller, Fedor Radmann, in charge of sports promotion, and Hans-Jörg Bauer, heading up the textile operation, wrote a letter to the Dasslers demanding that Horst should return to Herzogenaurach without delay. They were fed up with the family's dithering.

So was Horst. Less than a year later he informed Becker that he had entered talks with several investment banks. He had drawn up an offer to buy out his sisters, valuing the company at roughly DM2 billion. By then, however, Käthe Dassler had resolved to remove any obstacles to her son's return. After a cerebral attack her health faded fast, and she was desperate to ensure that her children wouldn't tear each other apart after her death. Her relationship with Horst warmed considerably in her last years, as he showed patience and compassion for his mother. She was particularly sensitive to the understanding her hard-headed son unexpectedly displayed when it came to her private life.

Shortly after the amorous rebuff she had suffered in Brazil, Käthe had entered an intimate relationship with an Austrian shoe producer, who was subsequently placed at the head of Adidas Austria. A long-time supplier of Adidas, he was much younger than the widow. The relationship caused consternation among the Dassler daughters, and many German managers who watched the pair together also felt distinctly uneasy. 'It was obvious that this man was exploiting Frau Dassler's loneliness,' one of them said.

The Dassler daughters stood united for once and determined to undermine the relationship. They were wary of the Austrian's motives and feared that he would manipulate their mother into a second marriage. Convinced that Käthe Dassler had to be extracted from this relationship for her own good, several family members asked Klaus-Werner Becker to broach the subject with her. But she was unimpressed by this show of concern and furiously barred Becker from the Villa.

Horst Dassler was just as outraged by the Austrian's behaviour, but instead of chastising his mother, he openly encouraged her to enjoy the relationship. This considerate attitude certainly prompted Käthe Dassler to push ahead with planned reforms at Adidas – ignoring the predictable protests from her daughters. Hans-Jürgen Martens, head of legal affairs, was thus instructed to alter the statutes of Adidas. From 1982 it was to be gradually transformed into a foundation, Stiftung Adi Dassler & Co KG, with an informal family board at its head. But Käthe Dassler had clearly informed Horst that he would have a free rein in the management.

Horst Dassler agonized long over his decision. He assembled his managers in Landersheim and informed them of his prospective return to Herzogenaurach. 'I'm at a crossroads,' he told them, visibly distraught. He could sell his Adidas shares and embark on other projects, in which case he wanted to make sure that his trusted managers in Landersheim would follow, or else he could return to Herzogenaurach, in which case he had to warn them, in all honesty, that the influence of Landersheim would be sharply curtailed. 'Of course we would all have followed him with our eyes closed,' said Jean Wendling, then head of Sarragan France. 'But of course we all encouraged him to return.'

As far as Horst Dassler was concerned, one of the prerequisites for his return was that his sisters should be evicted from the management. He would head the board himself and beef it up with several managers recruited from other companies. His mother and sisters would exercise their shareholders' rights only as members of an unofficial family board. In exchange for their withdrawal, the Dassler sisters obtained an amazingly generous reward. Horst gave each of them a stake in Sporis, a holding company that owned just over half of ISL, his sports rights agency. When ISL was established, it was controlled equally by Horst Dassler and Dentsu. Shortly afterwards, Dassler convinced the Japanese advertising conglomerate to give him a 51 per cent majority in the venture, which he placed in Sporis. As part of the deal with his family, he gave each of his sisters a share of about 16 per cent in Sporis. Although he retained a larger holding of 36 per cent in Sporis, he could still be overruled if three of his sisters stood in his way. In other words, he relinquished sole control of ISL.

Walter Meier, Horst Dassler's lawyer, was startled by the gesture. In the course of the negotiations, which lasted more than one year, the Dassler sisters apparently turned down 'countless reasonable proposals'. But the ISL shares were a seemingly disproportionate concession, given the fact that Dassler had built ISL entirely by himself. 'For me that was hard to understand,' Meier was quoted as saying. 'He gave his sisters a very valuable present.'

The legal arrangements were finalized on 19 December 1984. A few days later, Käthe Dassler left Herzogenaurach to spend Christmas with her Austrian friend. While her poor health called for medical care, she was left for several days in an apartment in Klagenfurt. When Käthe's daughters realized the situation they sent a private plane to pick her up. It was too late. On 31 December *die Cheffin* passed away in a hospital in Erlangen, at the age of 65. The coroner's verdict was coronary failure. Others called it a broken heart.

Horst Dassler barely waited until his mother was in the ground to place his call to Austria. The man who forged a dubious relationship with Käthe Dassler was summarily dismissed. Gerhard Prochaska, the former marketing manager who replaced him at the head of the Austrian operation, was of the opinion that he had blatantly abused the relationship for his own commercial ends.

Since his mother had become weaker, in the last two years before her death Horst had shuttled between Herzogenaurach and Landersheim. But after she passed away, he immediately took the helm. His sisters cleared out their last belongings and Horst took full control of the management floor, surrounding himself with a handful of trusted managers. As he settled into his executive chair, Adidas appeared to be thriving. It had just chalked up an unprecedented turnover of nearly DM4 billion and it remained omnipotent in the sports business. But Horst was fully aware that this picture was deceptive. While he had been bickering with his sisters, Adidas had come under severe attack.

19

Collapse

Bill Closs slammed his fist on the table. Sitting in Herzogenaurach for his meeting with German managers in the early seventies, the Adidas distributor for the American West Coast was hugely frustrated. Over the previous years, they had repeatedly shrugged off his warnings about a smalltime operation called Blue Ribbon Sports, up in Oregon. Their Nike running shoes were popping up on more and more Californian shelves. Unless Adidas reacted swiftly, there was no telling what kind of damage these people could inflict on the Adidas business. 'You have to kill them right now,' Closs hammered. To illustrate the phenomenon, he brought back several pairs of Nike shoes and handed them over for inspection by the Germans. But to his dismay, the sneakers were cast aside with disdain. 'I told them they were selling like crazy, but they didn't care,' Closs recalled. 'They just didn't want to build running shoes. They said their shoes were as good as they could make, and that was it.'

The same happened to international managers who attempted to draw attention to Nike. Günter Sachsenmaier, export manager in Landersheim, spotted the brand on his US travels and thought that the technicians would be interested, but the response was invariably dismissive. The Waffle, the trainer designed by former coach Bill Bowerman in his kitchen, provoked outright hilarity. 'They inspected the sample as if it was a piece of dirt, pulled at it and threw it over their shoulder,' Sachsenmaier recalled. 'They thought it was all a big joke, these lunatics who designed shoes with a waffle-iron.'

The Nike managers themselves had to admit that their early production was far below the German standards. They faced an embarrassing series of mishaps, with shoes falling apart and parts coming unglued. Yet Phil Knight and his small crew relentlessly improved and pushed their product until they had conquered a group of hardcore runners. Then they began to snatch shelf space from Adidas.

Seen from Herzogenaurach the Nike problem didn't seem all that urgent, because the Adidas distributors themselves continued to clamour for more products. Yet the dearth of supplies which they had to endure strongly played into the hands of Nike. In the exploding American market, retailers became so weary of the haphazard Adidas deliveries that they could not afford to turn down an alternative brand.

To push its advantage, Nike introduced a shrewd mechanism known as futures. The principle was that they convinced retailers to place firm orders and to guarantee payments in advance. With these commitments, Nike could increase its orders from Asian manufacturers without gambling too much. In other words, they shifted some of the financial risk to the retailers. In return, the retailers who took part in futures trades would obtain a sizeable rebate on their orders and they could rest assured that they would actually obtain the goods. In a market driven by wild demand, this was an irresistible argument.

With the jogging boom in the seventies, Nike's advances turned into a tidal wave. At the forefront of the movement, Bill Bowerman led many thousands of otherwise unathletic Americans on daily jogs, and millions more followed all around the country. The Oregon coach had discovered jogging during an encounter in 1963 with Arthur Lydiard, a renowned New Zealand track and field coach. Upon his return, Bowerman took up the habit and set up jogging classes in Oregon. A guide which he published in 1967, praising the advantages of jogging as a form of light exercise, turned into a national best-seller. As he rightly predicted, it was so easy and practical that it would spread like wildfire. America's newly formed army of joggers turned to Nike en masse.

In Herzogenaurach, the German technicians generally dismissed the jogging trend by contending that 'jogging is not a sport'. When they finally gave in to the pleas of the American distributors, they still couldn't bring themselves to turn out what the customers wanted. While Germans tended to run on forest trails, the Americans jogged on roads and pavements; they needed plenty of cushioning. The Adidas distributors clamoured for soft shoes, but their pleas were placated with anatomical drawings, showing the alleged damage which such shoes could inflict on ankles and knees.

Desperate to get their say in product development, the American distributors forced the setting up of the Shoe Committee. Adidas technicians and export managers were to get together with representatives of the four US distribution companies to brainstorm on products that would be suitable for the US market. But with more than thirty participants, the meeting usually produced only brainache.

When Adidas responded to the jogging boom at last, it was too little, too late. In the late seventies the company came up with a training shoe called SL, which sold about 100,000 pairs during its first year in the US. Looking at the explosion of the market, the distributors pushed their orders up to at least a million pairs for the second year, which would have forced Adidas to increase its capacity. 'Adidas refused to make the required adjustments, because that would have entailed considerable investments,' said Horst Widmann, Adolf Dassler's personal assistant at the time. 'It turned out to be a bad mistake.'

Horst Dassler was equally guilty of aloofness when it came to Nike. Absorbed by the setting up of his sports rights business, he didn't display much concern about the Nike issue. His French managers had come up with a soft running shoe called Country, but the effort was half-hearted.

RUIN A WAFFLE IRON.
START A GLOBAL SPORTS REVOLUTION.

JUST DO IT

26. At Adidas, they couldn't stop laughing when they heard that Nike designed shoes with a waffle iron. The two men behind the operation were Bill Bowerman (pictured here), the inventive coach of the US track and field team, and Phil Knight.

Larry Hampton, former marketing manager at Adidas France, long struggled to convince Horst Dassler that he should learn more about Nike. He eventually agreed to meet Phil Knight and some other Nike executives at a trade show in Houston in February 1978. Hampton was disappointed by the meeting, which he deemed utterly uneventful. But the Nike men couldn't believe what they had just heard: Horst Dassler had let it slip that a strong Adidas shoe sold about 100,000 pairs each year in the United States. Blue Ribbon Sports was selling roughly the same number of Waffle trainers a month.

Until the mid-eighties, Adidas continued to report double-digit sales hikes in the United States each year. The Dasslers failed to grasp that, in this ballooning market, Nike was growing much faster still, grabbing market share at a staggering pace. Blinkered by their competition with Puma, the Adidas technicians were not prepared to regard any other company as a serious contender.

Just months before his death, Adolf Dassler finally acknowledged that Adidas had dozed through a complete overhaul of the sports market. He gathered his closest lieutenants and spoke with uncharacteristic virulence. He finally understood that, regardless of its early technical flaws, Nike was taking over the market. He even scheduled an unprecedented journey to the United States, but died before the set date.

For the marketing men at Nike, the Los Angeles Olympics in 1984 were the perfect stage to show what they were all about. Eight years earlier, in Montreal, the brand was barely on the international market. Four years earlier, as an American company, Nike was unwanted in Moscow. But for Los Angeles, Nike was all set.

The company's executives had marked the city as their territory. Among their most spectacular displays was a painting that stretched more than eight metres wide, covering two buildings at the heart of Los Angeles. It was a lifesize picture of Carl Lewis, the American runner and long jumper, flying over the sandpit. Drivers who cruised along the Marina del Rey Freeway could not fail to spot it.

As usual, Adidas had meticulously prepared for the Games. Horst Dassler had personally taken part in the diplomatic kow-towing that preceded the event, as the Soviet Union decided to boycott Los Angeles. He flew to Havana to meet with Fidel Castro but could not persuade the Cubans to send their team. On the other hand, Horst was widely credited for the participation of Romania, the only east European country to ignore the Soviet-ordered boycott. The presence of the three stripes was somewhat diminished by the absence of all the other east European teams, but before the competition started it was almost guaranteed that Adidas would claim the highest number of medals.

Horst Dassler's marketing men had extensively advised Peter Ueberroth, head of the Los Angeles organizing committee. Unfazed by the financial debacle at the preceding Olympics in Montreal, Ueberroth had decided to run the Games like a commercial enterprise, using mostly private funds. In exchange for Dassler's expertise, he granted Adidas a licence to make products bearing the Olympic mascot: Sam the eagle.

Overall, Adidas had set aside a budget of $15 million for the Games. The company had its own vault at a bank in Los Angeles, where Joe Kirchner, a former textile manager, and other trusted employees deposited several million dollars in cash. Old habits die hard, and the Olympic athletes, supposedly amateur as always, still preferred their payments not to appear on their bank statements.

Bill Closs, responsible for the West Coast, spent several months making other arrangements for Adidas. Premises were rented near the university for athletes and reporters while Horst Dassler and his closest lieutenants stayed at the Hilton hotel, to network with scores of Olympic officials. Adidas, Horst Dassler and the Olympics just belonged to each other.

The Nike men had other plans. They openly despised the elderly European aristocrats who ruled over world sports. They portrayed their athletes and themselves as mavericks, intent on upsetting the sporting establishment. While the Adidas people shared cocktails with the notoriously crooked honchos of the athletics world, Phil Knight and his crew raided the beach for impromptu beer parties.

By then, Nike had changed its marketing tack. It had conquered the American market from the track and long supported hundreds of runners. But in the early eighties, Nike felt that the benefits of such small endorsements were diffuse. They decided to spend more money on advertising and on endorsement deals with a restricted number of athletes and players with whom they could build the Nike brand. For the Olympics, the Nike men made their presence felt in the streets of LA through dramatic advertising, featuring some of the most inspiring US athletes. While Carl Lewis jumped through the Californian sky, John McEnroe towered over the city in a leather Nike jacket. During the Games the same cast appeared in a striking sixty-second commercial. To the sound track of Randy Newman's 'I Love L. A.', the ad contained clips of other US star athletes such as marathon runner Alberto Salazar and Mary Decker, a middle-distance specialist. Such commercials were completely unprecedented in the sports business. Adidas had yet to run ads that were not entirely dedicated to their products.

When the medals were counted at the end of the Olympics, the first ever to return a profit in the modern era, Adidas claimed a predictable victory. Adidas athletes had reaped 259 medals, against 53 for Nike. Salazar failed to get a medal. Mary Decker fell in the 3,000-metre final, the only distance in which she competed in Los Angeles, after a tussle with Zola Budd, a South African athlete who ran barefoot for Great Britain. Nike had put on a 'costly and ephemeral show', Horst Dassler sniggered.

Yet the marketing people at Adidas knew that Nike was on to something. No matter how many more athletes Adidas outfitted, Nike had hijacked the Games in Los Angeles. Although Converse paid $5 million to be the official partner of the organizing committee, consumers were under the impression that Nike had sponsored the Olympics. All but three of the men's gold medals in track and field had been won by Nike athletes. Their beach house party was the talk of the town.

For those who witnessed it that summer in California, it suddenly became clear that Adidas was under serious attack. As one Adidas man recalled, 'Los Angeles was a massive wake-up call.'

The Adidas trump card in the United States was an energetic Italian by the name of Angelo Anastasio. He had emigrated with his parents in the sixties and settled in New York. Once he finished college, he went on to play soccer for New York Cosmos, on the same team as Pelé and Franz Beckenbauer. But towards the end of the seventies, he moved to Los Angeles and obtained a job with Adidas officially in charge of entertainment promotion.

Such a position was more or less unprecedented, yet Anastasio knew exactly what he was doing: he became chummy with emerging American celebrities and convinced them to wear the three stripes. If Adidas was getting thrashed on the courts and in the streets, at least it could still get exposure by being seen on the hips and feet of prominent citizens.

Anastasio was perfectly cut out for the job. An easy talker, he was known in Los Angeles for his Ferrari, which had 'Adidas I' on the licence plates. He happily hung around at pop concerts to meet upcoming stars, he shared drinks with Sylvester Stallone and rode his Harley-Davidson with Mickey Rourke. His breakthrough came with Rocky Balboa. The brainless boxer played by Stallone seemed to permanently wear three stripes. Adidas sold about 750,000 units of the black fleece warm-up suit worn by Stallone in *Rocky IV*, with the Italian flag's colour on the shoulders. The practice would become known as product placement, keeping squadrons of public relations people busy in Los Angeles. But it was still so fresh at the time that Stallone never asked for a cent to appear in Adidas. Anastasio just made sure that his muscular friend would never have to go barefoot.

The Italian had a budget of only up to $8,000 in merchandise to hand out each month, but he promptly became known in Los Angeles as 'Mr Adidas'. Under this guise he bumped into Ziggy Marley, son of the late Bob. From then on, Marley regularly appeared on stage with three-striped clothing that conspicuously clashed with the rest of his attire. In exchange, Adidas agreed to sponsor the football team he supported in Jamaica.

But the most talked-about celebrity tie-up came about in 1985, when Anastasio was attending a concert in New York's Madison Square Garden. On his way out, he spotted three young black men who were break-dancing on the street, watched by scores of onlookers. He was perplexed to see that they were wearing Adidas pants known as 'rainsuits', made of shiny material. Once they had finished dancing and Anastasio introduced himself, they explained that the rainsuits helped because they were slippery – which happened to be practical since the young men were dancing on cardboard.

The Italian closely followed the three men over the next years and continuously sent them Adidas gear. It paid off when they became known as Run-DMC. The rappers eagerly adopted the Superstars, the Adidas basketball shoes, as an original alternative to other sneakers. They liked the shell toe design and preferably wore their Superstars without laces. When the band agreed to turn up at the 1986 Supershow, a huge sports trade fair in Atlanta, they were stormed by thousands of fans.

'I gave them one million dollars but they ended up generating sales of more than $100 million over the next four years,' said Anastasio. 'At a time when Nike was growing like crazy, it gave Adidas exposure and kept the brand alive in the eye of the public.' On the back of the endorsement, Anastasio estimated that Adidas sold an extra half a million pairs of Superstars. Another fast-selling product was a pair of black leather trousers with three stripes as worn by the rappers.

The deal came at a time when street fashion was becoming increasingly influenced by music and the media that carried it. It was fabulous advertising for Adidas to have several pairs of Superstars fill MTV screens for close to twenty seconds, as part of a clip shot by Run-DMC in 1986 when they recorded 'Walk This Way' in collaboration with the song's originators, Aerosmith.

The endorsement was the first of its kind between pop music and a sports company. It went so far that Run-DMC and Anastasio jointly composed a song, called 'My Adidas', for their album *Raising Hell*:

> Me and my Adidas do the illest things
> We like to stomp out pimps with diamond rings.
> We slay all suckers who perpetrate
> and lay down law from state to state.

> We travel on gravel, dirt road or street.
> I wear my Adidas when I rock the beat,
> on stage front page every show I go,
> it's Adidas on my feet, high top or low.

It became such a hit that, when Run-DMC began to sing it on stage, thousands of enthusiastic spectators waved three-striped shoes and shirts.

Still, the exposure could not make up for the company's weaknesses when it came to products and marketing. Just as Adidas was waking up to Nike's strength, the Oregon men were mulling over plans to take their brand further. They had decided to shrink payments to athletes, and they went ahead with yet more radical cutbacks in basketball: they wanted to make a splash with a talented and inspiring player, one who could overhaul the entire American business.

By the early eighties Adidas had almost been swept off American basketball courts. Just as it had crushed Converse with the Superstar in the late sixties, it had itself been hammered by Nike in the late seventies. While Adidas rested on its Superstar laurels, Nike had come up with an invention known as Air, consisting of visible air cushions that were inserted into the soles. Adidas didn't even grant an interview to Frank Rudy, the man behind the Air concept, but the Nike men could easily picture the marketing line.

By the mid-eighties, nearly half of the players in the NBA, the American basketball league, had switched to Nike, while most of the others had returned to upgraded Converse shoes. All of these players were paid up to $100,000 per year to wear the Swoosh, which added up to a considerable sum for the company. The Nike marketing men wanted rid of these individual basketball contracts to build one all-encompassing endorsement deal.

The project was led by Rob Strasser, one of the most rambunctious characters in Phil Knight's crew of go-getting executives. As a lawyer he had fought alongside Nike to win the thorny court case after Knight's break-up with Onitsuka in 1973, and had decided to stay with Phil Knight. In other companies Strasser might have been described as a marketing manager, but at Nike he was known as 'Rolling Thunder'.

Shortly before the Los Angeles Olympics he heard about Michael Jordan, a player from North Carolina. Sonny Vaccaro, Nike's basketball scout, was enraptured by the boy: the way he described Jordan, he made such spectacular jumps that it looked as if he could fly. The problem was that Michael Jordan described himself as an 'Adidas nut'. He always wore Adidas while training and when a game was on he reluctantly laced up his Converse, which was part of his university team's uniform. Michael Jordan bluntly made it clear to Nike that he would favour the three stripes over any other brand. 'I don't want to go anywhere else,' he defiantly told Nike executives, after his mother had dragged him out to Oregon. But Jordan changed his mind when Adidas offered him just $100,000, the same deal as they had with Kareem Abdul-Jabbar. With Nike he stood to earn about $2.5 million, with royalties on sales of shoes and garments that bore his name.

Air Jordan propelled Nike to new heights. The shoe was initially banned by the NBA because it was red and black, which departed too much from the mostly white shoes worn by the other players, yet it generated sales of more than $100 million for Nike in the first year. In the long run, Air Jordan accelerated the spread of basketball shoes in the United States as streetwear. Basketball would come to represent about 60 per cent of sales in the American market – and it was Nike territory.

As the eighties progressed, Adidas's Nike problem was aggravated by another one called Reebok. The brand was derived from Joe Foster, the British company which had been selling track and field shoes since the beginning of the century. As the business dwindled in the fifties, some of Joe Foster's heirs set up another company that came to be known as Reebok and teamed up with distributors to spread it beyond England. In 1979, Paul Fireman, an entrepreneur in Boston, acquired the rights for the United States.

Fireman's business got off to such a slow start that he nearly went bankrupt. To keep it afloat he sold 55 per cent of the venture to Stephen Rubin, a British investor, but Fireman's fortunes picked up dramatically when he introduced a shoe called the Freestyle. This was designed for aerobics, another form of exercise that was spreading like wildfire in the United States.

The Freestyle actually originated from a mistake by Reebok's manufacturing partners in Asia, who had erroneously used the sort of soft leather intended for gloves. When they sent the samples to Reebok they apologised for the wrinkles, promising to iron them out before line production. Back in Boston, however, the Reebok managers were thrilled. With the ultra-soft shoe, they raided the women's market. The Freestyle drove the most spectacular rise ever witnessed in the sports business. From global sales of about $300,000 in 1980, Reebok exploded to $12.8 million in 1983.

As might be expected, the Adidas managers were oblivious. German technicians threw Reebok's Freestyle over their shoulders just as they had done with Nike's Waffle trainer a few years earlier. But the Nike men were guilty of precisely the same error, deriding aerobics as 'a bunch of fat ladies dancing to music' and contending that the Freestyle was not a sports shoe. By 1987, Reebok sales had reached $1.4 billion.

Nike and Reebok created the most spectacular upset ever witnessed in the industry. Before they came along, Adidas owned more than half of the American market. But by the mid-eighties, the three stripes were in free fall. They had not just lost their leadership, they had been relegated to fourth position, behind Nike, Reebok and Converse. The time had come for drastic action.

The American distributors stared at each other in disbelief. Assembled for the Supershow in Atlanta, they had just heard, seemingly out of the blue, that Adidas intended to buy them out. Gary Dietrich, distributor for the Midwest, was stunned. 'We had devoted our lives to this thing and all of a sudden it was taken from us,' he lamented. Bill Closs, who had helped Horst Dassler through rough patches, was angry and hurt. As for Ralph Libonati, the East Coast distributor, he was so furious that he vowed to sue.

Back in Herzogenaurach, the plans had been germinating for several months. Sure, Adidas owed the American distributors a large part of its international reputation. They had been consistently faithful, and their orders generated an increasing and relatively easy stream of revenue for Adidas. But Horst Dassler slowly became convinced that, given the seriousness of Nike's assault, the set-up was no longer adequate. To bite back, he would have to take the American market in his own hands.

One of his arguments was that the split of the market hampered hard-hitting marketing investments. From the beginning, the distributors had been asked to contribute about 4 per cent of their turnover to a marketing fund for promotion and nationwide advertising. Each of them further invested in regional marketing. Yet Horst felt that the efforts remained disconnected. The situation called for a much more vigorous and tightly steered counter-attack.

Another problem was that the US competition rules prevented the distributors from offering the same prices for Adidas products on their respective territories. That would have been construed as price fixing. The discrepancies between the distributors were small but they still encouraged retailers to shop around.

Meanwhile, the explosion of the sports business had given rise to fast-growing chains of specialist retailers, which Adidas could not service properly. Sports gear, which was previously sold in small independent stores whose interiors were often permeated with the smell of sweat, could suddenly be found in specialist chains, with outlets all around the country. Foot Locker was among the retail conglomerates that popped up in the seventies, to accompany the rise of jogging and the spread of trainers as ordinary streetwear. They opened their first store in California two years after Nike started out, in 1974; ten years later the retailer had 619 outlets across the United States.

The problem was that Foot Locker bought their products centrally. Whether they were located in New York or Los Angeles, the stores all ordered their products through a buyer at their head office. The same went for department stores, which increasingly stocked sports products. The Adidas distributors therefore decided to split the large accounts among them and share the revenues pro rata. This set-up worked relatively smoothly, but Horst figured that it would still be easier to take care of the emerging retail behemoths from a central Adidas office.

In the early eighties, the case was studied extensively by Rich Madden. An independent entrepreneur and Harvard graduate, he had been hired by Käthe Dassler in 1982 to tighten Germany's grip on the company's American operations. Madden was recruited as chief executive of Adidas USA, a structure based in Mountainside, Pennsylvania, that covered joint textile and marketing activities. As he saw it, the American distributors had become complacent. They had amassed considerable fortunes on the back of Adidas and had lost the impetus to fight back. Madden was taken aback that the distributors refused to increase their marketing budgets. He was even more incensed that they turned down a joint order scheme, which would have enabled them to pool some of their stocks. Madden could not fathom why the distributors should reject such a suggestion, at a time when their warehouses were clogged with millions of dollars' worth of obsolete inventories. He regarded them as smalltime businessmen who could just not deal with the demands of the modern sports business.

This harsh diagnosis was paired with a radical proposal: Rich Madden suggested that the Dasslers could buy out the distributors and float Adidas USA on Wall Street. Instead of disbursing cash, Adidas could pay out the distributors in shares of the floated company. Called Plan-X, the proposal was studied in depth by financial experts Lehman Brothers and Merrill Lynch. They envisaged one of the largest public offerings in the country at the time, to raise at least $200 million. 'Adidas would not have to deplete its cash. It would get about $110 million and I would have kept $90 million for comprehensive marketing and retail plans,' Madden explained. 'And the distributors would have stayed in there with large minority shares.'

Yet Plan-X was swept under the carpet. The distributors deemed it 'preposterous' to be offered shares in a company that barely existed. They were angry that Madden had barged in and ignored the decades-long relationship they had built up with the Dasslers. The plan was far too bold for Hans-Jürgen Martens, the company's haughty and conservative chief financial officer in Herzogenaurach. The Dasslers were just not prepared for such an audacious move, and Rich Madden was summarily dismissed. But over the following years, the Adidas business began to stagnate and frustrations continued to mount on all sides. While Horst had no interest in a stock-market launch, he became convinced that he would quickly have to seize control of the brand's sales and marketing in the United States. The knot was cut at the Supershow in Atlanta.

After the shock of their meeting with Horst, the distributors went into conclave. Doc Hughes, the Texan trader who covered the South, had already thrown in the towel and his territory had been carved up between Bill Closs and Gary Dietrich. The two believed that the writing was on the wall, and both accepted an invitation to discuss the sell-out in Herzogenaurach. But Ralph Libonati was still fuming and firmly intent on suing.

Horst Dassler had retained Dick Pound, a Canadian lawyer, to advise him on the matter. The fact that Pound was on the IOC's executive board, in charge of television rights, didn't seem to strike anyone as a conflict of interest. A Canadian swimming champion, Pound was one of Juan Antonio Samaranch's most loyal aides when it came to raising revenues for the IOC. He had worked closely with ISL, Horst Dassler's sports rights agency, when it embarked on its Herculean project to bring back control of the Olympic rings to the IOC.

The talks went awry, as Dietrich and Closs both felt that the opening offer of the Germans was insulting. That evening, Dietrich called Closs to his room at the Sportshotel. He vividly recalled the day when, in the same hotel, one of his sales people had tuned in his radio to catch the US Armed Forces station and heard conversations at the bar. If the bar was bugged, they could be certain someone was listening to their discussion, too. Conscientiously articulating each word, for the benefit of any eavesdroppers, Dietrich told Closs that they should return to the United States and file a lawsuit against Adidas. 'The next day their attitude changed completely,' Dietrich recalled. 'Horst called us into his office and handed us a little piece of paper with seven points on it. That was our deal.'

The negotiations still lasted for several months, as Adidas and the distributors debated the value of their inventories. Adidas agreed to take them over entirely. Ralph Libonati was persuaded not to sue, but all of his bad stock was purchased by Adidas at full value. After nearly two years of haggling, Adidas wound up with tons of obsolete goods, four warehouses and a sales force of mixed quality. For Ralph Libonati alone, Adidas forked out an estimated $35 million for stock that should have been written off. The final bill was huge for Adidas, estimated at over $120 million. To make matters worse, the value of the dollar reached an all-time high against the Deutschmark.

The men who made Adidas in the United States walked off with more millions than they could ever spend. Ralph Libonati was the least fortunate of the three: he agreed to take over the helm at Pony, the American brand which was partly owned by Horst Dassler, and some of the company's shares. He was unable to redress the ailing Pony, and he died prematurely. Gary Dietrich retired to a plantation in North Carolina and a breathtaking forest mansion in Montana. Bill Closs continued to dabble in the tennis business with Nike, otherwise enjoying his stupendous view on Lake Flathead, Montana. But for Adidas, the cost of the American buy-out precipitated a vertiginous collapse.

20

The Emperor Strikes Back

Shortly after Horst's return to Herzogenaurach in the early eighties, the fifth floor of the Adidas management building was entirely reconstructed. He ruled over it from an imposing office situated at the centre of the floor. In the adjacent offices he installed some of his trusted managers from Landersheim and a batch of impressive recruits.

By then in his late forties, Horst Dassler envisaged a complete overhaul of Adidas. The company would officially acquire the operations that had been picked up as it went along, such as Arena, Pony and Le Coq Sportif, all to be integrated under one umbrella. It would shed some of the ludicrous habits that had been holding it back over the previous years. The dispersion was to make way for a finely honed, international organization.

Among the slipshod arrangements that Horst Dassler was no longer prepared to tolerate was that in the United Kingdom. Smart as it may have been in the early years, the collaboration with Umbro was causing increasingly painful headaches for Adidas. The tensions had been building ever since Adidas entered the clothing sweepstakes in the seventies. The conflict of interest was so obvious that Horst Dassler repeatedly offered to buy Umbro, but he could never reach an agreement with the Humphreys.

Under their deal, Adidas was still handled by a separate unit in Poynton and it had a secondary agreement with Blacks in Yorkshire to take care of some large-scale retailers. This had worked well for several years, but the Adidas business began to dwindle in the late seventies. The Blacks deal scattered its marketing effort and it appeared to lose its way after Robbie Brightwell resigned to take charge of Le Coq Sportif in 1976. Several other leading executives left Adidas in his wake – mostly for Nike.

Just like the Dasslers several decades earlier, Phil Knight had begun to send off a few consignments of Nike shoes to European distributors who requested them. Some of them quickly threw in the towel, but others continued to preach until the message came across loud and clear. Not only had Nike snatched the market leadership in the United States, it was beginning to gnaw at the Adidas business in Europe as well.

The earliest British recipient of Nike boxes was Ron Hill. A leading long-distance runner, he was the first Briton to win the Boston Marathon, in 1970, and he briefly held several world records. In the early seventies he set up his own business, Ron Hill Sports, somehow convincing the British track and field authorities that he was not breaching the amateur rules because the capital used for the company was all his. A textile chemist by education, Hill began by marketing running shorts in synthetic fabrics which he developed himself.

Then, as he was leafing through *Runner's World*, Hill was intrigued by a Nike ad. He wrote them a letter and convinced Phil Knight to send him a small consignment. Hill began by placing the trainers on the shelves of his sports store in Lancashire, Running Wild, but he was such a well-known runner that he easily introduced the brand in other specialist stores. He soon ran an entire warehouse, which was used for deliveries in several other European countries. Still, the business was weakly funded and Nike quickly realized that it would need a more established partner in the United Kingdom.

Just like Ron Hill, Mike Tagg had taken part in the 10,000 metres races at the Mexico Olympics in 1968, but he pursued a career in business as a sales manager at Adidas. Then, shortly after the departure of Robbie Brightwell, Tagg left the company to set up Reliance Sportswear, a specialist unit in Reliance plc, a large-scale supplier of underwear and socks.

To begin with, 'Taggo' sold Viga, his own brand of sportswear, but after six months Reliance was recruited as British distributor for Nike. The former Adidas manager had heard about Nike from his American friends in the tight-knit running community and had been immediately struck by their enthusiasm. They sounded like converts, taking time fervently to explain the merits of their trainers. Mike Tagg became convinced that Nike could shake up the British market and he poached an entire pack of his erstwhile Adidas colleagues to make it happen.

When Tagg called them about Nike, they weren't sure what to think. 'We had just never heard about Nike,' said Mike Chapman, former Adidas sales manager. 'We never cared much for competitors, because we felt that Adidas was way above the rest. We could have put stripes on anything and sold it. We were constantly told that we were the bee's knees and nobody could touch us.'

British retailers were just as ignorant about Nike, but the salesmen recruited from Adidas knew all the right moves to obtain shelf space. By far the best-selling Nike shoe was the Waffle trainer: while Adidas were laughing it off, British retailers were welcoming it as a genuine improvement on the stiff Adidas counterpart. 'They immediately took up the Waffle trainer because they could see that it was something else,' said Tagg. The name itself was a departure from the Adidas style, and Nike pushed its advantage by coming up with a children's trainer called the Wally Waffle.

At the same time, Nike burst onto the British running scene with Brendan Foster. A middle-distance runner, Foster was the only Englishman to bring back a track and field medal from the Montreal Olympics in 1976, where he broke the world record for 5,000 metres and took bronze in the 10,000. The ex-Adidas wearer was recruited by Nike to spread the word among upcoming runners. At the time British athletes were allowed to accept gifts of shoes from manufacturers.

As it happened, British athletics was entering a golden age, with two outstanding athletes battling it out at the front of the international pack: the smooth Sebastian Coe and the angular Steve Ovett. Their rivalry became the drawing card of many athletics meetings, and it was a tremendous show for Nike, since they both agreed to endorse the brand.

Mike Chapman was on his rounds in Sheffield when Mel Batty, a runner and Nike agent, introduced him to Seb Coe. When the two men turned up on the Coes' doorstep, the runner was unpacking several boxes of Adidas gear which had just been delivered to him, but Coe was happy to listen to the Nike men and ended up signing a juicy endorsement deal. Steve Ovett was recruited through Andy Norman, a controversial agent who aggressively fought to abolish the amateur principles in athletics, organizing many commercial events.

The clashes between the two British runners culminated at the Moscow Olympics in 1980. Since the United States had boycotted the Games, Nike's hopes were pinned on the two pending showdowns between Coe and Ovett, who were both in strong shape. An entire chunk of the grandstand was swathed in Union Jacks as the two runners headed for their first confrontation, in the 800 metres. Sebastian Coe was regarded as the favourite at this distance. His supporters would be bitterly disappointed.

As he said later, it had been 'the worst race of my life'. He left his finishing kick too late and was unable to catch up with the triumphant

Ovett. Six days later, however, Coe put on a stunning performance in the 1,500 metres. He had picked himself up remarkably after his disappointment and beat Ovett comprehensively, leaving his rival trailing in third place. His elation at the finishing line remains one of the most enduring pictures in British athletics, and a superb advertisement for Nike.

By then, the Nike men in Oregon had picked the United Kingdom as a beachhead for their conquest of Europe. Although the European business was still relatively small, Nike felt in tune with the British culture. To tackle the market more aggressively, Nike bought out Reliance Sportswear in 1980 and set up its first European subsidiary in Halifax, to be headed jointly by Mike Tagg and Brendan Foster.

Over the next few years, Nike's expansion in the United Kingdom would be largely fuelled by rising enthusiasm for running. Chris Brasher, who took gold in the 3,000 metres steeplechase at the Melbourne Olympics in 1956, contributed to the craze by helping to inaugurate the London marathon. As his running days faded, Brasher embarked on a glowing career in journalism and business. As he prepared for the debut race in March 1981, he was expecting about 4,000 entrants, but more than 7,000 started at Greenwich Park and the marathon went on to become a London institution.

Brasher himself benefited from the trend through Fleetfoot, his distribution company. In 1979 he had obtained a deal with New Balance, an American brand that specialized in running shoes. They were most widely known for the comfort and support of their trainers, derived from the arch which had become their trademark. New Balance later distinguished themselves by opening a shoe factory in Cumbria, at a time when others were closing theirs, and stubbornly refusing to take part in the endorsement game. They prided themselves on being 'Endorsed by No One' – because they preferred to spend the money on technological research that would benefit all buyers.

The running boom took on such proportions that Nike and New Balance both trounced Adidas. While the Germans were still reluctant to cater for this business, Nike and New Balance inundated the market with their trainers. By 1983, Nike had become the predominant running brand in the United Kingdom.

Adidas received another painful blow from a foul-tempered American. A hugely talented tennis player, John McEnroe became known as the

27. *The battle between Sebastian Coe and Steve Ovett dominated international tracks in the early eighties, propelling Nike to new heights in Europe.*

man who stomped on rackets and swore at umpires. The Nike men, who liked to portray themselves as the rebels in the sports business, eagerly signed McEnroe in 1978 and produced matching commercials. When the player turned up for Wimbledon in 1981, they ran ads with their tennis shoes and a headline that said: 'McEnroe Swears by Them'. Another one spelled out 'McEnroe's Favorite Four-Letter Word'. The tag worked perfectly as McEnroe went on to win the tournament, beating the otherwise unflappable Björn Borg. Most importantly for Nike, the McEnroe tennis shoes enabled them to move beyond the running business.

The Adidas managers consoled themselves with the thought that they still had football. Yet in the early eighties, this had become the largest bone of contention between Adidas and Umbro. The Adidas managers were no longer satisfied with the crumbs thrown to them by the Umbro men. They felt that Umbro was holding them back, by keeping deals with football clubs to itself. They were clamouring for a club of their own. 'Every football team ended up causing a conflict,' said Stuart Humphreys, the younger of the brothers who owned Umbro.

After several years of begging, Umbro resolved to hand over one of its teams to Adidas. At the time the British brand outfitted nearly all of the country's most inspiring teams, including Liverpool and Arsenal. Adidas got Ipswich Town, then a mid-table First Division side. Umbro managers were delighted to have placated Adidas without relinquishing any of their leading teams – until, a few months later, Ipswich's 1977/78 FA Cup run climaxed in a 1–0 defeat of Arsenal at Wembley.

The premature death of John Humphreys in 1978 further weakened the relationship between Adidas and its British distributor. Umbro seemed rudderless, unable to cope with the pressure of the Adidas business and their rivals.

Nike had sent over Rob Strasser, a former marketing manager, to mastermind its European onslaught. The ebullient ex-lawyer was working from Nike's European head offices – which then consisted of a small apartment in a residential district of Amsterdam and a table at a Mexican cantina in the red light district. Strasser's brief was to concentrate on the UK, which Nike regarded as the most influential European market.

Once the brand had become strong in the British running and tennis business, Strasser felt that the time was ripe to attack the Adidas stronghold – football. When Tagg and Foster took the American to Anfield to watch Liverpool, Strasser had to admit that he had never seen a football game before. He was so enthused that he set up a plant in Heckmondwike, just a few miles from the CWS plant that once produced the Stanley Matthews range and run by the same man, Harry Blacker.

To wear them, Nike chose Peter Withe. The Aston Villa striker proved a remarkable catch for Nike. Just after he had signed their deal in 1982, Aston Villa unexpectedly reached the final of the European Cup. The stadium in Rotterdam was packed for the clash, which pitted Villa against the entirely three-striped Bayern Munich. Much to Nike's delight, it was Peter Withe, resplendent in Nike, who scored the winning goal. Unfortunately, Peter Withe's talents could not disguise the fact that his boots were falling apart.

Michel Lukkien, the Nike distributor in the Netherlands, was in an awfully embarrassing predicament. He had been pushing doggedly for Nike to enter Dutch football, and once the factory in Heckmondwike was up and running he excitedly signed up Volendam, a small but popular Dutch team. 'Six months later we turned into a laughing stock, because the soles kept flying off the boots,' sighed Lukkien. The Nike name would not return to the football pitch for almost a decade.

Notwithstanding Nike's embarrassment, Adidas appeared completely paralysed in the face of advances by the American brand. In the circumstances, Horst Dassler was not prepared to waste any more time on the wobbly partnership with Umbro, but to trigger a break-up he would have to provoke an unprecedented spat.

Umbro believed they were untouchable in British football, but Horst Dassler had his own ideas. He 'bumped into' club executives at international meetings and he invited some of them to the parties which he organized with a French football magazine for the Adidas Golden Boot award. Among Dassler's regular guests were executives from Liverpool FC, which was under contract with Umbro. Through his sharp antennae, Dassler heard that the club was deeply frustrated with its relationship with Umbro. John Humphreys had seen to it that Liverpool would get proper exposure – always at the ready to make new shirts and to set up deals that would enhance Anfield's revenues. After all, Liverpool were serial European champions, and the Reds stirred enthusiasm way beyond Merseyside, but since John Humphreys' death Umbro no longer appeared to have much time for Liverpool.

Horst Dassler began to sabotage the relationship between Liverpool and Umbro during the final of the 1984 European Cup, in Rome against AS Roma. Shortly before the start of the game, Liverpool managers were told that their players could not run out wearing their Umbro strip. 'Horst Dassler had convinced the Uefa chairman that, for some ludicrous reason, the Umbro diamond was illegal,' explained Stuart Humphreys. 'Since it was far too late to change shirts, the players had to cover up the Umbro sign with sticking tape.' Just as Horst intended, this caused yet more friction between Liverpool and Umbro.

Over the next months, the Adidas chief stepped up the pressure. As part of Umbro's deal with Liverpool it had been agreed that the club would use Adidas balls. Suddenly, Horst Dassler cried foul, for no obvious reason claiming that Umbro was trying to edge Adidas out of the deal and to build up its own ball-making business. As he saw it, this justified the opening of talks with John Smith, Liverpool's chairman, and Peter Robinson, its long-time general manager.

When the Umbro managers learned of the discussions, they weren't best pleased. They pointed out that the company had just opened a new plant in Ellesmere Port, close to Chester, which risked closure if Umbro lost its Liverpool deal. Scores of people would be made redundant, and

Liverpool would have to shoulder the blame. This was a powerful argument, especially to men already unsure of the reaction they might provoke by signing with a German company, but still they were unable to resist Horst Dassler's advances. 'He invited us over, gave us his personal phone contacts and pledged to take a personal interest in Liverpool,' said Peter Robinson. The deal was settled in 1985 when Horst Dassler assured the Liverpool board that Adidas would produce football shirts in the United Kingdom, for British sales at least.

That May Liverpool again reached the final of the European Cup. In theory, the Reds should still have worn their Umbro shirts, but the Adidas managers had convinced the players to switch to the three stripes for the final, offering Umbro hefty compensation. Tragically, the enduring image of that night at the Heysel stadium in Belgium has little to do with football.

Thereafter the relationship between Adidas and Umbro became untenable. Umbro was supposedly selling Adidas, yet the German brand dwarfed its British distributor. While they were meant to be partners, Horst Dassler craftily elbowed Umbro out of the most enticing deals. They were heading towards a break-up that would enable Adidas to take full control of its influential British business, from February 1986.

This plan was perfectly in line with Dassler's global thinking. At a time when fax machines still had to make an appearance in most offices, multinationality was by no means commonplace. There were only a handful of brands that handled their business on a truly global scale. With its unparalleled distribution and the might of its brand, Adidas was well placed to be in the vanguard.

Horst Dassler nodded approvingly. The Frankfurt office of Young & Rubicam, an international advertising agency, had come up with an inspiring concept: 'The Adidas factor: It's either for you or against you,' ran the tagline. The executives at Y&R, one of the last two agencies in the running for the Adidas account, listened nervously as Horst delivered his verdict. Adidas was any creative director's dream, and for all they knew Adidas would have an enormous budget.

Horst had become convinced that Adidas needed to invest in international advertising – like all the high-profile brands he dealt with at ISL, his sports rights agency. Until the mid-eighties most Adidas advertising was provided by Fick, the small design office in Nuremberg which Adi Dassler had retained in the fifties. They came up with a variety of ideas and each subsidiary could decide the type of campaign it wanted to run. Horst could see that the times had changed: he wanted to switch to a harmonized, international message.

Young & Rubicam obtained the contract but they were in for some nasty surprises. To begin with, they found out that Adidas invested very little in advertising, as their marketing budget still went mostly on deals with athletes and federations. Ingo Kraus, head of Y&R in Germany, could not believe the numbers: the budget on which he was supposed to promote Adidas worldwide was smaller than Ford's in Germany alone. Worse still, the agency discovered that Adidas was completely out of sync with its international reputation as a brand. Steeped in their provincial ways and preoccupied by their internal problems, the Dasslers had quite neglected to adjust their business to its increasingly international marketplace. The managers at Y&R had their own line to summarize the problem: 'Great brand, dumb company.'

The brand had travelled without regard for national borders, but the company's international business was a maze of independent distribution and licensing deals. The smalltime traders who had once knocked on the Dasslers' door in Herzogenaurach had since turned into local industry chieftains who were preventing Adidas from imposing an orchestrated marketing effort. They were not about to let slick advertisers in Frankfurt decide what consumers were told in Argentina or Taiwan.

The lack of control over the Adidas advertising budget was just as amazing. For Procter & Gamble, another of their customers, Young & Rubicam produced roughly one print ad per year. The company demanded regular insights and updates on the agency's spending. But at Adidas each of the subsidiaries demanded their own versions. Two months after they obtained the contract Y&R had prepared nearly fifty print ads, and the company didn't seem to care about the soaring cost.

When the agency finally came up with the concept for Adidas's first global television commercial, as requested by Horst, it faced yet more opposition. Unlike the hard-hitting Nike commercials, the Y&R production had an arty touch, based on a cloud motif. The principle was that the clouds didn't require translation. They could be used anywhere in the world. But national managers still requested so many adjustments that Y&R ended up producing four versions of the commercial – English,

French, German and 'international'. 'It basically defeated the purpose that Horst Dassler wanted, of having a global campaign,' said Tom Harrington, then account manager at Y&R.

The commercial was eventually introduced in August 1986 at ISPO, an international sports trade fair in Munich. The company's assembled distributors and country managers listened expectantly as Horst Dassler outlined the concept. 'We now have a global advertising campaign by a global advertising agency,' he said. 'And this is not negotiable.' But the negotiations started as soon as the presentation ended.

One of the loudest protests came from France. Bernard Odinet, general manager in Landersheim, flatly refused to run the commercial, saying it reminded him of a Nazi production by Leni Riefenstahl – using the same ethereal mix of perfect bodies and cloudy skies. He was backed by many other country managers, who didn't care for a campaign based on an image: they wanted the commercials to feature products, products that would do well in their particular country. 'It was the most hostile environment I've ever had for any sort of presentation,' said Ingo Kraus. As the advertisers lamented, their global concept turned into a product catalogue.

This patchy advertising was compounded by a series of costly marketing failures. The most damaging flop resulted from Horst Dassler's drive away from performance sports. As he remarked, Nike had begun to expand at staggering pace when trainers became part of the leisure uniform of the United States. Nike had redefined the sports business in the United States: Adidas could do the same elsewhere. 'I want to be a leisure brand,' Horst told startled executives.

To get his point across, Horst Dassler produced a drawing of a pyramid. The peak represented the sports market, he said, while the wide bottom part symbolized the mass leisure market. It didn't take an elaborate marketing study to conclude that Adidas would be well-advised to target the base market.

The company was further encouraged by creeping changes in German dress codes. Germans were still more stifled by formality than people in the United States, but trainers were beginning to appear in more and more places that would previously have banned such casual attire. Joschka Fischer, a Green Party politician, made the top story on German news bulletins in 1985 when he outraged the establishment by taking his oath as regional environment minister in a pair of Adidas high-tops. Unfortunately, the Adidas response was ill-conceived. The company introduced a range of street shoes, called 'City', that departed entirely from sports. It contained a puzzling array of boat shoes, walking shoes with thick plastic soles, and even some women's pumps.

'There were crazy things,' said Peter Rduch, then in charge of footwear development. He had ordered a study on the leisure business and come to the conclusion that Adidas had no competence in this field. Yet the company was under such pressure to break into leisure that it went ahead anyway, recruiting a batch of fashion-oriented designers.

It worked well on the clothing side, enabling Adidas to sell millions of colourful T-shirts and sweaters. But the company was far less savvy about its footwear, allowing the Adidas name to be affixed to the most improbable concepts. 'Our catalogues and flyers looked wonderful, but some of the shoes could only have been launched out of desperation,' sighed Rduch. Among the most embarrassing products were shoes with flavoured laces.

The misguided move caused huge confusion: it alienated sports retailers, who watched Adidas diluting its appeal as a sports brand; it baffled fashion retailers, who wondered what Adidas products were doing on their shelves; and it caused frictions in the company, where lifelong sports designers suddenly had to mingle with the fashion set. They couldn't stop staring when one of the fashion designers turned up in a black cape.

'Horst Dassler tried to emulate Nike but did it precisely the wrong way round,' said Tom Harrington, still at Young & Rubicam. 'Nike was selling a sports product and ended up reaching the masses. Adidas was presenting itself as a fashion product, which it wasn't, and it was still selling mostly to sports people.'

Adidas could barely afford such costly failures. It was already badly weakened by the buy-out of its American distributors and under increasing attack in the European market, where Nike was beginning to make its presence felt. Still unimproved by Horst Dassler's reforms, the company's financial situation was increasingly precarious.

When Horst Dassler boarded the little aeroplane, his companions noticed that he looked strained. Settling for the short flight from Herzogenaurach to Landersheim, he unfolded his newspaper. His fellow travellers looked at each other in dismay as they distinctly heard, behind the paper, the sound of their unshakeable chief sobbing.

'It was such a shocking sight that I felt compelled to ask him what was up,' recalled Blago Vidinic. 'Horst then explained that he had just taken one of the toughest decisions in his business life. He would have to close down a plant in the Alsace, which he had acquired himself as a young man. He knew full well that several families would lose more than one job, and it was such a desolate village that they would never find others. This genuinely distressed him.'

The French plant closure would be followed by many others. As much as it pained him, Horst Dassler acknowledged that Adidas could not maintain large-scale production in Europe. Cheaper Far Eastern supplies enabled Nike to work with gross margins of more than 40 per cent, while Adidas was stuck closer to 25. The differential enabled Nike to pump money into advertising. There was no way that Adidas could counter-attack unless it aligned its production costs.

Over the previous years, Adidas had already shifted much of its footwear production to eastern Europe and the Far East. By the mid-eighties the Taiwanese Riu brothers turned out about half of all Adidas footwear, roughly 40 million pairs, with several factories in Taiwan and China. To speed up the shift, Horst Dassler hired Uwe Breithaupt, a footwear production specialist.

However, Adidas still wasn't prepared to relinquish control of its production. While Nike dealt with entirely independent Far Eastern manufacturers, most Adidas production took place in plants that were at least partly owned by the company. Breithaupt led a group of German technicians who were paid at expatriate rates to run Adidas plants first in Korea, then in Malaysia, Thailand and China. Under these conditions Adidas could not take full advantage of the cheaper production, and the result was an infuriating mess. As Adidas failed to deliver, the company was confronted with irate customers and growing losses.

Under Horst Dassler's oligarchic regime, only a couple of managers were fully aware of the company's troubles. While Horst orchestrated far-reaching cutbacks and other badly needed reforms, he knew it would take several years for the measures to pay off. The American buy-out had punched a gaping hole in the company's balance sheet, and the ensuing problems generated yet more red ink. The company struggled to integrate four distribution fiefdoms into one smooth-running operation.

Steve Tannen, the manager recruited to head Adidas USA, seemed at a loss to halt the brand's vertiginous slide. Then there were all the auxiliary interests that Horst Dassler had accumulated under Sarragan: his rights to Le Coq Sportif, Pony and Arena were all bought by Adidas for a symbolic sum, but they burdened the company with further losses and operating headaches.

By the end of 1986, Horst's second year at the helm, the Dassler sisters began to doubt their brother's ability to steer the family company out of its dire straits. Their suspicions were aroused most persistently by Christoph Malms, husband of the youngest sister, Sigrid. Since he had completed his studies at Wharton business school and joined McKinsey management consultants, Malms made his voice heard with increasing firmness at family meetings.

Although Horst Dassler rarely talked about his family, he made it abundantly clear to his aides that he didn't have much time for Christoph Malms' words of wisdom. As he told several managers, he could barely stand his brother-in-law's cockiness, and he wasn't about to take advice from a fresh-faced consultant. Unwilling to confront Horst directly, Malms convinced the Dassler sisters to let an independent consultant study the company. They picked Michel Perraudin, a partner at McKinsey in Düsseldorf who specialized in operations management. At the beginning of 1987, he agreed to a discreet meeting with Christoph Malms at the Hilton hotel in Zurich. 'This felt like a conspiracy, because nobody was supposed to know,' said Perraudin. He was asked to prepare a brief study of Adidas, to be presented to the board in May. He could not have guessed that, by then, there would no longer be any need to hide from Horst.

Just before the opening of the 1986 World Cup in Mexico, Horst Dassler told some of his closest managers that he was slipping off to attend an unscheduled meeting in New York. He didn't tell them that the appointment was with a medical adviser, who advocated surgery to remove cancerous cells behind Dassler's left eye.

One of the few people Horst Dassler called during his hospital stay in New York was Pat Doran, a former reporter for *Sportstyle*. The two had got to know each other when Doran reported on Adidas, and she ended up joining the US operations of Le Coq Sportif. She was thoroughly impressed by Dassler, whom she regarded as far ahead of his time. He, in turn, appreciated her flair, and he increasingly sought advice from her on the American fashion scene.

Over the years, Pat Doran had often been confronted with Horst Dassler's workaholic habits and his paranoia. Still, she was stunned to watch Horst run Adidas from a New York hospital bed. 'While he was waiting for the magnet therapy that would reduce the tumour, he was making calls around the world to people who thought he was at one of his offices,' she recalled. One of the reasons he cited for the secrecy of his stay was that he didn't want his cousin Armin to find out. 'He really believed that Armin had spies following him everywhere,' Doran observed.

When he returned to Herzogenaurach with a patch over his eye, Horst Dassler resumed his harrowing schedule. He sometimes left meetings early, apologizing that he felt tired or dizzy. One of his old friends was puzzled when Horst Dassler turned down a business dinner, choosing to spend the evening with his wife instead. Others noticed that Dassler's eye was weeping. But he brushed aside any concerned queries, and none of the Adidas board members or other high-profile executives realized the seriousness of Dassler's health problems.

With at least one close friend, Horst Dassler shared feelings of personal unhappiness: his relationship with his sisters remained strained, his marriage had all but dissolved, he said, and he was uncertain that his children, Adi and Suzanne, possessed either the will or ability to build on his achievements. Several managers had been asked to act as mentors for Adi Jr, taking Dassler's son into their department for several weeks. Their observations weren't all too encouraging: Adi was a fine lad but he showed more interest in partying than in Adidas, often skipping work in the mornings or dozing off at his desk.

Increasingly short-tempered, Horst Dassler began to take out his frustration on some of the people with whom he had worked most closely. Among them was Jean-Marie Weber, Horst's bagman. For many years Dassler had relied entirely on Weber to keep track of his financial affairs in a maze of company holdings and undercover payments. This had turned into a mess, and Horst readily identified the culprit. Dassler called Weber 'incompetent' and firmly intended to get rid of him. Another target of his scorn was Sepp Blatter, the Fifa general secretary. Since Horst Dassler had been instrumental in his gaining that position, Blatter had not always displayed as much gratitude as Dassler expected.

The two continued to celebrate their near-simultaneous birthdays together in Landersheim, but their business relationship quickly deteriorated. Dassler was furious when he heard that Blatter was spotted playing tennis in Puma gear. More seriously, Dassler was enraged by Blatter's perceived dithering at Fifa. While others criticized Blatter for blatant collusion with Dassler and ISL, the Adidas chief felt that the Swiss wasn't helpful enough.

By early 1987, it had become clear that the treatment had failed and that Dassler's disease had spread. He rapidly lost weight and began to look emaciated. Managers who had not seen him for a long time were shocked by his sagging cheeks and his bilious complexion. However, Horst Dassler continued to run Adidas with unwavering firmness, as if he had many years ahead of him.

At the end of March 1987 he issued instructions in a six-page memo for the company's board members. 'Unfortunately my illness will drag on a little longer than originally expected,' he wrote. 'To make sure that these intestine and stomach problems don't become chronic, I will have to rest and to stay on a diet for another two months.' But in his tone there was a sense of urgency, coupled with a touch of irritation.

Among the last files handled by Horst Dassler was the Adidas contract with Steffi Graf. The steady German tennis champion had long been covered in trefoils and three stripes, but the talks between Adidas and the player's representative to increase her earnings from the contract were dragging on. As instructed, Tomas Bach, then in charge of sports promotion, negotiated hard, until he received an unsettling phone call from Horst Dassler. 'He had previously asked me to hold on, to get the price down, but all of a sudden he wanted me to sign right away,' Bach recalled.

As Horst lay dying, he might have acknowledged to himself that he failed to clean up the company. Horst had partly managed to mend its fractured family structure, bringing all the brands under the same roof and instilling a truly international approach, and Adidas just about remained the market leader in 1987, with international sales that would reach almost precisely DM4 billion, compared with roughly DM900 million for Puma. But this amounted to a decline for both of them, as Nike and Reebok were making their way to Europe. The measures advocated by Horst Dassler to reduce costs had certainly not sufficed to make Adidas as sharp and lean as its American foes.

On the other hand, Horst Dassler could rest assured that ISL had turned the corner. In spite of his tussles with Sepp Blatter, the sports rights agency continued to ride high in the football business, and it had pulled off an amazing coup with the Olympics. Since nearly all national Olympic committees had agreed to surrender their rights to the rings, ISL executives had been roaming the world to convince international companies to pump their marketing dollars into the Olympic programme (TOP) for the 1988 Games in Seoul.

To begin with, and to their dismay, ISL executives found that international companies weren't rushing to buy into the Olympics at all. By late 1985, Dassler had guaranteed millions of dollars but they had just two partners on board. They gave themselves another six months to find more – otherwise they would have to give up. Fortunately, the situation suddenly improved when another two companies committed themselves. Horst Dassler could proudly tell the IOC that the Olympic marketing plan had raised about $95 million from nine international companies, from Philips in the Netherlands to Visa in the United States and the Japanese Brother Industries. Sadly, he would not live to savour ISL's accomplishments.

Horst Dassler died on 9 April 1987, barely a month after his fifty-first birthday. When they arrived for work the next day, thousands of German employees were stunned to learn of their chairman's death. Those who had not seen him for several months could not have guessed that he had been unwell. An international sales meeting was interrupted and the board members gathered to discuss the disaster.

The German response was relatively muted, however, compared with the scenes that unfolded in Landersheim. When they heard the news over the loudspeaker that morning, scores of grown men and women erupted in tears. 'It was a gripping sight,' as one of them recalled. 'There were people wailing down the corridors, others collapsed in their office, crying desperately for hours on end.'

The obituaries published by the German press praised Horst Dassler as 'an unostentatious, modest man', who steered the international growth of a company with sales of DM4.1 billion. Others referred to him as 'the most powerful man in sports'. He was 'a tireless, but not selfless genius', one reporter noted, while another portrayed Dassler as 'the man in the background, who pulled the strings'.

Monika Dassler led the small funeral cortège that brought her husband to his final resting place. Juan Antonio Samaranch and Sepp Blatter both

28. Sepp Blatter (with dark glasses), João Havelange and Juan Antonio Samarnach are among the mourners at Horst Dassler's funeral, walking behind his widow and two children.

walked behind the widow and her children. Adi and Suzanne had not seen much of their father, but they knew him well enough to know what touched him most. They had seen to it that, on his last journey, Horst would wear the watch he had gleefully received from his friend Ilie Nastase.

21

The Fall of Puma

Armin Dassler beamed as he shook the bankers' hands. As head of Puma since Rudolf's death he had suffered triumphs and setbacks, but this was undeniably his finest hour. That morning, 25 July 1986, Puma was to be listed on the Frankfurt stock exchange. While Adidas was still a private company, its smaller rival entered the select group of German firms that featured on the financial pages every day.

Puma's shares shot up immediately. In the eyes of the German public, they were closely associated with a freckle-faced tennis player who had burst onto the scene the previous year. In July 1985 the 17-year-old Boris Becker stunned the tennis world by winning Wimbledon – the Puma logo clearly visible on his shoes as he dived around the court.

Puma had been tipped off about Boris Becker by a Romanian former player, Ion Tiriac. With protégés such as Guillermo Vilas and Henri Leconte, two leading tennis players in the eighties, he had become an influential manager. On the tennis circuit, Tiriac was mostly known for his thick moustache and his threatening gaze. As one British reporter wrote, 'Tiriac has the air of a man who is about to close a deal in a back room behind a back room.'

In this case it was the Puma boardroom in Herzogenaurach. After a rejection by Adidas, Tiriac convinced Puma to fork out DM300,000 in 1984 for a shoe contract with Boris Becker, then completely unknown. It paid off in spades as Boris went on to become 'Boom Boom' Becker, a hugely popular and extremely successful player. The hype reached its peak in July 1986, just days before the Puma float, when Becker won his second Wimbledon title in a row, beating the three-striped Ivan Lendl in straight sets. The company claimed that the Becker effect had nearly tripled the sales of its tennis rackets. Puma was so closely associated with the player that the company's public offering was dubbed 'the Becker float'.

By then, the split of the shares between the Dassler brothers had somewhat changed to the benefit of Armin. He had agreed to take over an extra 10 per cent from his brother Gerd, when the latter suffered some financial troubles. The Dassler brothers floated 28 per cent of their shares, while retaining the majority of the stock and all of the voting rights. As Armin Dassler explained, the sale of the shares would be useful to raise cash, but it had been partly motivated by his acute health problems. Several years after a Kenyan safari, Dassler had been felled by a severe bout of malaria. It nearly cost him his life. Armin told reporters that the stock market listing might ease inheritance problems. If he died prematurely, his children could easily draw on outside capital to keep the company afloat.

The deal crowned a triumphant run for Puma. Since Armin Dassler had taken over from his father in 1974, the company's turnover had shot up to nearly DM820 million in 1985. Rudolf Dassler's sons had inherited a brand which had an inspiring heritage but still couldn't compete with the international exposure of its much larger rival and derived most of its sales from German football. When he took control, Armin began to issue a throng of licences and distribution deals that beefed up the brand's international sales, and he strove to cultivate its position as a snappy underdog.

The most thrilling rewards came from Latin America, where Armin continued to benefit from the connections of Hans Henningsen, Puma's agent in Brazil. He delivered much of the Argentine team that won the 1978 World Cup. Among the endorsees was César Luis Menotti, the Argentine trainer. When he spotted a chubby attacker at Boca Juniors, he sent the teenager straight to Armin Dassler. Diego Maradona was still so young that the contract had to be signed by his father.

This caused Puma many headaches over the years, as Maradona became increasingly capricious. When he once deigned to travel to Munich for an appearance at the ISPO trade fair, the Dasslers had to book several adjoining hotel suites for him. He would not move without his entire family, consisting of about twenty people. Other demands were attributed to superstition, which was hard to counter. But the deal secured continuous exposure for Puma, as Maradona shone on international pitches. He became part of the European football elite in Barcelona and Naples, and his football career was crowned at the World Cup in 1986 – won by Argentina after Maradona's infamous 'hand of God' goal in the quarter-finals against England.

At the same time, Armin Dassler continued to run Puma as a family business. For many years he entered the company through the factory floor and greeted all of the workers. He endeared himself to the employees through his open door and his generous behaviour. John Akii-Bua, a Ugandan hurdler, experienced it in the seventies when he fled the political turmoil in his country. Dassler and Akii-Bua had got to know each other at the Munich Olympics in 1972, where the Ugandan won a gold medal for the 400-metre hurdles. When Armin heard that Akii-Bua was in trouble he put him up in one of his properties in Herzogenaurach, together with his family, and offered him a job in Puma's sports promotion department.

Compared with Horst, Armin Dassler still had the air of a provincial entrepreneur, more comfortable with a plate of dumplings than sushi. Yet he had become established in the sports business as the chairman of the World Federation for the Sporting Goods Industry (WFSGI), lobbying in favour of free trade on behalf of the sports companies. The

29. *Armin Dassler* (left, with check jacket) *is persuaded to sit down briefly at the same table as his enemy cousin, Horst, at an industry meeting in Japan.*

appointment came about in 1986, when the federation's board convened in Tokyo. The chairmanship was then in the hands of Kihachiro Onitsuka, the Asics chairman. But under the federation's rules it had to rotate between executives from different continents, and it was Europe's turn. Since Armin Dassler already headed the European sporting goods federation, Onitsuka thought he would be the obvious choice.

Still, the shrewd Japanese knew that the move was bound to anger Horst Dassler. Therefore, the night before the announcement, Onitsuka went to the Adidas chief's room in Tokyo and politely informed him. 'Horst was very upset and issued all sorts of threats. He said it was completely unacceptable to him and he would leave the federation, but I still managed to appease him,' Onitsuka recalled. 'I taught him the Buddhist proverb which says that the one who leads the attack will get the punch back in his own face.'

Horst eventually agreed not to intervene against his cousin at the next day's meeting. Shortly afterwards, he could even be persuaded to shake hands with Armin and to be pictured sitting at the same table as his cousin. Again, it was Onitsuka's wisdom that did it: 'I told him about another Buddhist proverb, which says that it is one's duty to get on with one's family,' he chuckled.

On the other hand, Armin's impulsive behaviour sometimes landed Puma in dire straits. One of his most damaging outbursts was the sudden dismissal of Beconta, Puma's long-time and exclusive distributor for the whole of the United States, in June 1979. The decades-old relationship worked reasonably well until Armin began to feel that the company was holding him back, because it didn't have the resources to suitably push Puma all across the country. Another problem was that, unlike the Adidas distributors, the Beconta managers were entitled to source their own Puma shoes in Asia. On these sales Puma Germany would pocket only royalties, instead of the full price they received for product sourced by the German organization.

The arrangement was unsatisfactory, but instead of working out a compromise or organizing a smooth transition, Armin Dassler fired Beconta in a huff. 'There was no need for the mayhem which my brother caused by breaking up with them from one day to the next,' said Gerd Dassler. 'I don't know why Armin flew off the handle this time. From then on, the United States was a mess for Puma.'

Armin Dassler asked Dick Kazmaier, a former Converse distributor, to replace Beconta quickly with four separate distributors. Their orders and marketing activities were to be supervised by a central office, Puma USA, set up by Kazmaier in Boston. Kazmaier himself took up distribution for the East Coast and found three other partners to cover the rest of the country. The transition was handled as quickly as possible, but Puma deliveries were still heavily disrupted for at least a year at a time when the market was undergoing drastic changes.

Over the next few years, the chosen partners struggled to convince Puma that their hard shoes were no longer adequate for the American market. Just like their competitors at Adidas, they failed to get the message across and muddled along with 'shoes that felt like bricks'. But the Puma brand suffered an even more damaging blow when Armin Dassler encouraged Kazmaier to sign a massive deal with an American discounter.

As Dick Kazmaier recalled, he received an urgent call from Armin in August 1983, as he was heading towards the World University Games in Edmonton, Canada. Armin explained that he was in a quandary. 'He told me he needed more volume and receivables, therefore he wanted to sell two million pairs by the beginning of September,' Kazmaier recalled. 'Two million pairs were a whole lot of shoes at the time. There was no way to sell them over such a short period without entering the mass market.' This led to a large-scale deal with Meldisco, a shoe franchise of K-Mart, an American discounter. Armin Dassler apparently flew over to Boston just to pick up the written copy of the order.

Kazmaier felt uneasy about the deal, knowing that 'it would wreak havoc with the other distributors'. The deal may have been critical to Armin in the short term, because he needed orders to offset expenses on his balance sheet. But by selling to an offshoot of K-Mart, he was undermining his own marketing efforts. The fact that Puma could be found in discount stores would inevitably tarnish the brand, giving it a tacky reputation. The move was almost certain to alienate upscale retailers.

On the back of the Meldisco order, Puma started a programme to distinguish discount shoes from others: the pairs reserved for regular retailers were packed in green boxes, while the ones intended for discount merchants went in white boxes. By the mid-eighties, Puma began to suffer the consequences. Foot Locker, the most influential sports retailer in the United States, decided to scrap its business with Puma. If the brand was sold at K-Mart, they didn't want it on their shelves.

Just like his cousin before him, Armin Dassler then decided to buy out his company's remaining American distributors. Two of them had already given up on Puma, but Dassler still had to absorb Dick Kazmaier and Richard Voit, the Puma distributor on the West Coast. Puma USA, the office run by Kazmaier for joint buying and marketing, would be expanded into a full-fledged subsidiary. But Puma USA quickly ran into nightmarish problems. Three chief executives struggled to restore the brand's reputation, but none of them lasted more than a few months. They quickly became frustrated by the company's German leadership, which seemed oblivious to US market realities.

Armin Dassler then turned to his eldest son. Aged twenty-nine, Frank was still a law student. A bright and hard-working young man, he regularly turned up at Puma before his lessons in the mornings, and set up a research department called the Running Studio, which looked into the biomechanical aspects of running. However, his knowledge of the business remained limited and his managerial experience was non-existent. When Armin Dassler told the board that he wanted Frank to fix Puma's abysmal problems in the US, at the beginning of 1985, several managers attempted to convince him that it was wrong. He would not be doing the company a favour, nor his son. Frank Dassler himself felt that the request was 'kind of crazy'. But Armin flatly overruled.

For all his ardour, Frank Dassler was unable to stem the US collapse. At a meeting in February 1985, he warned the Puma board that the brand's American sales were crashing. But the full extent of the troubles became apparent towards October 1986, just months after the Puma float. By then, the value of the Puma shares had soared from an issue price of DM130 to more than DM1,400. As news of the company's US woes began to seep out, the shares fell back just as sharply. It became clear that Puma would end the year with a substantial loss, stemming mostly from the United States. Puma's American sales had nearly halved to $95 million for 1986, down from $180 million the previous year. The loss suffered by the American operation, which would reach around $27 million, would plunge the entire company into the red.

To make matters worse, Boris Becker became a millstone round Puma's neck. Once hailed as a German role model, he was suddenly perceived as an arrogant brat. His performance on the court waned as fast as his tabloid infamy grew. A German tennis magazine wrote that Boris Becker was 'the most exciting but least attractive of tennis players, before Lendl and McEnroe'. He triggered nationwide outrage when he moved to Monte Carlo in an apparent attempt to avoid German taxes and to duck out of obligatory military service. 'The retailers told us the Boris Becker products would sell much better if they didn't have the name on them,' sighed Uli Heyd, Puma board member.

But Puma was stuck with a huge contract which Tiriac had negotiated in 1986, shortly after Becker's second Wimbledon victory. Apparently blinded by the euphoria and hypnotized by the hirsute Romanian, Armin Dassler had signed a delirious deal to outfit Boris Becker from shirt to racket: the player would pocket at least $5 million for each of the next five years, as well as a hefty commission on the sales of Puma products in the Boris Becker range. It would have taken staggering sales to make the deal worthwhile for Puma at the best of times. In the circumstances it was a permanent embarrassment and a growing liability.

The problem assumed such proportions that, in January 1987, Armin and Gerd Dassler resolved to inject DM62 million into the company, through a private subordinated loan. Unfortunately that failed to quell the unrest among the shareholders. Two months later rumours were doing the rounds that, to reimburse their loan, Armin and Gerd Dassler had put the company up for sale.

Puma shareholders were up in arms over the next few months, as auditors went through the company's numbers. Under the German rules at the time, Puma did not have to consolidate the results of its American and British subsidiaries (take them up fully in their accounts). Under the headline of 'Current business and prospects', the Puma prospectus indicated that 'the order backlog shows a clearly declining trend in the American business'. However, disgruntled shareholders accused the Puma management of disguising the extent of its American troubles, thereby misleading the market. The Deutsche Bank, which had arranged the float, was clearly targeted by the critics.

Although he was just weeks away from death at the time, Horst Dassler apparently couldn't refrain from making a personal dig. After a press meeting in Budapest in March 1987, he lashed at his cousin with vicious remarks. Horst had called the conference to discuss the opening of an Adidas store in Budapest, but he stayed behind to rail at Armin Dassler and Puma's financial situation. 'Puma is looking for a buyer that needs high tax-deductible losses,' he sniped. Puma's stock market troubles were bringing disrepute to the entire industry, he said, denouncing 'an absolute bank scandal'.

The shareholders, mostly private investors, became yet more agitated as several months went by and Puma was unable to hold its shareholders' meeting, pending the approval of their accounts. The assembly should have taken place in May, but by the end of the summer the shareholders still hadn't received their invitations. To quell the unrest, Armin Dassler came up with an amazingly generous offer to the shareholders: to replace the expected dividends, he would pay them out of his own pocket.

As its reputation was dragged through the mud, Deutsche Bank seized control at Puma. Alfred Herrhausen, then chairman of the bank, felt personally responsible for the file. After all, he was the one who had signed the agreement to underwrite the Puma public offering, which was turning into a disaster. Deutsche Bank had been denounced by angry shareholders, but Alfred Herrhausen knew that the abuse would get much worse if he pulled the plug on Puma. Thousands of discomfited small investors and redundant employees would point an accusing finger at the bank.

Jörg Dassler, Armin's second son, distinctly recalled the evening in

September 1987 when his father crashed on the couch in a state of utter despair. He had just returned from a meeting with bankers at the Deutsche Bank. They said that they were preparing to remove him from the company. 'You have lost your business,' Armin was apparently told. This was a devastating blow for Armin, who had dedicated his life to Puma. He had weathered the humiliations inflicted by his cousin and worked tirelessly to make sure that Puma could continue to compete. It was hard for him to comprehend how anonymous bankers could take this family heirloom away from him, and it was a blow from which he never fully recovered.

Shortly afterwards, his two oldest sons were called in for a meeting with the bankers. By then, Frank Dassler had returned from the United States to pursue his law studies, but he still squeezed in some Puma assignments. Jörg, in his thirties at the time, had long been in charge of the department dealing with 'entertainment promotion' – encouraging the likes of Elton John and The Scorpions to wear Puma shoes when they were touring or being interviewed on television. Both sons were bluntly asked to clear out their desks. 'As the bankers put it,' Frank Dassler said, 'they thought it unacceptable that we should be paid just for being Armin's sons.'

The Dasslers were deeply distressed by the bankers' methods and allegations, but they were not in a position to protest. Because of the loan which the Puma Dasslers obtained from the Deutsche Bank earlier that year, their shares were virtually in the hands of the bankers. Another reason behind their apparent resignation was the fast deterioration of Armin's health. Perhaps due to the malaria he suffered two years earlier, his liver was badly damaged. He reluctantly agreed to a liver transplant but he became increasingly tired and irritable.

The company's long-delayed shareholders' meeting was finally scheduled for 19 October 1987, at the Sheraton Hotel in Munich. The worst criticism was targeted at the bankers on the supervisory board. Due to his illness and his generous gesture, Armin Dassler was largely spared. The shareholders were told that he would leave his company over the next weeks.

His replacement was Hans Woitschätzke, an experienced manager in the sports business. The lanky German had previously taken over Kneissl, a ski company, when it went bankrupt in the early eighties. Woitschätzke agreed to meetings with Manfred Emcke, supervisory board chairman, and Alfred Herrhausen, the Deutsche Bank chairman, who convinced him to take over the helm at the ailing Puma. 'This company will not go bankrupt,' Herrhausen promised.

Without this commitment, the odds were that Puma would have been forced to file for bankruptcy. As Hans Woitschätzke discovered over the next months, Puma's former management had not been overly rigorous when it came to accounts. 'The books were filled with questionable dealings, from weird expenses to bad receivables that were parked in an off-shore company,' said Woitschätzke. 'The Deutsche Bank evidently hadn't done its homework as an underwriter. Otherwise it would have come to the conclusion that Puma was heading towards disaster.'

The wrongdoings partly reflected the informal methods of the former management board. Under Armin Dassler, many contracts had been sealed on the back of personal relationships. Armin's huge office was fitted with a bar, which he regularly used when meetings dragged on until late. Other restraints imposed on the board members appeared to have been relaxed over the years. Each of the six board members had a driver and, judging from their expense sheets, Woitschätzke thought that 'they must have known every bar from Flensburg to Garmisch-Partenkirchen'. In a letter to Armin Dassler, the Deutsche Bank apparently issued further accusations of 'misappropriation of profits'. In other words, the bankers felt that the chief executive had used some of Puma's money for purposes other than to further the company.

Yet more disturbingly, it seemed that the company's assets had been grossly inflated. To help him sort out the wreckage, Hans Woitschätzke recruited a well-regarded financial manager, Bernd Szymanski. Shortly after his recruitment in early 1988, he hired an external audit firm to write an unofficial report on the company. The document painted such a stark picture of Puma's hidden liabilities that Woitschätzke and Szymanski decided to destroy it. 'If the contents of this report had become known, we would have had no choice but to file for bankruptcy,' said Woitschätzke. 'We decided this should be avoided at all cost, because it would have had deadly repercussions for the brand.' The two held endless meetings with their bankers, who were rushing for the door. As promised by Alfred Herrhausen, the Deutsche Bank staunchly backed up the managers. It permanently put pressure on the other banks to uphold their credit lines.

In his efforts to redress the company, Hans Woitschätzke began by cleaning up Puma's management. Out of the six former board members, Uli Heyd, in charge of legal affairs, was the sole survivor. At the same time he embarked on what he called a 'creeping clean-up'. Out-of-control expenses were slashed through a 'zero-based budget'. Since Puma's gross margins had slipped below 30 per cent the improvement of its cost structure was given priority over sales growth. Woitschätzke rounded off the closure of French and German production plants, keeping just a pilot plant in Herzogenaurach. And he strove to move Puma out of the downmarket retail outlets which had damaged its reputation.

The disproportionate Becker contract was another burning issue. Woitschätzke braced himself for a tough meeting when he invited Ion Tiriac to discuss changes in the deal. The Romanian stood firm, insisting that Puma should stick to its contract. But Woitschätzke convinced him to relent. 'We went through the whole spectrum, from begging to threats,' he said. His strongest argument was that 'Becker's reputation would take another painful hit if it turned out that Puma had been driven into bankruptcy, just because Boris demanded $5 million from us each year.' Under the new contract, Puma still had at least $20 million to fork out. Tiriac agreed to a cash payment of $4 million, coupled with an 'improvement clause'. If Puma managed a profit over the next five years, Becker would be entitled to a maximum of 20 per cent of that income.

Meanwhile the Deutsche Bank was negotiating the last details for the sale of Puma. It was to be acquired by BTR, a British conglomerate that owned Dunlop, Puma's long-time distributors in the United Kingdom. A final meeting was set up at the Vierjahreszeiten hotel in Munich. But as the Germans pulled out their negotiated contract, the British negotiators demanded one more concession. Manfred Emcke, the supervisory board chairman, whom Deutsche Bank had entrusted with the sale of the company, was so furious that he sent them all packing, killing the deal.

Several months later, Hans Woitschätzke came to the Puma building with an unfamiliar guest. He was introduced to the Puma board members as Herr Muller, a foreign banker who had requested details about the company's strategy and prospects. After the presentation, Uli Heyd fetched the banker's hat and spotted two initials embroidered on the inside, KJ. 'Ha, Herr Muller, I didn't realize that you stole hats,' Heyd quipped.

Klaus Jacobs forced a smile, wondering if the Puma board member had seen through his fake identity. The German investor, owner of Jacobs Suchard, a Swiss confectionery group, had agreed to assume it at the request of Emcke and Woitschätzke. They feared virulent reactions because Klaus Jacobs controlled a chain of discount outlets. Other German retailers would rightly assume that they would lose out on Puma business if the company were taken over by Jacobs. Woitschätzke didn't want to provoke any unrest by publicly holding talks with him. The disguise turned out to be unnecessary, however, as Jacobs turned down the offer, apparently deeming Puma's prospects too shaky.

After several other rejections, the Deutsche Bank was becoming restless. Woitschätzke then came forward with another suggestion: Cosa Liebermann, the Swiss holding that held the Puma licence for Japan and took care of manufacturing arrangements in the Far East. Before his recruitment at Puma, Woitschätzke had been an influential member of the company's board (he resigned to avoid a conflict of interest). In the interval, Cosa Liebermann's sourcing deals with Puma had been cancelled, but Puma's Japanese sales still made up a large chunk of its business.

Two years into the clean-up, the company was still loss-making, on artificial life support. The bankers had faced so many rejections that they had to turn to smaller partners to pull themselves out of this quagmire. In May 1989, they gladly offloaded the Dasslers' 72 per cent stake in Puma to Cosa Liebermann, at an estimated price of $43.5 million, to be split equally between a cash injection into the company and compensation for those selling their shares.

As the Deutsche Bank saw it, the second part of the payment should have been transferred straight to their account, to pay off the Dasslers' remaining debts from the loan they had contracted in early 1987. However, Hans Woitschätzke convinced the Deutsche Bank that the Dasslers should receive at least some of the money from the sale. Once they had sealed a compromise, the Puma Dasslers were apparently left with little more than DM20 million between them.

With that, the Deutsche Bank had severed the last remaining ties between Puma and the Dasslers. Frank and Jörg, Armin's two eldest sons, would not return to the company. While Frank set up a law firm in Herzogenaurach, specializing in sporting-goods matters, his brother ran a printing business. Michael Dassler, Armin's son by Irene, was still studying when Puma was sold off, and none of Gerd's children were given a chance to pursue a career at Puma. It was no longer a family-owned business, and it seemed that the new proprietors could barely wait to erase the family's legacy at the company.

Armin Dassler became increasingly prone to depression. His 'liver trouble' turned out to be cancer, and it was quickly spreading to his bones. After a short bout of chemotherapy, he was advised to return home. He died in the early afternoon of Sunday 14 October 1990, at the age of 61. Although it was the cancer that destroyed his body, Armin Dassler's family remains convinced that he was mortally shattered by the loss of his company. 'Put it this way,' said Irene Dassler, 'he didn't fight.'

Since the two Dassler heirs had passed away, the battles between Adidas and Puma had lost their personal sting. They had spent several decades mostly fighting each other, but they had begun to falter under intense pressure from other market forces, which brought them to the edge of the precipice.

22

Extra Time

Scores of reporters were preparing to rise from their red velvet seats in the meeting room of Rome's Forum Olimpico as João Havelange was wrapping up his press conference. It was the eve of the 1990 World Cup final and they had all gathered to watch the end game, pitting the freshly united Germany against Argentina.

To their surprise, Havelange, still chairman of Fifa, asked them to remain seated, because Adidas had an 'important message' to convey. As the reporters settled back in their seats, the Fifa logos on the screen were replaced with the Adidas trefoil and three beaming men appeared on the stage. Some of the French reporters gasped as they recognized Bernard Tapie, the maverick owner of Olympique Marseille.

Sporting a beige suit with a trefoil pinned to his lapel, the Frenchman hijacked the stage. 'Save for the birth of my children, this is the most beautiful day of my life', he crowed. He explained that he had just taken control of Adidas and its legendary three stripes: a couple of days earlier,

30. *The two most influential Dassler daughters: Inge Bente with her husband,*
Alf, a long-serving second-in-command at Adidas Germany; and Brigitte
Baenkler, in charge of relations with east-European partners.

the four Dassler sisters had signed over their 80 per cent shareholding
in the German company.

Over the previous years, Bernard Tapie had permanently elbowed his
way into the limelight. Starting off as a small-time electronics dealer, he
had risen to prominence by taking over near-defunct companies and
turning them around. He shook up the French establishment with his
charisma, verbosity and go-getting attitude, which earned him a slot as
a the host of a prime-time television show. But Tapie's name became
truly ubiquitous in 1989 when he won a seat affiliated to the socialist
group in the French parliament in a tough district in Marseilles. Nobody
in France could remain indifferent to Tapie. Some regarded him as
the country's answer to the swashbuckling self-made men who ripped
through corporate America with their leveraged buy-outs in the eighties.
He was lionised by business students who yearned to get rid of the
country's staid business establishment. On the other hand, he was reviled
by many alumni of the French elite schools – the ones who ran State-
controlled companies, rarely made a speech without quoting obscure
poets and abhorred insolent outsiders. To them, Bernard Tapie was a

31. *All four daughters held equal shares in Adidas: Karin Essing (left) supervising the marketing department; and Sigrid Malms, the youngest of the daughters, briefly in charge of textiles.*

charlatan, an impudent dare-it-all: a former TV salesman who had twice filed for personal bankruptcy.

While the sports reporters in Rome remained dumbfounded, the news hit business newsrooms like a bombshell. Here was Bernard Tapie, the controversial Frenchman with a swagger and a seventy-four-meter yacht, who had just seized control of a German institution. The deal had been sealed just three days earlier on the drab morning of 4 July 1990, in a meeting room at the Röhm chemicals company in Darmstadt. Brigitte Baenkler, the third Dassler daughter, had struggled to retain her composure that morning as she handed over her father's heritage with the blessing of her three sisters. They would all come to regret it immensely.

Since the sudden death of their brother, Adidas had been rudderless. After several months of chaos, the sisters had entrusted the company's leadership to René Jäggi, a smooth Swiss manager who had worked alongside Horst as a marketing manager. His ordinary youth had taken an unexpected turn when he bought a one-way ticket to Tokyo to prepare for the 1972 Olympics in Munich, in which he hoped to take part as a judoka. Although Jäggi never made it, he returned from Japan with very sharp insights into business and human nature.

As he explained, he conquered the leadership of Adidas by constantly keeping on the move. 'Think of a shark. It is the only fish that cannot keep still, otherwise it sinks. This gives the shark an unbelievably elegant swimming movement', he told the German edition of *Playboy*. 'The type of person that I am is a shark.'

As he took over the reins, René Jäggi was plagued by many aspects of Horst Dassler's legacy – from the production that had stayed largely in Europe, while competitors produced at a fraction of the cost in the Far East; to the bitter rivalries between Herzogenaurach and Landersheim; the lack of zest in the marketing of Adidas; a series of payments made to people he could not even identify, let alone the services they were meant to perform for Adidas; not to mention the bickering Dassler sisters, to whom he had to report.

By 1989, the humiliation of Adidas was official. The brand which had once defined the sports business had not only been thrashed by Nike, it was trailing in third position behind Reebok. To make matters worse, losses suffered in the United States and the United Kingdom were bleeding the company dry.

Jäggi struggled to close down European factories and to inject some marketing chutzpah. He convinced Peter Überroth, former organizer of the Los Angeles Olympics and a celebrated businessman, to steer Adidas in the United States. Yet the ebullient Swiss quickly came to the conclusion that he could not reverse the brand's fortunes without a massive cash injection, which the Dassler sisters were not in a position to provide. With a mix of realism and deal-making enthusiasm, he convinced the Dassler sisters that they didn't have a choice. If they didn't sell, the company was bound to sink.

While René Jäggi attempted to seduce several weighty investors, a French banker discovered the file and ran it by Bernard Tapie. The Frenchman immediately realized that this was his chance to shine. While he had impressed with his other takeovers, they were all small beer compared with Adidas. Without consulting his bankers, he convinced the emissaries of the Dassler sisters that he was the man to restore Adidas to its former glory. But, as the company was on the verge of collapse, they should count themselves lucky to get DM 110 million each.

The deal was extraordinary in many ways. The price of the transaction, DM 440 million for 80 per cent of the shares (while another 15 per cent of the shares had already been sold off to German investors by Horst Dassler's two children, who retained just 5 per cent) valued the whole of Adidas at just DM 550 million. This was far less than the estimates of business reporters who covered the sale in July 1990. Once again, Bernard Tapie had displayed irresistible charm and walked away with a golden deal.

On the other hand, the turnover of Adidas was ten times higher than the sales of all his other holdings combined, and Tapie's coffers were empty. Therefore he had to borrow the entire sum of the takeover and his negotiations with his friendly bankers weren't nearly as sharp as his dealings with the Dasslers: the loan would have to be entirely repaid in two years.

Still, Tapie had no doubts that he could redress Adidas fast enough. He didn't need any marketing consultants or long-term plans, because he had it all sussed out. 'A first-year business student would have grasped the company's problems', he railed. To sum up the company's troubles he pointed to Ivan Lendl, the Adidas-sponsored Czech tennis player who was taking one trophy after the other with a spectacularly joyless game. 'I mean, who on earth would want to look like this guy?' he asked.

When he acquired Adidas, Bernard Tapie kept René Jäggi at the helm. However, the Swiss encountered many of the same problems under Tapie as he had before: the most painful headache was the lack of cash, as Jäggi struggled to pay the bills due for factory closures and marketing investments. Since Tapie urgently had to reimburse his loans, he certainly didn't have money to pump into the company.

And if Jäggi thought that the Dassler sisters were making his life a misery, he didn't have much more joy with Bernard Tapie. While he refused to settle down in Herzogenaurach, the Frenchman loved to tell Jäggi – and the whole world – about his fantastic new ideas for Adidas, which often blatantly contradicted those of the company's management.

Just one year after the acquisition, in July 1991, Bernard Tapie was stuck. He had to repay part of the Adidas loan but he had failed to sell off any of his other assets and didn't have any cash available. The Frenchman therefore convinced his banks, led by the Crédit Lyonnais, to swap some of the debt for Adidas shares. At the same time he raised some cash by selling just over 20 per cent of the Adidas capital to Stephen Rubin, chairman of the Pentland group, a British footwear and sporting goods conglomerate.

Another year down the road, and Bernard Tapie still didn't have any money to repay the second part of his loan, and he couldn't sell any more shares without losing control of Adidas. But at this point he had long forgotten that the Adidas deal had once given him the most beautiful day of his life. In the meantime he had become a government minister, and his business interests were holding him back. So Tapie made it abundantly clear that he would part with Adidas without a fuss.

The obvious candidate to walk away with the prize was Stephen Rubin, yet he was a shrewd deal-maker. He wasn't about to declare his interest, because he knew that Bernard Tapie was driving Adidas into the wall, and he could easily pick up the pieces after the crash. 'In all the deals we did with Tapie, one of the techniques was to sit back and wait, because it seemed likely that he would dig a hole and fall in it', Rubin explained.

Adidas employees were holding their breath as the company was fast heading towards collapse, and there didn't seem to be many investors around who believed it could pull through. They breathed a sigh of relief when, early in the morning on 7 July 1992, Rubin's lawyers declared that he would take over Bernard Tapie's shares in Adidas. Unlike the Frenchman, Rubin had a decades-long track record in the footwear business. Even more convincingly, he was the investor who had made a fortune on the back of Reebok.

But much to the annoyance of Adidas management, the due diligence that was to be completed before the final acquisition dragged on for several months. Stephen Rubin's team kept coming back with more questions, and in the end the bankers and management agreed to issue Rubin an ultimatum. To their amazement, Rubin didn't respond. On 15 October 1992, he declared that he had given up on Adidas, ominously citing 'a number of matters of which Pentland was not previously aware'.

The Rubin episode made it even trickier for the bankers to find another suitor, despite Bernard Tapie breathing down their necks. The financial situation had become so tight that Axel Markus, chief financial officer, knew Adidas was just days away from bankruptcy. Preparing for the worst, Markus walked down to the office of Herbert Hainer, then in charge of Adidas Germany. 'How do you think our German employees would feel,' he asked, 'if we failed to pay salaries on time for October?'

The nightmarish situation came to an end in the middle of a cold night in February 1993. In the plush offices of Banque du Phénix, near

35. Robert Louis-Dreyfus anxiously watches the performance of his team, Olympique de Marseille. He had more joy with Adidas, pushing through reforms that brought the brand back on track.

the Arc du Triomphe in Paris, an army of lawyers and bankers put the finishing touches to a complicated agreement that would seal the fate of Adidas. The deal centred around two French investors, Robert-Louis Dreyfus and Christian Tourres. As their lawyers haggled over the last details, the two men slipped off to the all-night Brasserie Presbourg round the corner for a juicy steak. They couldn't be bothered to stay in the room because they had already got what they wanted: Adidas – and it had been virtually given away.

As part of the deal, which would give rise to an unprecedented damages claim by Bernard Tapie, the Crédit Lyonnais heavily sponsored the two gentlemen and some of their friends to acquire a small stake in Adidas (15 per cent of BTF GmbH, a holding company which itself controlled 95 per cent of Adidas), while the rest of Tapie's shares went to offshore funds. The price of this transaction valued Adidas at about 2.1 billion French francs. However, unbeknownst to Tapie, there was a very generous side-deal: if Robert Louis-Dreyfus and Christian Tourres managed to turn round Adidas, they could buy most of the remaining shares for a fixed sum that valued the three stripes at about 4.4 billion

French francs. If they failed and wanted rid of their 15 per cent package, that wouldn't be a problem either. In fact, they wouldn't even have to reimburse the original loan!

For Herzogenarauch, the upside was that Adidas was now firmly in the hands of hard-hitting managers. Robert Louis-Dreyfus didn't need money since he was the heir to one of France's trading and banking dynasties, but he had still, together with Christian Tourres, amassed a fortune with the sale of IMS, an American market research company. He then made a name for himself as an occasional date for Kim Basinger, star of 9 1/2 *Weeks*, but he was chiefly known in business circles as the somewhat eccentric chief executive who managed to turn round Saatchi & Saatchi, the British advertising company.

What wasn't quite as well-known was that Robert Louis-Dreyfus was also a sports freak, who could recite the exact score and line-up of most international football games since the sixties, not to mention the Olympics. If anybody could take Adidas in the right direction, it would be him.

As the two Frenchmen settled into their executive chairs, a young German manager was parachuted into the hot seat at Puma. Coming after an embarrassing series of failures and continuing losses, the appointment didn't exactly send investors into ecstasy. As for Puma's bankers, they were downright wary when Jochen Zeitz was introduced to them, in June 1993. At thirty, he was the youngest man ever to take over the reins of a listed German company. Tall and athletic, with preppy blond hair, he looked as if he had walked in straight from his graduation ceremony. Sure enough, there would be yet another restructuring plan, and yet another bill for the bankers.

But those at Puma who had worked with Zeitz over the two previous years, when he had been marketing manager, could have testified that he was something special. Focused to the point of coldness, he always knew exactly where he was going – and so far, he had always got there. Zeitz had all the hallmarks of a wunderkind. He began by studying medicine before switching to the European business school and was fluent in six languages. During a stint at Colgate-Palmolive, in Hamburg and New York, he had learned the ropes of marketing. But it was his determination and steely personality that set him apart.

Predictably, Zeitz began by wielding a sharp axe. 'There will be no sacred cows,' he said, and steered Puma back into the black in less than two years. Then, he turned the sports industry on its head by inventing an entirely new business, which he defined as 'sports lifestyle'. His Pumas were not meant to be worn on the pitch, yet they kept the aura of the brand's sports heritage, while also having the flair of high fashion. This was a merger that was good for the margins.

To make it all a little more glamorous, Zeitz teamed up with Arnon Milchan of Regency Enterprises, the film production company behind such blockbusters as *Pretty Woman*. American retailers couldn't believe their luck when they were invited to the brand's US relaunch in 1996 and ended up on a Hollywood studio set. There was a full roster of stars to greet them – invited by Milchan as well as Fox, the television network belonging to News Corp, Rupert Murdoch's media empire, which was a shareholder in Regency.

Gwyneth Paltrow and Brad Pitt were spotted with a formstripe around their heels. As she embarked on her World Tour, Madonna ordered an entire batch of Mostros – the ones with the velcro and picots, inspired from climbing shoes. Zeitz himself felt that the brand had turned the corner when he spotted people queuing up at Jil Sander stores to snatch a pair of the trainers she had designed exclusively for Puma. 'It was an unbelievable sight,' said Zeitz.

Across town, Robert Louis-Dreyfus and Christian Tourres barely had time to watch the progress of their much smaller rival. They were busy closing yet more factories, ending absurd distribution deals and rebuilding the reputation of the three stripes. Much of the foundation work had begun before the two men even set foot in Herzogenaurach, but in the end they were the ones who reaped the rewards.

At the end of 1994, they happily exercised their option to acquire the remaining Adidas shares at a price that valued the company at 4.4 billion French francs. The Crédit Lyonnais was there to finance the deal yet again. They all cashed in on 17 November 1995, when Adidas was launched on the Frankfurt stock exchange. The flotation valued Adidas at the equivalent of 11 billion French francs.

Just like Jochen Zeitz, Robert Louis-Dreyfus invested most in the United States. He settled a deal with Rob Strasser and Peter Moore, two of the men who had made Nike in the early years. They were the odd couple behind the Air Jordan, yet they had left Nike on a sour note and they eagerly took on the daunting Adidas job – establishing new head offices for Adidas USA on the outskirts of Portland, Oregon, just across town from Nike.

As Peter Moore saw it, the three stripes had virtually disappeared from the American market. 'They seemed to be kind of lost in space, and nobody cared,' said the designer. With the rambunctious Strasser at the helm, Adidas USA was duly shaken out of its lethargy, and the brand took off again within months. Sonny Vaccaro, the American agent who had spotted Michael Jordan, joined the team and delivered Kobe Bryant, the Los Angeles Lakers star. Even the New York Yankees would seal an unprecedented deal with Adidas, provoking the wrath of the baseball commissioner.

Those were halcyon years for Adidas. After all the time of chaos and uncertainty, the three stripes were conquering football pitches all over again. Louis-Dreyfus knew that this would have to be a priority when Franz Beckenbauer admitted that Bayern Munich was on the verge of signing with Nike. If he'd allowed the Bavarians to play wearing American shirts, Adidas would have lost its crown jewel: the most prestigious football club in Germany and a long-term Adidas partner. Louis-Dreyfus therefore convinced Beckenbauer to give him one last chance. He had a team work on the presentation flat out for two weeks. The 'Kaiser' was a bit grumpy when he arrived at the Munich planetarium for the pitch, but he was quickly swept up in Adidas' enthusiasm. As soon as the presentation ended he jumped to his feet and told the team, 'You've got it!' The same trick worked with AC Milan, and while they were at it, the Adidas men deployed their charms in Spain as well, winning over Real Madrid.

The three stripes were also on a roll in the United Kingdom, worn by everyone from the Gallagher brothers to Prince Naseem. And there was an obscure young football player from Manchester United. David Beckham had been spotted by one of the Adidas scouts and given a measly contract back in 1993. The managers who welcomed him at the Adidas offices in Stockport were almost embarrassed by the shyness of the teenager.

All of this changed on 17 August 1996, when Manchester United made their way to Selhurst Park for a game against Wimbledon. For the first time that afternoon, David Beckham had agreed to wear a pair of Predator boots. Adidas managers watched intently as he prepared to take a free kick, and they couldn't believe what they saw next: Beckham scored from inside his own half with a stupendous shot that sent the ball soaring over the defenders and right into the corner of the net. 'We had never seen anything like it,' said Aidan Butterworth, the former Leeds player dealing with marketing at Adidas UK. 'It wasn't just the talent but the attitude, just to try it. Then we knew for sure that we had something special on our hands'. As the free kick was replayed over and over, it didn't seem to matter that the tongues of the Predators Beckham was wearing were inscribed with the name of Charlie Miller, a player from Glasgow Rangers.

That 'something special' which Beckham displayed would end up costing Adidas an estimated €4 million each year, but it would reap invaluable publicity as the charismatic player went on to monopolize magazine covers as well as the pitch – epitomizing modern sports marketing as a heady mixture of sport, celebrity and style.

Robert Louis-Dreyfus decided to bid farewell to Adidas shortly after the French victory at the 1998 World Cup, which crowned the return of the three stripes. 'La victoire est en nous,' the slogan devised by Adidas France to inspire some confidence in the French team, turned into a national motto after Zinedine Zidane twice headed the ball into the net, defeating the Nike-clad Brazilians.

Other managers took the Adidas ball and ran with it, led by Herbert Hainer. He was a Bavarian butcher's son, who financed his studies by playing for the second league team of Landshut and began his career at Procter & Gamble. In other words, he had been brought up to look after the pennies, knew all he needed to know about football and learned about marketing from some of the masters in the art.

By the time the Athens Olympics opened in July 2004, Adidas had regained such strength that Paul Fireman, chairman of Reebok, invited Hainer for a coffee on his yacht *Solemates*. Only a few years earlier Reebok had humiliated Adidas by cruising in ahead of them in financial results. But by 2004, Fireman felt he could no longer sustain the fight against Nike on his own, and he called on Hainer to join forces. One year later, Adidas announced that it had swallowed Reebok.

The sports business had gone a long way since Adi Dassler turned up with his duffel bag at the Berlin Olympics. It had turned into a huge industry, run by a handful of sporting-goods titans which fought each other with slick advertising and marketing campaigns, transforming the world's largest sporting events into marketing extravaganzas.

But the ultimate battlefield was still the football pitch. Since Nike had become part of the game in the nineties, tournaments had turned into marketing duels as well as football ones. The 2006 football World Cup was the backdrop for a multimillion dollar battle of the bootmakers, pitting Adidas squarely against Nike.

The American brand made original use of its stars: in the 'Joga Bonito' commercials that toured the world many times over by way of the internet, Ronaldinho could be seen displaying his amazing talent and his toothy laugh as a kid playing indoor football, while Zlatan Ibrahimovic showed how to kick around a piece of chewing gum. Unfortunately the Nike players didn't perform quite as impressively on the pitch.

The campaign orchestrated by Adidas, at a cost of an estimated €250 million, bore all the hallmarks of a military operation: the public were bombarded at regular intervals for several months, all around the world, as the company launched its latest boots and balls. The centrepiece was a massive advertising campaign that told everyone 'Impossible is nothing.' The campaign even had its own monument, the Adidas World of Football, a smaller but otherwise exact replica of the Berlin Olympic stadium, erected on the lawn of the Reichstag, the country's Parliament building.

After all the build-up, the end game was a repeat of the fiercest derby in the sports business, featuring the three-striped French team against the Puma-clad Azzuris. Jochen Zeitz had saved Puma as a sports lifestyle brand, and it had rebounded so strongly that Puma had narrowed the gap between it and its competitors. It confidently claimed its position among the leading sports brands in world, leaning on its rich football heritage. Pelé was wheeled out for commercials, and Puma secured its presence on the pitch by obtaining the endorsements of many African teams. In the end, with a mixture of luck and flair, the smallest of the large contenders lifted the trophy with the Italian players.

There was no way that anyone catching a glimpse at the event could escape the hoardings lining the pitch or the pervading presence of the sponsors. Since Horst Dassler had opened the floodgates, international companies continued to pour their money into sport – and on an ever larger scale.

The zealots who roamed around Olympic villages in the seventies to track down and remove any corporate logos would have had a fit at the latest edition of the Games and there was worse to come: Adidas spent an estimated $80 million to outfit officials and the Chinese team at the opening and medal ceremonies of the 2008 Olympics – a combination which Horst Dassler himself could only have contemplated in his wildest dreams, and the ultimate example of collusion between the interests of sports, business and politics.

The sports business has changed beyond recognition since the Dasslers invented it. Long gone are the days when a sneaky employee could just leave a pair of boots in the locker room with a couple of banknotes. Hushed conversations have been replaced by the shuffling of lawyers' loafers in the corridors of huge sports agencies. And some of the unassuming athletes who were grateful just to go along for the ride have turned into millionaire superstars who, under pressure, might just about agree to tie their own laces.

Adi and Rudolf Dassler could never have begun to picture it all.

Epilogue

The Sportsmen

Jesse Owens returned from Berlin to a tickertape parade in New York, but was banned for life from the American Athletics Union because he refused to take part in one of the exhibition races it organized in Europe after the Berlin Olympics. Owens embarked on a string of short-lived business ventures, making ends meet by racing horses and dogs. He died of lung cancer in March 1980. At the suggestion of Nazi hunter Simon Wiesenthal, the avenue leading to the Olympic stadium in Berlin was named after him.

Fritz Walter remained true to his club in Kaiserslautern, turning down numerous appetizing foreign offers until he hung up his boots in 1959. Many German pundits regard Walter as the most talented player their country has ever produced. He endeared himself to a wider public with his modesty and down-to-earth attitude. Fritz Walter died in June 2002, shortly after his beloved wife, Italia. Two members of the 1954 Hungarian team attended the memorial ceremony for Walter in the Kaiserslautern stadium that bears his name.

Armin Hary retired from athletics shortly after the Rome Olympics, where he was the first runner blatantly to exploit the rivalry between the Dassler brothers. This exit was partly prompted by a ban by the German athletics federation. He was accused of unfairly criticizing German sports officials and cheating the federation with inflated expense claims. Hary later spent some time in jail for his role in a property swindle.

Uwe Seeler remained with Adidas as a sales representative for north Germany until the early nineties. He never regretted his decision to turn down Milan's exorbitant offer, judging that 'I'm a down-to-earth kind of guy'. He disapprovingly watched the young football players who took their comfort for granted. The attitude would have been anathema to Adi Dassler. 'He would have been happy to throttle a few of them,' Seeler thought. He lives in Hamburg with his wife, Ilka.

Gordon Banks went on to be celebrated as one of the most remarkable goalkeepers in football. His club, Leicester City, amazingly placed him on the transfer list just months after England's 1966 victory, but he continued to shine at international games. His most stupendous save occurred at the 1970 World Cup, when Banks lunged at an apparently unstoppable header by Pelé. In 1972 his career in England was halted by a car crash in which 'Banks of England' lost an eye.

Franz Beckenbauer consolidated his position as the German football Kaiser, heading up the organizing committee for the 2006 World Cup. It did not seem to strike anyone as a conflict of interest that, at the same time, the smooth-talking Beckenbauer remained on the Adidas payroll as a lifelong ambassador.

Günter Netzer managed to retain his wild mane, but he swapped his Puma boots for more businesslike loafers. He had a long career as a sports columnist before assuming a leading role in the sports business by taking part in the buy-out of the rights that belonged to the Kirch empire. Backed up by Robert Louis-Dreyfus, among others, he helped to set up a new sports marketing company called In Front, that handled the television rights for the 2006 World Cup.

Pelé became the most prestigious advertisement for football in the United States when he ended his career at the New York Cosmos. He went on to become Brazilian sports minister. In this position, he lashed out at the alleged corruption in football and pushed through the Pelé Law, designed to emancipate players from greedy and inept club managers. He acts as an ambassador for the United Nations, Unicef and Puma.

Ilie Nastase remains a familiar sight at international tennis tournaments, where he enjoys playing seniors competitions. He briefly embarked on a political career, culminating in a failed campaign to be elected mayor of Bucharest. Since the country opened up he has invested in Romanian media and real estate. Nastase admits that he has calmed down a little since his sporting heyday, 'otherwise I would be mad by now'. He lives in Paris and Bucharest with his third wife, Amalia, and their daughter.

The Family

Inge Dassler and **Karin Essing** both retired from business after the sale of their stake in Adidas. While Karin Essing remained in Franconia, where she suddenly died of cancer in 2006, Inge Dassler moved to the Bahamas. Her former husband, **Alfred Bente,** who ably steered much of the company's expansion in Germany, started a new life in the south of Portugal.

Brigitte Baenkler continued to run the Herzogspark hotel, which she bought back from Bernard Tapie. She turned it into a highly rated establishment, with a wide range of sports facilities and pictures of her illustrious parents adorning the walls.

Christoph Malms, husband of Sigrid Dassler, was placed at the head of ISL, the sports marketing company founded by Horst Dassler. This triggered the departure of the firm's two leading executives, Klaus Hempel and Jürgen Lenz, who went on to found a competing company, Team Marketing. ISL was declared bankrupt in May 2001. A Swiss prosecutor spent several years investigating the circumstances of the failure and indicted six people linked with ISL. By then the Malms couple had disintegrated. **Sigrid Dassler** moved to the Bahamas with their children.

Suzanne Dassler, daughter of Horst and Monika Dassler, lost her last interest in the family's business with the bankruptcy of ISL. When Sepp Blatter alleged that the Dasslers had been behind illicit payments in the sports business, she forced a gag order on the Fifa chairman. She moved to Switzerland and decided to reconcile with the rest of the family. Her brother, **Adi Dassler Jr,** briefly owned a Los Angeles restaurant and set up a small sneaker-making company called AdiOne. Like his father, Adi Jr. died prematurely, defeated by cancer at the age of just forty-three, in October 2006.

Gerd Dassler retired and remained in Herzogenaurach, where he is described as the town's highest-paid golfer. He resides on the Christoph Dassler Strasse with his second wife, Lydia. They live in the house that Gerd inherited from his father, Rudolf, as part of the acrimonious settlement with his late brother Armin – the one with the large garden, where Pelé and Eusebio once kicked about with the children. He admits that the family disputes still give him nightmares.

Frank Dassler caused a furore in Herzogenaurach, when it was announced that he had been appointed head of legal affairs at Adidas, in June 2004. He courageously broke the absurd taboo that made it unthinkable for a Puma heir to cross the river. Longtime Puma employees fumed that Frank's father, Armin Dassler, must be turning in his grave. **Irene Dassler**, Armin's widow, expressed the same views in a local tabloid. She privately retracted her statements and congratulated Frank on his prestigious appointment. He lives in Herzogenaurach with his wife and son.

The Brits

Robbie Brightwell still spends many of his evenings around the track as a high-level coach of the British athletics team, grooming a brood of promising young sprinters and middle-distance runners (no lack of motivation with the London Olympics in sight). He left Le Coq Sportif to head up several other sports companies but remained in Congleton. 'Meet my girlfriend,' he says, introducing Ann Brightwell-Packer, the stunning Olympic medallist in Tokyo. All their three sons are high-performance sportsmen.

Stuart Humphreys continued to run Umbro with several outside managers after both his brother, John, and his brother-in-law, Jim Terris, died. It declined sharply after the split from Adidas, encouraging Stuart to sell off the entire company to Jack Stone, an American partner, in 1992. Seven years later the buyer was in trouble and Umbro was passed on to a group of hard-nosed English managers, supported by a private equity firm. They revived Umbro as an international brand specializing in football, still endorsed by the England team. Stuart Humphreys died in the spring of 2005.

Derek Ibbotson continued to hand out Puma shoes and bonuses until the early nineties. When the brand's British business was transferred to Slazenger in 1974, Armin Dassler demanded that Ibbotson should be part of the package. Among his most prominent catches were Olympic gold medallists Jonathan Edwards (triple-jumper) and Linford Christie (sprinter), who agreed to wear contact lenses with an imprinted Puma logo. Ibbotson left Puma in 1992 to retire in Ossett, Yorkshire.

Patrick Nally long struggled to keep his business going in sports marketing, after Horst Dassler had declared him persona non grata. He moved on to other forms of entertainment, investing in musicals and the construction of football arenas, but his business outlook changed dramatically after the demise of ISL, when several of Horst's companions exited the stage. 'A cloud lifted and people who had ignored me for years began to recognize me again,' said Nally. Among many other projects he is involved in raising funds for Unicef.

The Chief Executives

Gilberte Beaux runs an investment company in Paris, but she spends much of her time in Argentina, where she steers several investment projects and runs a large *estancia*. Her holding company, Basic International Holdings, is involved in an array of other companies. Beaux is also at the forefront of a French women's group that is striving to organize an international women's forum, along the lines of Davos or Porto Alegre.

René Jäggi continued to dabble in the sports business, reversing the fortunes of FC Basel and jumping to the rescue of FC Kaiserslautern. He put together an intricate package to salvage the club, which was on the brink of insolvency and under financial investigation. Partly owing to his arrangements with Bernard Tapie when he left Adidas, Jäggi has invested in a string of other companies, from the Anfi Palace in Mürren to Romika, the defunct German shoe company. He likes to be portrayed as a charismatic and hard-hitting turnaround manager. He lives in Kaiserslautern and Basel, with his wife and two children.

The Investors

André Guelfi continued to cultivate his skills as a wheeler-dealer. This briefly landed him in jail, when he was arrested in connection with the Elf bribery scandal of the late 1990s. He was accused of acting as an intermediary for the French oil company in its efforts to secure exploration deals. Horst Dassler's former sidekick was initially given a three-year suspended sentence but the prosecution appealed, successfully requesting a custodial term.

During his stay at La Santé prison in Paris, Guelfi occupied a cell adjacent to Bernard Tapie. The two got chatting when Tapie noticed that Guelfi could not walk comfortably around the courtyard and offered the older man the loan of his Adidas trainers. They later concocted deals together in Russia.

Bernard Tapie was incarcerated for his part in a bribery scandal at Olympique de Marseille. Due to his personal bankruptcy, he could not return to business and switched to acting, obtaining a lead role as Inspector Valence in a French TV cop series and starring in a play titled *Un beau salaud* (a neat bastard).

At the same time, Tapie led a crusade against Crédit Lyonnais, claiming that he had been fleeced in the sale of Adidas. He argued that, as part of the arrangements with Robert Louis-Dreyfus, the bank had virtually sold Adidas to itself. He further claimed that Crédit Lyonnais had sold Adidas on the cheap, as part of a crooked deal that would enable the bank to reap a large portion of the profits in a subsequent sale.

French judges provoked an outcry in September 2005 when they deemed Crédit Lyonnais to be guilty and awarded unprecedented damages of €135 million to Tapie (to be paid for by French taxpayers). The French government referred the case to the Court of Cassation and Tapie tasted victory in October 2006 as its chief prosecutor vigorously backed him up – stating that the Crédit Lyonnais had committed a 'massive fault', and suggesting that Tapie's damages should in fact be raised to more than €145 million. Just three days later, however, the Court of Cassation dashed Tapie's hopes of a spectacular financial recovery by rejecting the Appeal Court's verdict and the prosecutor's judgement, and referring the case back to the Appeal Court.

Robert Louis-Dreyfus briefly hired Bernard Tapie as a manager at Olympique de Marseille. However, this startling partnership was short lived. Louis-Dreyfus remained the owner of Olympique de Marseille, which brought him nothing but losses and harassment. At the same time, and while continuing his battle with illness, he built up a thriving telecommunications arm in the Louis-Dreyfus family empire. He often works from a palazzo on the lake of Lugano, where he welcomes guests in a pair of Adidas flip-flops.

Notes

CHAPTER 1: The Dashing Dassler Boys

p. 5 'English weed': *Deutsche Turn Zeitung*, German gymnastics newspaper, as quoted in Dirk Bitzer and Bernd Wilting, *Stürmen für Deutschland (die Geschichte des deutschen Fussballs von 1933 bis 1954)*, Campus Verlag, 2003.

p. 5 'These two were inseparable': conversation with Klaus Zehlein, 8 July 2004, Herzogenaurach.

p. 7 Background on Karhu provided by Jani Pösö, who is compiling a book on the company's history, September 2005.

p. 10 'Rudolf was a bit of a peacock': Betti Bilwatsch (née Strasser), interview 8 July 2004, Lauf an der Pegnitz.

p. 12 Registration for NSDAP membership: Bundesarchiv Berlin, NSDAP-Zentralkartei.

Details in this chapter not specifically noted above are drawn to a large extent from several excellent articles by a number of local historians.

CHAPTER 2: The Owens Coup

p. 13 Background on sports under Nazism is drawn from several referenced sources, predominantly Gerhard Fischer and Ulrich Lindner, *Stürmer für Hitler*, Verlag die Werksatt, 1999.

p. 15 Max Schmeling anecdotes: Donald McRae, *In Black and White: the untold story of Joe Louis and Jesse Owens*, Simon & Schuster, 2002, and George von der Lippe (ed.), *Max Schmeling: an autobiography*, Bonus Books, 1998.

p. 17 Background on British team at the Berlin Olympics from the above noted books as well as research kindly shared by specialist British historians Don Anthony and Philip Barker.

p. 18 'We woke up' and all other quotes from Dorothy Odam: telephone conversation with Dorothy Odam-Tyler, June 2005

p. 18 Background on Foster mostly provided by David Foster, who relaunched the Foster brand in 2004.

p. 19 'animal qualities': as quoted in McRae, *In Black and White*.

p. 20 'These are outstanding shoes': American track and field coach as quoted in the 1939 Adidas catalogue featuring the 'Friedenskollektion', Nuremberg state archive.

p. 22 'She was a serious person' and 'Her brother-in-law's family': from Hermann Utermann, 'Der Mann der Adidas war', unpublished ms., 1983.

p. 22 'Käthe had learned to stand up': interview with Betti Bilwatsch, 8 July 2004, Lauf an der Pegnitz.

p. 22 'Heil Hitler': correspondence as part of an investigation by the finance authorities into suspected illegal profits, in May 1944, which led to a fine of 4,000 Reichsmarks (State Archive of Nuremberg, Regierung von Mittelfranken, 78/3930–1).

p. 22 'It was Adi Dassler': telephone conversation with Hans Zenger, March 2005.

CHAPTER 3: Two Brothers at War

p. 23 Assignments of shoe companies under the Nazi regime: files of the Wirtschaftsgruppe Lederindustrie (Bundesarchiv Berlin R13, XIII).

p. 23 Details regarding Adi Dassler's assignment in the Wehrmacht: Utermann, 'Der Mann der Adidas war'.

p. 24 'Kampf' and 'Blitz': price list included in the wartime investigation of Gebrüder Dassler by the finance inspectorate, State Archive of Nuremberg.

p. 25 Request for Russian workers: correspondence, Fachgruppe Schuhindustrie der Wirtschaftsgruppe Lederindustrie, Landersarbeitsamtsbezirk Bayern (Bundesarchiv Berlin, R13 XIII, 250).

pp. 26, 27 'Rudolf bluntly rejected her pleas', 'Here are the bloody bastards' and anecdote: interview with Betti Bilwatsch, 8 July 2004, Lauf an der Pegnitz.

pp. 27, 28 'I will not hesitate', 'My brother-in-law apparently had some high-placed contacts' and the details on the parachuting boots patent: extract from a letter written by Rudolf Dassler, as quoted by Käthe Dassler in her statement to the denazification committee on 11 November 1946 (Adolf Dassler denazification file, Archiv Amtsgericht Erlangen, Akte 625/VI/14B46).

pp. 28–9 'My disapproval of Himmler's police rule' and 'I expected that': statement by Rudolf Dassler to the American authorities, dated 1 July 1946, Hammelburg (Rudolf Dassler file, United States Army Intelligence and Security Command, Fort George G. Meade).

p. 28 Rudolf Dassler's war tale: compiled from his written description of his wartime activities; his more formal statements to the US authorities; the denazification file of Adolf Dassler; and the investigations of the US authorities into the wartime activities of Rudolf Dassler, archived by the intelligence service of the US army and declassified for the purpose of this book under the Freedom of Information Act.

p. 30 'Liberation of Herzogenaurach: Kriegsende und Neubeginn, Herzogenaurach 1945', booklet compiled by Klaus-Peter Gäbelein and published by Heimatverein Herzogenaurach.

p. 31 Tale of Rudolf's last war months: unofficial statement by Rudolf Dassler, 'Politische Zuverlässigkeit', dated 6 September 1945, written on Dassler-headed paper.

CHAPTER 4: The Split

p. 33 American internment camps: Lutz Niethammer, 'Allierte Internierungs-lager in Deutschland nach 1945', in Christian Jansen (comp.), *Von der Aufgabe der Freiheit*, Akademie Verlag, 1995.

p. 34 Testimony of Friedrich Block in a statement to the American authorities in Hammelburg, 30 June 1946, included in the US Intelligence Service file.

p. 34 Findings of US investigating officer in US Intelligence Service file.

p. 36 All arguments and witness accounts put forward by Adolf Dassler are extracted from a letter to the Spruchkammer (the jurisdiction in charge of the denazification file), Höchstadt a.d. Aisch, dated 22 July 1946, and appendices (Adolf Dassler's denazification file).

p. 38 'Rudolf Dassler further accuses my husband' and 'The speeches held inside and outside': Käthe Dassler's statement to the denazification committee, 11 November 1946.

p. 38 Mitläufer verdict: issued by Spruchkammer Höchstadt a.d. Aisch, Sitz Herzogenaurach, on 22 November 1946, Adolf Dassler's denazification file.

p. 41 Registration of the three stripes confirmed in a letter by Dr Wetzel, patent lawyer, dated 31 March 1949.

p. 43 Background on Zatopek: David Wallechinsky, *The Complete Book of the Olympics*, Aurum Press, 2000.

p. 44 The Karhu three stripes: anecdote recounted by Jani Pösö, Karhu company historian.

p. 44 Puma ads featuring Josy Barthel: *Rudolf Dassler 70*, privately published by the Dassler family to mark Rudolf Dassler's seventieth birthday.

CHAPTER 5: Screw Them On!

p. 45 Rudolf Dassler's remark to Sepp Herberger: 'Deutschlands grösster Famili-enkrach', *Neue Illustrierte Revue*, 2 February 1968.

p. 45 'The Führer is very excited': from Goebbels' diaries as translated in Simon Kuper, *Ajax, the Dutch, the War: football in Europe during the Second World War*, Orion, 2003.

p. 46 More background on German football during the war: Ulrich Hesse-Lichtenberger, *Tor! The story of German Football*, WSC Books, 1992, and Fritz Walter's autobiography *3:2, Die Spiele zur Weltmeisterschaft*, Stiebner Verlag, 2000.

p. 47 Details on early English football boots: Ian McArthur and David Kemp, *Elegance Borne of Brutality: an eclectic history of the football boot*, Two Heads Publishing, 1995.

p. 49 Details on Sepp Herberger in Switzerland: Jürgen Leinemann, *Sepp Her-berger: Ein Leben, eine Legende*, Rororo, 1998, and the feature film *Das Wunder von Bern* by Sonke Wortmann.

p. 51 'What a Dassler!': *Daily Sketch*, July 1954, as quoted in Adidas-Salomon Group, *Making a Difference*, Adidas-Salomon Group, 1998.

p. 51 Puma's claim is contained in an ad placed before the 1954 World Cup, in which they boasted that the winners of that year's German league champion-ship, Hannover 96, had won the title in Puma boots with screw-in studs.

p. 52 Details on Stanley Matthews' boots: Stanley Matthews, *The Way it Was*, Headline, 2000.

p. 53 'If Adi felt': interview with Horst Widmann, 13 January 2005, Herzog-enaurach.

p. 53 'He was particularly prolific': interview with Heinrich Schwegler, 5 February 2004, Herzogenaurach.

p. 54 'He was completely obsessed': interview with Uwe Seeler, 4 February 2005, Hamburg.

p. 55 'Sometimes we made mistakes': interview with Peter Janssen, 3 July 2003, Herzogenaurach.

p. 56 Anecdotes of Sporthaus Löhr and lawsuit on Adidas slogan: Utermann, 'Der Mann der Adidas War'.

p. 57 'If there had been a hole left': quote published in unknown British news-paper, as cited by *Sports Illustrated*, 10 March 1969, in its cover article 'The $100,000 Payoff: No Goody Two-Shoes', by John Underwood.

p. 57 'Puma attempted to paralyse us': Utermann, 'Der Mann der Adidas War'.

p. 57 'with active support from Adi Dassler': Möbus company brochure.

CHAPTER 6: Olympic Handouts

p. 59 'My father wasn't exactly bubbly': Paulheinz Gruppe, *Revolution im Welts-port*, Hase & Koehler, 1992, which provides most of the details on Horst Dassler's childhood.

p. 59 'Rudolf wanted a child': interview with Betti Bilwatsch, 8 July 2004, Lauf an der Pegnitz.

p. 60 'The relationship was not easy': interview with Peter Janssen, 3 July 2003, Herzogenaurach.

p. 61 Details on the Sports Depot: correspondence with Ron Clarke, June 2005, and from his book, *The Measure of Success: a personal perspective*, Lothian Books, 2004.

p. 62 'They were relatively expensive': telephone conversation with Chris Chataway, June 2005.

p. 63 'We all trailed over': interview with Derek Ibbotson, 27 October 2004, Ossett.

p. 63 'None of the American companies': telephone conversation with Al Oerter, November 2004.

p. 63 'It was a blessing and a problem' and other Severn quotes in this chapter: telephone interview with Chris Severn, June 2005.

p. 63 'They were just': telephone conversation with Bobby Morrow, March 2005.

p. 66 The Hary precedent is particularly well-documented in Adidas-Salomon Group, *Making a Difference*.

p. 68 'I gave him shoes' and 'It was truly hurtful': interview with Werner von Moltke, 29 July 2003, Nieder Olm.

CHAPTER 7: The Alsatian Plot

p. 70 'For our company': telephone conversation with Georges-Philippe Gerst, who supplied many of the details on the early days of Adidas France, January 2005.

p. 71 'He just didn't care': interview with Alain Ronc, 20 June 2003, Boulogne.

p. 71 'Three groups of people': correspondence with Pat Doran (see chapter 20).

p. 72 'He asked if my prospective wife': interview with Alain Ronc, 20 June 2003, Boulogne.

p. 73 'It was exhilarating': interview with Johan van den Bossche, 30 January 2004, Clichy.

p. 74 'They pressured the retailers': telephone conversation with Just Fontaine, 7 June 2005.

p. 74 Anecdote on the Spanish balls: interview with Peter Lewin, 3 June 2003, Madrid.

p. 75 'Otherwise he asked': interview with Jean-Claude Schupp, 30 April 2004, Monaco.

p. 77 'The old man' and 'We offered to have him chauffeured': interview with Irene Dassler, 13 January 2005, Nuremberg.

CHAPTER 8: England Scores, Germany Wins

p. 79 Barney Goodman anecdote: interview with Ron Goodman, his son, 2 November 2005, London.

p. 79 'They didn't look like' and 'I ignored the jibes': telephone conversation with Jimmy Gabriel, 27 October 2005.

p. 79 Roy Gratrix anecdote: Jimmy Armfield, *Right Back to the Beginning*, Headline, 2004.

p. 80 Umbro history: interview with Stuart Humphreys, interviewed 25 October 2004, Wilmslow, and telephone conversation with Charles Humphreys, 22 November 2005.

p. 81 'He was a Humphrey Bogart figure': telephone conversation with Charles Humphreys, 22 November 2005, and ensuing correspondence.

p. 81 'We were always fishing': telephone conversation with Bobby Robson, June 2005.

p. 81 Relationship between Umbro and Adidas: further details provided by Jackie Wood, former management secretary who produced the minutes of some meetings between executives of the two companies.

p. 82 'My father was gone for six weeks': telephone conversation with Charles Humphreys, 22 November 2005.

pp. 82–4 Arrangements made by Jim Terris, 'These people had never heard' and 'I thought of him': interview with Ron Goodman, 2 November 2005, London.

p. 84 Puma's preparations for the competition: interview with Derek Ibbotson, 27 October 2004, Ossett. All Derek Ibbotson quotes in this chapter issued from the same interview.

p. 85 'If you managed to withstand': letter from dean of Hamburg University as quoted in Hesse-Lichtenberger, *Tor!*

p. 85 Telephone conversation between Adi Dassler and Uwe Seeler: interview with Uwe Seeler, 4 February 2005, Hamburg.

p. 86 'There was a cobbler': interview with Franz Beckenbauer, 25 September 2003, Kaiserslautern.

p. 87 'It was a very awkward situation': interview with Stuart Humphreys, 25 October 2004, Wilmslow.

p. 87 'I'm sure they were not very happy': telephone conversation with Eusebio, June 2005.

p. 89 Gordon Banks' observations about the relatively poor earnings of the player in Gordon Banks, *Banksy: my autobiography*, Michael Joseph, 2002.

p. 89 'Imagine that': Alan Ball, *Playing Extra Time*, Sidgwick & Jackson, 2002.

CHAPTER 9: Dirty Tricks in Mexico

p. 91 'It's time for black people': McRae, *In Black and White*.

p. 92 'They got the money': Underwood, 'No Goody Two-Shoes'.

p. 94 'The whole container' and 'They came to fetch us': interview with Peter Janssen, 3 July 2003, Herzogenaurach.

p. 94 'I placed it in my handbag': interview with Irene Dassler, 13 January 2005, Nuremberg.

p. 95 'She cried her eyes out' and 'The detention was dreadful': Art Simburg as quoted in Paul Zimmermann's version of the story in the *New York Post*, 3 May 1972.

p. 95 'Why should I sit around . . . ?': Underwood, 'No Goody Two-Shoes'.

p. 96 David Hemery anecdote and quote: telephone conversation with him, 6 June 2005.

p. 98 Dick Fosbury anecdote related to me at the World Athletics Championships in Paris, August 2003.

CHAPTER 10: The Overgrown Son

p. 99 'All that mattered was size': interview with Klaus Hempel, 7 April 2004, Lucerne.

p. 99 'Forget Puma and the other brands': interview with Günter Sachsenmaier, 23 November 2004, Ottersthal.

p. 100 Details on the Spanish situation: interview with Peter Lewin, 3 June 2003, Madrid.

p. 101 Details on the history of Adidas in the United States: in part from interview with Peter Rduch, former export manager, who began to study this area for the company, 6 February 2003, Herzogenaurach.

pp. 101, 102 'The growth was exponential' and 'We were ordering': interview with Gary Dietrich, 12 August 2004, Condon, Montana.

p. 102 'I once requested an entire container': interview with Bill Closs Sr, 13 August 2004, Big Fork, Montana.

p. 103 'The internal competition': interview with Charles Hesse, 23 November 2004, Eckartswiller.

p. 103 'Once we had finished': interview with Peter Rduch, 6 February 2003, Herzogenaurach.

p. 104 'Horst thoroughly prepared': interview with Gerhard Prochaska, 10 August 2002, La Baume de Transit.

p. 104 Most details on the launch of the Superstar and quotes from Chris Severn: telephone conversation with Chris Severn, June 2005.

p. 107 'It was damned complicated': telephone conversation with Robert Haillet, April 2005.

p. 108 'I got really annoyed': telephone conversation with Stan Smith, 5 April 2005.

p. 109 'My friend Horst': interview with Ilie Nastase, 9 December 2004, Paris.

pp. 110, 111 'Horst asked us', 'Horst told us' and 'When they came to Landersheim': interview with Günter Sachsenmaier, 23 November 2004, Ottersthal.

p. 111 'The next day': interview with Peter Lewin, 3 June 2003, Madrid.

CHAPTER 11: From Head to Toe

p. 114 'Every athlete in Munich': telephone conversation with John Bragg, March 2005.

p. 115 Details on the early days at Nike: drawn to a large extent from J. B. Strasser and Laurie Becklund, *Swoosh: the unauthorized story of Nike and the men who played there*, Harcourt Brace Jovanovich, 1991, notably the anecdote on Bill Bowerman in Munich.

p. 116 Guzzling contest anecdote: telephone conversation with John Bragg, March 2005.

p. 118 'Horst, you won't spare me anything!': Grupe, *Horst Dassler*.

p. 118 'You must be out of your mind': interview with Günter Sachsenmaier, 23 November 2004, Ottersthal.

p. 119 'He had it all in his head': interview with Alain Ronc, 20 June 2003, Boulogne.

p. 119 'This gave the impression': correspondence with Georges Kiehl, who further provided the details on Cali.

p. 120 'They were putting the squeeze': interview with Bill Closs Sr, 13 August 2004, Big Fork, Montana.

p. 121 Anecdote on Borsumij Wehry: interview with Jan van de Graaf, former head of the Adidas unit at the company, 18 April 2005, Etten-Leur.

p. 121 'In our frenetic drive': interview with Alain Ronc, 20 June 2003, Boulogne.

p. 121 'The situation was crazy enough': interview with Peter Rduch, 6 February 2003, Herzogenaurach.

pp. 121–3 Details on the English and quotes: interview with Robbie Brightwell, 26 October 2004, Congleton.

p. 123 'The retailers would have': telephone conversation with Joe Kirchner, 21 March 2005.

p. 124 'When German managers': interview with Jean Wendling, 23 September 2003, Bitschoffen.

p. 124 'The boss sometimes told us': interview with Uwe Seeler, 4 February 2005, Hamburg.

CHAPTER 12: The Pelé Pact

pp. 125–6 Many details of the Pelé pact: interviews with Helmut Fischer, former advertising manager at Puma, 5 February 2004, Herzogenaurach, and Hans Nowak, formerly in sports promotion at Puma, 4 July 2003, Munich.

p. 126 'the situation was just too ridiculous': correspondence with Hans Henningsen, June 2004 to March 2005.

p. 127 The anecdotes surrounding Cruyff's contracts with Cor du Buy stem from the former distributor's files, including numerous press clippings, original contracts, correspondence and internal memos.

p. 127 'complete codswallop': correspondence with du Buy's lawyer in the Cruyff case.

p. 128 'The truth of the matter': quoted in nearly every national Dutch newspaper, 4 September 1968.

p. 128 'We would be grateful': letter to Johan Cruyff in the du Buy files.

p. 129 'Lieber Horst': letter from Horst Dassler in the du Buy files, along with the reply.

p. 130 Further details on the Cruyff dispute with the KNVB: interviews with Jan van de Graaf, head of the unit that distributed Adidas in the Netherlands at the time, 18 April 2005, Etten-Leur, and Jan Huijbregts, secretary general of the KNVB, 19 April 2005, Leusden.

p. 130 'elegance', 'inventiveness' and 'genius': various foreign newspapers as quoted in Hesse-Lichtenberger, *Tor!*

pp. 132, 133 'He didn't want to know' and 'some extra money': interview with Horst Widmann, 10 February 2005, Herzogenaurach.

p. 133 'It was phenomenal': interview with Gerd Dassler, 2 July 2003, Herzogenaurach.

p. 134 'It was a thorny matter': interview with Irene Dassler, 13 January 2005, Nuremberg, and for all quotes from Irene Dassler in this chapter.

p. 135 Anecdote of secret meetings between Adi and Rudolf Dassler: interview with Horst Widmann, who remembered arranging them, 10 February 2005, Herzogenaurach.

CHAPTER 13: Politics

p. 139 'I'm fine, John': interview with John Boulter, 25 September 2002, Saverne.

p. 141 'There were these general secretaries' and 'The gold service': interview with Gerhard Prochaska, 10 August 2002, La Baume de Transit.

p. 142 'Those who had never': interview with André Guelfi, 30 July 2003, Paris.

p. 142 'Once they had finished': telephone conversation with John Bragg, March 2005.

p. 142 Anecdotes on the Terrasse Hotel: interview with Jacky Guellerin, 3 May 2004, Courbevoie.

p. 143 'He had the amazing ability' and 'At the end of an evening': interview with Patrick Nally, 22 July 2003, London.

p. 144 Karl-Heinz Huba on the payroll: memo by René Jäggi to Adidas managing directors, dated 18 May 1992, in which he writes that: 'For many years K.-H. Huba was on the secret "sport politics" payroll of one of our employees in France, who obviously was highly regarded by Huba. Despite much internal "sport political" resistance, I put an end to all such payments. Since then I have been the target of continuing attacks.'

p. 144 'On the rare occasions': telephone conversation with John Bragg, March 2005.

p. 144 Most details on Christian Jannette's involvement: interview with Christian Jannette, 23 September 2003, Illkirch.

p. 146 'Others had to wait': interview with Georg Wieczisk, 15 January 2004, Berlin.

p. 146 Walter Cierpinski story: Kees Kooman, *Kinderen van Pheidippides: de marathon, van Abebe Bikila tot Emil Zatopek*, Tiron Sport, 2005.

p. 147 'My opinion is that': Stasi reports into the activities of Horst Dassler and Adidas, by informant 'Möwe'. Quote extracted from a report titled 'Adidas und Einfluss auf verschiedene Organisationen und Wahlen in den internationalen Sportgremien', undated. (Zentralarchiv, der Bundesbeauftragte für die Unterlagen des Staatssicherheitsdienstes der ehemaligen Deutschen Demokratischen Republik, archive number 15825/89.) Other quotes from this informant in this chapter are ibid.

p. 148 'There was nothing we could do': interview with Gerd Dassler, 2 July 2003, Herzogenaurach.

p. 148 'I was somewhat shocked': interview with Johan van den Bossche, 30 January 2004, Clichy.

p. 149 'When a sports official': interview with Gerhard Prochaska, 10 August 2002, La Baume de Transit.

p. 149 Morocco anecdote: interview with Blago Vidinic, 22 November 2004, Strasbourg.

p. 150 Description of *Champion d'Afrique* culled from the full collection of the magazine at the Bibliothèque nationale in Paris.

p. 151 'Horst always helped Ollan': telephone conversation with John Bragg, March 2005.

p. 151 Other details about the American arm of the sports political team described by John Bragg and Margaret Larrabee, Mike's widow, in correspondence.

pp. 151–2 Ali anecdote and 'Horst had an incredible intellect': telephone conversation with John Bragg, March 2005.

CHAPTER 14: The Bountiful Game

p. 155 'the struggle was between': Keith Botsford, *Sunday Times*, 16 July 1974.

p. 156 'I left the celebrations early': interview with Blago Vidinic, 22 November 2004, Strasbourg, wherefrom issued the entire anecdote.

p. 156 Most details on the early days at West Nally: interview with Patrick Nally, 22 July 2003, London.

p. 158 'He fired instructions': interview with Patrick Nally, 22 July 2003, London.

p. 160 'He didn't have anyone around him': interview with Didier Forterre, 30 January 2004, Paris.

p. 160 Most of the background on the early dealings of SMPI: interview with Patrick Nally, 22 July 2003, London; investigations by German news magazines, particularly *Stern* and *Der Spiegel*, added some details.

CHAPTER 15: The Clandestine Empire

p. 161 Le Coq Sportif history: drawn to a large extent from Emile Camuset, *Le Coq Sportif*, privately published, n.d.

p. 161 Details of the court tussles between Le Coq and Adidas: drawn from published French judicial rulings.

p. 163 'I went over': interview with André Guelfi, 30 July 2003, Paris.

p. 164 André Guelfi's life story: compiled from his autobiography, *L'Original* (Robert Laffont, 1999), as well as articles in *Le Monde*, and *Forages en eaux profondes*, by Airy Routier and Valérie Lecasble (Bernard Grasset, 1998), regarding the Elf bribery scandal. Fatima Oufkir has described her ordeal in *Les Jardins du Roi*, Michel Lafon, 2000.

p. 166 'Between the two of us': interview with André Guelfi, 30 July 2003, Paris.

p. 167 'When someone came': interview with Johan van den Bossche, 30 January 2004, Clichy; also the source for the Heller anecdote that follows.

p. 167 'Horst sometimes pretended': interview with André Guelfi, 30 July 2003, Paris.

p. 168 'In such a jumble': Grupe, *Horst Dassler*.

p. 168 Le Coq Sportif's story in the United Kingdom: interview with Robbie Brightwell, 26 October 2004, Congleton.

p. 170 'It was the pink-shirted-sissies': interview with Jacky Bloch, 14 May 2003, Paris.

p. 171 Background on Roberto Muller: interview with him, 16 August 2004, New York.

p. 171 'flashes of genius': interview with Larry Hampton, 23 July 2003, Wimbledon.

p. 172 Anecdote on the white-powder from, among others, interview with André Gorgemans, 5 July 2005, Munich.

p. 172 'Sarragan became': interview with Jean Wendling, 23 September 2003, Bitschoffen.

p. 173 Le Coq Sportif racket details: interview with Gerhard Prochaska, 10 August 2002, La Baume de Transit.

p. 173 'Sometimes I wondered': interview with Robbie Brightwell, 26 October 2004, Congleton.

p. 173 'She completely flew off': interview with Dieter Passchen, 5 February 2004, Herzogenaurach.

p. 174 'But Herr Dassler' and what follows: interview with Alain Ronc, 20 June 2003, Boulogne.

p. 175 'Ask him tricky questions': interview with Klaus Hempel and Jürgen Lenz, 7 April 2004, Lucerne.

p. 176 'Adi Dassler was livid' and the Juantorena anecdote: interview with Horst Widmann, 13 January 2005, Herzogenaurach.

p. 176 'One day he was walking': interview with Karl-Heinz Lang, 11 January 2005, Scheinfeld.

CHAPTER 16: Olympic Friends

p. 178 'A Cuban delegation': correspondence with Hans Henningsen, June 2004.

p. 178 Details on Steve Prefontaine's relationship with Nike: Strasser and Becklund, *Swoosh*.

p. 178 Details on Asics: Kihachiro Onitsuka's biographical booklet, 'My life history', originally published in the Japanese economic newspaper *Nikkei*, July 1990.

p. 179 Details on the set-up at the Montreal Olympics: telephone conversation with John Bragg, March 2005, and interview with Patrick Nally, 22 July 2003, London.

p. 180 'Pavlov was like a kid': interview with Christian Jannette, 23 September 2003, Illkirch.

p. 181 Details on Samaranch's intimate relationship with the Franco regime: Andrew Jennings, *The Great Olympic Swindle: when the world wanted its Games back*, Simon & Schuster, 2000, and *The New Lord of the Rings*, Simon & Schuster, 1996.

p. 181 'He distinguished himself': interview with Christian Jannette, 23 September 2003, Illkirch, who further recounted the details of the encounter between Samaranch and Dassler in Barcelona.

p. 182 'For every task': interview with Gerhard Prochaska, 10 August 2002, La Baume de Transit.

p. 185 'We were convinced': interview with Patrick Nally, 22 July 2003, London.

p. 185 Anecdote of Sportshotel bugging: interview with Gary Dietrich, 12 August 2004, Condon, Montana.

p. 186 'And all of a sudden': interview with Jörg Dassler, 24 September 2003, Herzogenaurach.

p. 187 'He was permanently hiding': interview with Klaus Hempel, 7 April 2004, Lucerne.

p. 187 'He quizzed me' and 'He told me he could not trust me': interview with Christian Jannette, 23 September 2003, Illkirch.

p. 187 'You could see': interview with Patrick Nally, 22 July 2003, London.

CHAPTER 17: Pitch Invasion

p. 189 'After several meetings': interview with Rolf Deyhle, 3 February 2005, Maria Woerth. Most of the anecdotes relating to Deyhle in this chapter emanate from him. The details of the clashes and the injunction against Fifa remain somewhat hazy because Deyhle has not kept any files on the subject, but the thrust of the dispute was confirmed by several protagonists and partly detailed in Thomas Kistner and Jens Weinreich, *Das Milliardspiel: Fussball, Geld und Medien*, Fischer, 1998.

p. 190 'Horst asked me': interview with André Guelfi, 30 July 2003, Paris.

p. 191 'From the beginning': extracted from Sepp Blatter's written replies to author's questions.

p. 191 'They held discussions': interview with Christian Jannette, 23 September 2003, Illkirch.

p. 191 'Horst openly talked': interview with André Guelfi, 30 July 2003, Paris.

p. 194 'He used to make', 'Then during the dinner' and 'He fired off letters': interview with Didier Forterre, 30 January 2004, Paris.

p. 195 'Horst Dassler had been infatuated': interview with Monique Berlioux, 14 May 2003, Paris.

p. 197 Most details about the genesis of the Olympic programme: interview with Jürgen Lenz, 7 April 2004, Lucerne, complemented by *Olympic Turnaround*, London Business Press, 2005, by Michael Payne, then at ISL, who went on to become marketing manager for the IOC.

CHAPTER 18: The Return

p. 201 'Herr Lenz': interview with Jürgen Lenz, 7 April 2004, Lucerne.

p. 202 'fell head over heels': interview with Roberto Muller, 16 August 2004, New York.

p. 203 Discovery of Guelfi's suspicious dealings: several telephone conversations with Marcel Schmid, April 2005.

p. 204 'I'm afraid you have nothing': interview with Blago Vidinic, 22 November 2004, Strasbourg.

p. 204 'international crook': telephone conversation with Marcel Schmid, April 2005.

p. 205 'One hour cost': interview with André Guelfi, 30 July 2003, Paris.

p. 205 Tales of disappearing documents and customs raids: various interviews with Patrick Nally, Didier Forterre, Klaus Hempel and several others whose offices were searched.

p. 206 'There were entire periods': interview with Günter Sachsenmaier, 23 November 2004, Ottersthal.

p. 206 'She had fire in her eyes': interview with Don Corn, 7 August 2004, Carlsbad, California.

p. 207 'The Spanish crowds': interview with Blago Vidinic, 22 November 2004, Strasbourg.

p. 208 'We haven't always', 'Don't mess things up', 'We wouldn't want' and 'The reception was ice-cold': interview with Bernard Odinet, 28 October 2002, Saint-Germain-en-Laye; the third is quoting Georges 'Jojo' Delbrun.

p. 209 Anecdote of the management ultimatum: interview with Klaus-Werner Becker, 6 April 2004, Basel.

p. 210 'I'm at a crossroads' and 'of course we would': interview with Jean Wendling, 23 September 2003, Bitschoffen.

p. 210 'countless reasonable proposals': Grupe, *Horst Dassler*.

CHAPTER 19: Collapse

pp. 211–12 'You have to kill them' and 'I told them': interviews with Bill Closs Jr, 8 August 2004, Palo Alto, and Bill Closs Sr, 13 August 2004, Big Fork, Montana.

p. 212 'They inspected the sample': interview with Günter Sachsenmaier, 23 November 2004, Ottersthal.

p. 213 'Adidas refused': interview with Horst Widmann, 13 January 2005, Herzogenaurach.

p. 214 Details of the meeting between Horst Dassler and Phil Knight: interview with Larry Hampton, 23 July 2003, Wimbledon, and in Strasser and Becklund, *Swoosh*.

p. 215 Horst Dassler's meetings in Havana and the Los Angeles bank vault: telephone conversation with Joe Kirchner, 21 March 2005; Rich Madden, then head of Adidas USA, contended that he had been dismissed at least partly because he refused to carry one of the suitcases stuffed with cash: interview with Rich Madden, 16 August 2004, Summit, New Jersey.

p. 216 Details of Nike's preparations for the Olympics and 'costly and ephemeral show': from Strasser and Becklund, *Swoosh*.

p. 217 'Los Angeles was a massive': interview with Günter Pfau, 6 February 2004, Herzogenaurach.

p. 217 Quotes and anecdotes relating to entertainment promotion: telephone conversation with Angelo Anastasio, September 2005.

p. 220 Details on the Michael Jordan endorsement: Strasser and Becklund, *Swoosh*.

p. 221 'We had devoted our lives': interview with Gary Dietrich, 12 August 2004, Condon, Montana.

p. 223 'Adidas would not have': interview with Rich Madden, 15 August 2004, Summit, New Jersey.

p. 224 'The next day': interview with Gary Dietrich, 12 August 2004, Condon, Montana.

CHAPTER 20: The Emperor Strikes Back

p. 226 Details on the earliest Nike operations in the United Kingdom: telephone conversation with Mike Tagg, June 2005.

pp. 227–8 Further details on the take-off of running and New Balance: telephone conversation with Hugh Brasher, Chris Brasher's son, who runs a chain of running shoe stores called Sweatshop, June 2005.

p. 229 'Every football team': interview with Stuart Humphreys, 25 October 2004, Wilmslow.

p. 230 'Six months later': telephone conversation with Michel Lukkien, May 2005.

p. 231 'Horst Dassler had convinced': interview with Stuart Humphreys, 25 October 2004, Wilmslow.

p. 232 'He invited us over': interview with Peter Robinson, 26 October 2004, Crewe.

p. 234 'It basically defeated' and much of the advertising anecdote: interview with Tom Harrington, 7 August 2002, Bruchkobel.

p. 234 'It was the most hostile': interview with Ingo Kraus, 29 July 2003, Frankfurt.

p. 234 'I want to be a leisure brand': interview with Tom Harrington, 7 August 2002, Bruchkobel.

p. 235 'There were crazy things' and 'Our catalogues and flyers': interview with Peter Rduch, 6 February 2003, Herzogenaurach.

p. 235 'Horst Dassler tried': interview with Tom Harrington, 7 August 2002, Bruchkobel.

p. 236 'It was such a shocking sight': interview with Blago Vidinic, 22 November 2004, Strasbourg.

p. 237 'This felt like a conspiracy': interview with Michel Perraudin, 3 July 2003, Herzogenaurach.

p. 238 'While he was waiting': correspondence with Pat Doran, October 2004.

p. 239 'Unfortunately my illness': memo to board members dated 31 March 1987.

p. 239 'He had previously asked me': interview with Tomas Bach, 28 July 2003, Tauberbischofheim.

p. 240 'It was a gripping sight': interview with Johan van den Bossche, 30 January 2004, Clichy.

p. 240 'an unostentatious, modest man' and 'tireless, but not selfless genius': *Abendpost*, obituary by Dieter Gräbner, date unknown.

p. 240 'the most powerful man in sports': *Düsseldorf Express*, date unknown.

CHAPTER 21: The Fall of Puma

p. 242 'Tiriac has the air of a man': John McPhee, *Wimbledon: a celebration*, Viking, 1972.

pp. 243–4 'Horst was very upset' and the rest of the WFSGI anecdote: as told by Kihachiro Onitsuka during an encounter at the ISPO fair in July 2005.

p. 245 'There was no need': interview with Gerd Dassler, 2 July 2003, Herzogenaurach.

p. 245 'He told me he needed': interview with Richard Kazmaier, who provided most of the details on the American fiasco, 18 August 2004, Boston.

p. 247 'kind of crazy': interview with Frank Dassler, 10 March 2003, Herzogenaurach.

p. 247 'The retailers told us': interview with Uli Heyd, 9 February 2005, Herzogenaurach.

p. 248 'Current business and prospects': 'Verkaufsangebot und Börsenprospekt', Puma AG Rudolf Dassler Sport, July 1986.

p. 248 'Puma is looking for a buyer': *Wirtschaftswoche*, 13 March 1987.

p. 249 'You have lost your business': interview with Jörg Dassler, 24 September 2003, Herzogenaurach.

p. 249 'As the bankers put it': interview with Frank Dassler, 10 March 2003, Herzogenaurach.

p. 250 'This company will not go bankrupt' and 'The books were filled': interview with Hans Woitschätzke, 14 March 2005, Barcelona.

p. 250 'they must have known' and 'misappropriation of profits': interview with Frank Dassler, 5 February 2004, Herzogenaurach.

p. 250 'If the contents': interview with Hans Woitschätzke, 14 March 2005, Barcelona, from which also issued the quotes and anecdotes that follow.

p. 253 'Put it this way': interview with Irene Dassler, 13 January 2005, Nuremberg.

CHAPTER 22: Extra Time

This chapter has been compiled from several chapters which were published entirely in the original version of *Pitch Invasion*, detailing the fate of Adidas and Puma after the death of the Dassler cousins. These chapters described the odd business dealings and marketing strategies which enabled the two brands to escape bankruptcy. They were based on scores of interviews with executives, bankers, investors, athletes and other sources, of which only a few are quoted below.

p. 253 'Save for the birth': as reported in several of the newspapers quoted in the sources.

p. 254 Details on Bernard Tapie from *Le Flambeur* and countless other books that have been written on his roller-coasting life.

p. 255 Details on the sell-out from interviews with numerous sources including Gerhard Ziener (then supervisory board chairman in charge of the sale) 22/09/03, Darmstadt; René Jäggi, interview 04/02/03, Neustadt an der Weinstrasse; and Laurent Adamowicz (then Paribas banker) telephone conversations on 04/05 and 05/05.

p. 256 'Think of a shark': René Jäggi interview in *Playboy*, 1990, issue n°10 (interview by Axel Thorer).

p. 257 'A first-year business student': interview Bernard Tapie, 03/03/04, Paris.

p. 258 'In all the deals we did': interview Stephen Rubin, 29/04/03, London.

p. 258 'a number of matters': press release by Pentland Group plc, dated 15/10/92.

p. 258 'How do you think?': Axel Markus quoted by Herbert Hainer, interview 10/02/05, Herzogenaurach.

p. 259 Details on the deal with Robert Louis-Dreyfus and Christian Tourres from numerous interviews including: Robert Louis-Dreyfus, 23/05/02, Caslano; Jean-Paul Tchang (general manager of Banque du Phénix), 11/10/04, Paris; Christian Tourres, 22/11/02, Paris.

p. 260 'There will be no sacred cows' and 'it was an unbelievable sight': interview Jochen Zeitz for an article in *Management* magazine, 25/04/02.

p. 262 'They seemed to be': interview Peter Moore, 09/08/04, Portland, Oregon

p. 262 'You got it', Bayern anecdote as relayed by Robert Louis-Dreyfus and Franz Beckenbauer, interview 25/09/03, Kaiserslautern.

p. 262 'We had never seen anything like it' and 'he had us adjust his boots': telephone conversation with Aidan Butterworth, August 2003.

p. 263 Reebok deal background from interview with Paul Fireman, Lancaster, Pennsylvania, 01/11/06.

Sources

This book is based on five years of research, entailing many days in dusty archives and interviews around Europe and in the United States. The interviews range from telephone conversations to repeated, day-long encounters. Some of the sources have kindly provided internal documents and personal correspondence, and I acknowledge here my debt to the authors of the listed bibliographical entries for a wealth of minor but illuminating detail scattered throughout the text.

The contents are further documented through clippings from *Die Süddeutsche Zeitung*, *Die Frankfurter Allgemeine*, *Handelsblatt*, *Bildzeitung*, *Die Zeit*, several regional German newspapers, *Stern*, *Spiegel*, *Wirtschaftswoche*, *Le Monde*, *Libération*, *Le Figaro*, *Les Echos*, *Le Quotidien de Paris*, *Le Nouvel Observateur*, *Le Parisien*, *De Telegraaf*, *Vrij Nederland*, the *Financial Times*, the *Wall Street Journal*, *Il Sole 24 Ore*, *Sports Illustrated*, *L'Equipe*, *Sportstyle*, *Sporting Goods Intelligence*.

The cinema, too, has played its part in documenting the history of sport. Among its output most relevant to this book are *Das Wunder von Bern* (Sönke Wortmann, 2004), *The Tokyo Olympiad* (Kon Ichikawa, 1964) and *Chariots of Fire* (Hugh Hudson, 1981).

Adidas and Puma both provided a wealth of annual reports, press releases and other company documents. I have drawn some early anecdotes from a manuscript written by Hermann Utermann, a German historian, about the life of Adi Dassler. This was never published and the rights were acquired by Adidas. The company itself published a substantial history of its beginnings – although it incidentally obliterated the forties.

Quotes that are not referenced in the endnotes below are taken from unrecorded conversations with sources who preferred to remain anonymous.

Bibliography

Adidas-Salomon Group, *Making a Difference*, Adidas-Salomon Group, 1998
Armfield, Jimmy, *Right Back to the Beginning*, Headline, 2004
Ball, Alan, *Playing Extra Time*, Sidgwick & Jackson, 2004
Banks, Gordon, *Banksy: my autobiography*, Michael Joseph, 2002

Beckham, David and Watt, Tom, *My Side*, Collins Willow, 2003

Bercoff, André, *Comment ils ont tué Tapie*, Michel Lafon, 1998

Best, George, *Blessed*, Ebury Press, 2001

Bieber, Christoph, *Sneaker-Story: der Zweikampf von Adidas und Nike*, Fischer, 2000

Bitzer, Dirk and Wilting, Bernd, *Stürmen für Deutschland (die Geschichte des deutschen Fussballs von 1933 bis 1954)*, Campus Verlag, 2003

Bouchet, Christophe, *Tapie, l'homme d'affaires*, Editions du Seuil, 1994

Bower, Tom, *Broken Dreams: vanity, greed and the souring of British football*, Simon & Schuster, 2003

Camuset, Emile, *Le Coq Sportif*, privately published, n.d.

Clarke, Ron, *The Measure of Success: a personal perspective*, Lothian Books, 2004

Conn, David, *The Football Business*, Mainstream Sport, 2001

Fischer, Gerhard and Lindner, Ulrich, *Stürmer für Hitler: Vom Zusammenspiel zwischen Fussball und Nationalsozialismus*, Verlag Die Werkstatt, 1999

Fryer, Daniel, *The Gola Years 1905–2005*, Jacobson Group, 2005

Geldner, Wilfried, *Adi Dassler*, Ullstein, 1999

Goldman, Kevin, *Conflicting Accounts: the creation and crash of the Saatchi & Saatchi advertising empire*, Touchstone, 1998

Grupe, Paulheinz, *Horst Dassler: Revolution im Weltsport*, Hase & Koehler, 1992

Guelfi, André, *L'Original*, Robert Laffont, 1999

Hesse-Lichtenberger, Ulrich, *Tor! The story of German football*, WSC Books, 2002

Hildred, Stafford and Ewbank, Tim, *There's only one David Beckham*, John Blake Publishing, 2002

Jansen, Christian (comp.), *Von der Aufgabe der Freiheit*, Akademie-Verlag, 1995

Jennings, Andrew, *The Great Olympic Swindle: when the world wanted its Games back*, Simon & Schuster, 2000

—— *The New Lord of the Rings*, Simon & Schuster, 1996

Les Jeux Olympiques, d'Athènes à Athènes, L'Equipe, 2003

Katz, Donald, *Just Do It: the Nike spirit in the corporate world*, Adams Media Corporation, 1994

Kistner, Thomas and Schulze, Ludger, *Die Spielmacher*, Deutsche Verlags-Anstalt, 2001

Kistner, Thomas and Weinreich, Jens, *Der Olympische Sumpf*, Piper, 2000

—— *Das Milliardenspiel: Fussball, Geld und Medien*, Fischer, 1998

Klein, Naomi, *No Logo*, Albert A. Knopf, 2000

Kok, Auke, *1974: Wij waren de besten*, Thomas Rap Amsterdam, 2004

Kooman, Kees, *Fanny Blankers-Koen: een koningin met mannenbenen*, L. J. Veen, 2003

—— *Kinderen van Pheidippides: de marathon, van Abebe Bikila tot Emil Zatopek*, Tirion Sport, 2005

Kuper, Simon, *Ajax, the Dutch, the War: football in Europe during the Second World War*, Orion, 2003

Lang, Karl-Heinz and Urban, Renate, *Adi Dassler, from the Beginnings to the*

Present: a history manual of the Adidas-Salomon Group, Adidas-Salomon Group, updated annually

Lecasble, Valérie and Routier, Airy, *Le Flambeur: la vraie vie de Bernard Tapie*, Grasset, 1994

Leinemann, Jürgen, *Sepp Herberger: Ein Leben, eine Legende*, Rororo, 1998

Maassen, Marcel, *De betaalde liefde*, Uitgeverij SUN, 1999

Mandell, Richard, *The Nazi Olympics*, University of Illinois Press, 1987

Matthews, Stanley, *The Way it Was*, Headline, 2000

McArthur, Ian and Kemp, Dave, *Elegance Borne of Brutality: an eclectic history of the football boot*, Two Heads Publishing, 1995

McPhee, John, *Wimbledon: a celebration*, Viking, 1972

McRae, Donald, *In Black and White: the untold story of Joe Louis and Jesse Owens*, Simon & Schuster, 2002

Nastase, Ilie and Beckerman, Debbie, *Mr Nastase: the autobiography*, Collins Willow, 2004

Netzer, Günter and Schümann, Helmut, *Günter Netzer: Aus der Tiefe des Raumes*, Rowohlt, 2004

Oufkir, Fatima, *Les Jardins du Roi*, Michel Lafon, 2000

Payne, Michael, *Olympic Turnaround*, London Business Press, 2005

Remnick, David, *King of the World: Muhammad Ali and the rise of an American hero*, Random House, 1998

Routier, Airy and Lecasble, Valérie, *Forages en eaux profondes*, Bernard Grasset, 1998

Rudolf Dassler 70, privately published by the Dassler family, 1968

Shirer, William L., *The Rise and Fall of the Third Reich*, Simon & Schuster, 1960

Simson, Vyv and Jennings, Andrew, *The Lord of the Rings*, Simon & Schuster, 1992

Stadtbuch Herzogenaurach, Aus der 1000-jährigen Geschichte Herzogenaurachs, Stadt Herzogenaurach, Kulturamt, 2003

Strasser, J. B. and Becklund, Laurie, *Swoosh: the unauthorized story of Nike and the men who played there*, Harcourt Brace Jovanovich, 1991

Sugden, John and Tomlinson, Alan, *Great Balls of Fire: how big money is hijacking world football*, Mainstream Publishing, 1999

Utermann, Hermann, 'Der Mann der Adidas war', unpublished biography of Adolf Dassler, 1983

von der Lippe, George (ed.), *Max Schmeling: an autobiography*, Bonus Books, 1998

Wallechinsky, David, *The Complete Book of the Olympics*, Aurum Press, 2000

Walter, Fritz, *3:2, Die Spiele zur Weltmeisterschaft*, Stiebner Verlag, 2000

Wattez, Eric, *Comment Adidas devient l'un des plus beaux redressements de l'histoire du business*, Editions Assouline, 1998

Winner, David, *Brilliant Orange: the neurotic genius of Dutch football*, Bloomsbury, 2000

—— *Those Feet: a sensual history of English football*, Bloomsbury, 2005

Acknowledgements

A few years ago, Adidas employees were sent out to clean an old storage room in Herzogenaurach. They were stunned to find, at the back of the hangar, boxes full of old shoes. Karl-Heinz Lang, a longtime Adidas technician, took upon himself the task of sorting through the rotting cartons and cleaning up the most valuable remains. The result is a row of cupboards in Scheinfeld, containing the spikes worn by Jesse Owens as well as the Muhammad Ali boots and many other treasures. Thanks to Karl-Heinz Lang for leading me through this superb display, which speaks more than a shelf full of books. To share this with a wider audience, he is working on the setting-up of an Adidas museum in Herzogenaurach. The project is steered by Frank Dassler.

Renate Urban, Lang's assistant in Scheinfeld, patiently helped me to visualize modern shoe production by leading me through the adjoining plant. This turns out small runs of standard football boots as well as handmade series for David Beckham and other high-maintenance players.

While this book remains entirely independent, I am most grateful to the leading executives of Adidas and Puma for their welcome and assistance. Because of the turbulent family history underlying the two companies, neither of them has comprehensive archives. However, both have kindly provided me with extensive access to all their public documents and arranged many interviews with current employees.

Much to their credit, the people in charge of press relations at Adidas and Puma accepted that I would portray their company's history as I uncovered it, with their controversial past and dubious dealings. Although they never attempted to influence the contents of the book, they apparently trusted me to make it clear that their current management could not be held responsible for such errings. I can only hope that I have not undermined their confidence in displaying such an unusually open attitude.

I am most indebted to Jan Runau and Anne Putz, in charge of media relations at Adidas, for their enthusiasm and co-operation. They have repeatedly welcomed me in Herzogenaurach, gone out of their way to dig up useful facts and opened doors that would otherwise have remained closed.

The night that I spent at the Puma head offices, holed up in a meeting room with scores of fascinating documents and an empty pizza box, oddly ranks as one of my fondest memories in five years of research. I still wonder how I resisted the temptation to roam through the empty corridors. Thanks to Ulf Santjer, head of media relations at Puma.

I owe the most thrilling moments of this project to all the people who agreed to share their memories for this book. For many of them, their time at Adidas or Puma was the most intense period in their professional lives. Their testimony was often fraught with the passion of times past – the excitement of the games, the ferocity of the battles with the other side. 'I have three stripes tattooed on my guts,' they would admit. I discovered some astonishingly forceful personalities, fascinating storytellers and amazingly kind individuals.

Many of the people I interviewed do not appear in this book. This is such a complex story, and there are so many facets of it, that I had to eliminate some of them. If you are frustrated about this I sincerely apologize, but you can be assured that the exercise was worse for me.

As I researched the company's war history, I was stunned by the diligence of German and American archivists. They spent hours answering my queries and came forward with invaluable advice.

More thanks are due to colleagues, friends, or both. Among those who provided guidance, encouragement or just a patient ear as I crashed in their living rooms on my travels, blabbering on about stripes and wildcats: Jeroen Akkermans and Annemieke Wapperom, Erin Barnett, Thierry Cruvellier, Alain Franco, Machteld van Gelder, Albert Knechtel, Simon Kuper, David Winner.

I was particularly impressed with the generosity of Andrew Jennings, the British journalist who uncovered large-scale corruption in Olympic circles. Andrew is so genuinely passionate in his disgust at such wrongdoings that he enthusiastically assisted the newcomer on his patch. My research on Horst Dassler's infiltration of sports organizations leaned heavily on his revelations.

David Luxton, my English agent and partner at Luxton Harris, took a risky gamble. After all, a Dutch woman residing in France, investigating two German sports companies and delivering an English-language manuscript did not seem an obvious proposal. I am most grateful for David's steadfast support, his quiet reassurances and his unwavering confidence in the project.

Preena Gadher, self-confessed trainer freak and publicist at Penguin, provided further encouragement through her enthusiasm for the subject and her creative efforts to promote *Pitch Invasion*.

I am greatly indebted to Helen Conford, my editor at Penguin, for her dedication to this book. She went to great lengths to draw attention to the project at Penguin, dressing up as a moustachioed Adidas fan and buying up officially fake dollars by the kilo. But I was even more privileged to benefit from Helen's sharp and patient guidance: while her twenty-four pages of dense comments looked daunting, they proved invaluable to improve my manuscript.

Still, the concept for this book might never have turned into a manuscript at all without Eugenio Di Maria, editor and publisher of *Sporting Goods Intelligence* in Europe. I met him in Munich about five years ago, when I first attended ISPO, the industry's international trade fair. As I reported for him over the next years, he patiently shared his unparalleled knowledge of the European sports industry.

He provided me with unique insights and introduced me to more people than I could have hoped to meet by myself. It has been an immense privilege to work with such a passionate and demanding editor. Eugenio should not be held responsible for the contents of this book, but I owe much of it to him.

Nîmes, November 2005

Index

PENGUIN POLITICS

HEAT
HOW WE CAN STOP THE PLANET BURNING

GEORGE MONBIOT

'A dazzling command of science and a relentless faith in people' Naomi Klein

Started to worry about just how hot our world is going to get, and whether you can do anything about it? What with the excuses, the lies, the fudged figures, the PR greenwashing and the downright misinformation on the power of everything from wind turbines to carbon trading, when it comes to saving the world most people don't know what to they're talking about. Luckily, George Monbiot does. Packed with killer facts and inspiring ideas, shot through with passion and underlined by brilliant investigative journalism, with a copy of *Heat* you really can protect the planet.

'I defy you to read this book and not feel motivated to change' *The Times*

PENGUIN PSYCHOLOGY

BLINK
THE POWER OF THINKING WITHOUT THINKING
MALCOLM GLADWELL

'Astonishing … *Blink* really does make you rethink the way you think' *Daily Mail*

'Trust my snap judgement, buy this book: you'll be delighted' *The New York Times*

An art expert sees a ten-million-dollar sculpture and instantly spots it's a fake.
A marriage analyst knows within minutes whether a couple will stay together. A
fire-fighter suddenly senses he has to get out of a blazing building. A speed dater
clicks with the right person …

This book is all about those moments when we 'know' something without
knowing why. Here Malcolm Gladwell, one of the world's most original thinkers,
explores the phenomenon of 'blink', showing how a snap judgement can be far
more effective than a cautious decision. By trusting your instincts, he reveals,
you'll never think about thinking in the same way again …

'Compelling, fiendishly clever' *Evening Standard*

'Brilliant … the implications for business, let alone love, are vast' *Observer*

'Superb … this wonderful book should be compulsory reading' *New Statesman*

'*Blink* might just change your life' *Esquire*

'Should you buy this book? You already know the answer to that'
Independent on Sunday

ECONOMICS

FREAKONOMICS

STEVEN D. LEVITT & STEPHEN J. DUBNER

'A sensation … you'll be stimulated, provoked and entertained. Of how many books can that be said?' *Sunday Telegraph*

'The book is a delight; it educates, surprises and amuses … dazzling' *Economist*

'Prepare to be dazzled' Malcolm Gladwell

What do estate agents and the Ku Klux Klan have in common?

Why do drug dealers live with their mothers?

How can your name affect how well you do in life?

The answer: Freakonomics. It's at the heart of everything we do and the things that affect us daily, from sex to crime, parenting to politics, fat to cheating, fear to traffic jams. And it's all about using information about the world around us to get to the heart of what's *really* happening under the surface of everyday life.

'If Indiana Jones were an economist he'd be Steven Levitt' *Wall Street Journal*

He just wanted a decent book to read ...

Not too much to ask, is it? It was in 1935 when Allen Lane, Managing Director of Bodley Head Publishers, stood on a platform at Exeter railway station looking for something good to read on his journey back to London. His choice was limited to popular magazines and poor-quality paperbacks – the same choice faced every day by the vast majority of readers, few of whom could afford hardbacks. Lane's disappointment and subsequent anger at the range of books generally available led him to found a company – and change the world.

'We believed in the existence in this country of a vast reading public for intelligent books at a low price, and staked everything on it'
Sir Allen Lane, 1902–1970, founder of Penguin Books

The quality paperback had arrived – and not just in bookshops. Lane was adamant that his Penguins should appear in chain stores and tobacconists, and should cost no more than a packet of cigarettes.

Reading habits (and cigarette prices) have changed since 1935, but Penguin still believes in publishing the best books for everybody to enjoy. We still believe that good design costs no more than bad design, and we still believe that quality books published passionately and responsibly make the world a better place.

So wherever you see the little bird – whether it's on a piece of prize-winning literary fiction or a celebrity autobiography, political tour de force or historical masterpiece, a serial-killer thriller, reference book, world classic or a piece of pure escapism – you can bet that it represents the very best that the genre has to offer.

Whatever you like to read – trust Penguin.